DOCTORING TOGETHER

A Study of Professional Social Control

DOCTORING TOGETHER
A Study of Professional Social Control

ELIOT FREIDSON

ELSEVIER

New York / Oxford / Amsterdam

ELSEVIER SCIENTIFIC PUBLISHING COMPANY, INC.
52 Vanderbilt Avenue, New York, N.Y. 10017

ELSEVIER SCIENTIFIC PUBLISHING COMPANY
335 Jan Van Galenstraat, P.O. Box 211
Amsterdam, The Netherlands

Library of Congress Cataloging in Publication Data

Friedson, Eliot.
    Doctoring together.

    Bibliography: p.
    Includes index.
    1. Group medical practice—Sociological aspects.
2. Physicians—Discipline. I. Title.
R729.5.G6F73   301.5   75-34210
ISBN 0-444-99017-8

Manufactured in the United States of America

Designed by Loretta Li

For MOUSE & MARYJANE

The war is temporary. But drawings
and chocolate go on forever.

—DONALD BARTHELME

Contents

Acknowledgments

Doing a study and writing a book is a collective activity. While I am the sole author and while I must take sole responsibility for this book's deficiencies, I must nonetheless acknowledge my debt to many people and record my thanks here.

For direct financial aid during the period in which the study reported here was carried out, and for some of the time during which I analyzed the data and wrote, I must acknowledge with gratitude the support I received from various agencies of the U.S. Public Health Service through grants RG-7882, GM-07882, CH-00025, CH-00414, and HS-00104. I must also thank the Center for Advanced Study in the Behavioral Sciences, Stanford, California, for its hospitality in providing me with an optimal setting for writing the final draft. My greatest institutional debt, however, is to New York University and its Department of Sociology which, by employing me over the years when I did not have direct grant support, and by allowing me to extend and deepen my education by teaching a variety of courses as my interests dictated, made an indispensable contribution to the ultimate intellectual product of the study.

The study itself could not have been completed without the collaboration and stimulation of my colleague, Buford Rhea, or without the literacy, conscientious skill and incredible energy of Helen Schulman, Project Secretary. A number of typists worked on various drafts of the manuscript, all with blinding speed and accuracy and good-humored tolerance for the slow pace at which I could provide them with material. I must especially thank Evelyn Shey, Florene Wiley, and Arlene Díaz, all of whom typed for me at New York University, and Helena Smith, who typed for me at the Center for Advanced Study in the Behavioral Sciences.

A number of people helped me with the substance of the manuscript. Jacqueline Rector Howard Garippa struggled valiantly to help me make better sense of a very crude second draft. Others provided helpful criticisms and suggestions for later drafts without which I would have lost all sense of proportion. These people were Arnold Arluke, Howard S.

Becker, Arlene K. Daniels, Avedis Donabedian, Helen Giambruni, Mary E. W. Goss, Wolf Heydebrand, David Mechanic, Derek Phillips, Richard Sennett, George A. Silver, Howard Waitzkin, and several anonymous reviewers of my final report to the federal funding agency. I thank them all and hope that they will not feel that they have worked in vain.

Finally, I must thank the physicians I studied for their cooperation and, I think the reader will agree, their thoughtful eloquence. During the course of the study, Buford Rhea and I came to respect and admire them greatly. Indeed, toward the end of our interviewing we noticed in the transcriptions that we were using the word "we" when we talked to the doctors. That was a sign both of the growth of our identification with them and of the necessity to end the study before we "went native." I hope that the critical nature of my analysis of their dilemmas, the perspectives they had, and the ways they coped with their problems will be taken to be what it actually is—respectful of their good intentions and sympathetic to their problems of doing what is very often hard and frustrating work.

The quotation on the dedication page is from "Engineer-Private Paul Klee Misplaces an Aircraft Between Milbertshofen and Cambrai, March 1916," reprinted with the permission of Farrar, Straus & Giroux, Inc., from *Sadness* by Donald Barthelme, Copyright 1970, 1971, 1972 by Donald Barthelme. The complete parable is a more compressed and stylish version of this book.

Preface

This book is about the underlife of social policy—about the men and women who carry out formal plans. Focussing on a medical organization which has served as a model for policy, it describes how the physicians who worked in it made sense of their problems of work, and how they attempted to deal with them. They tell their own story, for my method of study was one in which they were able to talk at length, without being constrained by fixed questions and categories, and one in which they could be observed talking to each other in their own way, informally, and on topics of their own choosing. In this book they discuss themselves, their work, their patients and their colleagues. They talk about when a mistake is "really" a mistake, how they decide whether or not someone is a "good" doctor, what they gossip about among themselves, what they feel about the value of the medical record, and how they think doctors should be rewarded or punished for the quality of their work. In telling their own story, they tell us how and why they act in ways that social policy does not plan.

My own analysis of the significance of the doctors' stories rests on both an ontological and a methodological base. Ontologically, I argue that the ultimate practical and moral reality of human society lies in what concrete people do and how they interpret their problems in the settings of everyday life. I argue further that the test of the value of any formal social policy is to be found in that everyday experience rather than in the highly selective abstractions of the statistics, accounting devices and indicators found in official documents. While all those devices are necessary tools for a large and complex society, they are only as useful as one's capacity to interpret them accurately. And one's capacity to interpret them accurately depends upon the depth of one's acquaintance with the everyday experience of those concrete people doing their work in their own way. Administrative statistics and accounts do not merely reflect the activity of those workers; they are *created* by them with their own purposes in mind. To interpret them wisely, one must know how and why they were created, as well as the broader context of activity from which they were selected. More reliable than inspired guesswork is direct, systematic qualitative study of the everyday settings of work or practice. That is my methodological argument.

This leads me, finally, to a policy argument. Essentially, I argue, it is inappropriate to approach the assessment of human services in the same way that one approaches the manufacture of goods. In the human services of medicine, education, welfare and law, the aim is not merely to "turn out" some measured product of a given quality at a given cost but to serve human beings in need of help. In manufacturing we do not concern ourselves with the tortures through which fibers, plastics, metals or the like are put in the course of the production process. But in the human services we are concerned that the course of providing help include some sensitive recognition of and responsiveness to the human quality of the structure of flesh and bone being processed. Responsiveness and recognition themselves may constitute the service and its benefit; without it, the encounter is dead and the service provided to a mere object, albeit not one of fiber, plastic or metal.

But the tendency in policy today is to finance, control and evaluate services as if they were provided to objects. For both determining and assessing policy, reliance is on formal administrative techniques drawn from industrial practices which reduce varied services to least common denominators of standardized technical and fiscal performançe. Broad economic and administrative frameworks are being built around services which do have the desirable virtue or providing assurance that they will be accessible to those in need. This is a distinct social advance over earlier times when there was no such assurance, but it is not enough. Only loosely constrained by that framework is the process by which the "workers"—in the case of health care, primarily physicians—provide and assess those services. There, however, in the nature of that process and not in the mere fact of a somehow provided service is the key to the difference between treating people who need help as objects or as human beings. The issue is not merely the quantity and technique of service, but the spirit in which it is provided. As I shall show, that can vary considerably within a single framework. The spirit of service is what distinguishes the problem of providing a human service from the problem of processing materials efficiently to produce an object.

The spirit of service, I argue, can be improved and extended only by changing the process by which those who provide them interact in concrete local settings with each other and with their clientele. If the nature of that interaction is such as to protect the self-serving and the indifferent, then the spirit of service will suffer accordingly, and the services themselves will do little to enhance the quality of human experience. If, on the other hand, those processes transform already existing commitments to personal career and professional technique by focussing them on devoted service to human beings in need of help, then the outcome will be markedly different. That transformation cannot occur if public policy assumes that so long as access to service is guaranteed, the spirit of service will take care of itself. It will occur only when a deliberate effort is made to mobilize and redirect the commitments of those who are engaged in doing the everyday work of doctoring.

ELIOT FREIDSON

Introduction

1:

Human Services and Professional Social Control

Just as every edition of newspaper must be published with an emphatic headline, so must every period declare itself in crisis. It seems to be a characteristic device of works competing for public attention to seek it by crying alarm, crisis, and imminent far-reaching change. But by the rapidity with which each proclaimed crisis is supplanted by another, one might assume that most are superficial, if not imaginary, in character. Institutional change may not be as slow as geological change, but it certainly takes longer to occur than the constant cry of crisis would lead us to expect.

Nonetheless, there are periods in history which are generally recognized as times of unusual turmoil, as turning points toward a new institutional order with profound importance to human life. Many thoughtful observers have seen the 1960s through 1970s as just such a period. Some observers see crisis in the ecological foundation of society—in the depletion of natural resources, in a severely limited capacity to produce sufficient food and energy to support a rapidly increasing population, and in the slow poisoning of the natural environment. Some see crisis in the economic foundation of society—in the exhaustion of capitalism's capacity to satisfy the needs of the underprivileged and in the imminence of revolution and rebirth. Others see the period as an economic, organizational, and technological turning point from which will evolve a new form of society, distinct from that which developed from the industrial revolution. At present there is talk of crisis and change in the whole spectrum of ecological, economic, political, and cultural life.

Among the events of this period worthy of close attention is the expansion in the United States of state-supported services designed to improve the well-being of the average citizen—expansion of what are called "the human services." This expansion took place in the 1960s, when public expectations for a better life rose dramatically and political pressure on government to supply it grew. At that time, the government extended its established programs, invented new ones, and increased its support to nongovernmental agencies. New ideas of the citizen's right to

3

health, education, legal, and welfare services were advanced, and many of these rights were given a legal foundation. Some programs even sought to mobilize the neglected to become a political force seeking their rights and control over their own services.

It was in the health services, however, that some of the most critical changes took place. For half a century the medical profession had successfully fought against broad public financing of health care (cf. Rayack, 1967; Somers and Somers, 1961). Traditional health care had been organized primarily around independent professional practice, on a fee rather than a salary basis. The client sought care as an independent individual, paying fees out of his[1] own pocket or obtaining his own health insurance to assist him to pay his fees. Health care institutions were organized around the needs of entrepreneurial medical practice, as were the vast majority of paramedical occupations. (cf. Freidson, 1970a). But in the middle of the 1960s there was instituted an unprecedented program of government financing of medical and hospital care for the elderly and indigent—Medicare and Medicaid (Harris, 1966; Marmor, 1973). This event created a radically different option for health care at the same time that consumer groups representing various segments of the population were seeking what they saw as their rights (Haug and Sussman, 1969). The established institutions of education, legal service, and welfare were shaken by the 1960s, but no similarly far-reaching change had taken place in their traditional economic foundation. Only in the case of health care could it be said that established traditions of payment and organization were breached.

THE PRESENT POLICY DEBATE

Government attention to and support of the expansion of all human services increased markedly in the 1960s, but so did the cost to the public treasury. Even before the end of the decade, it was felt necessary to restrict further expansion, and policy emphasis shifted to the reorganization of programs in such a way as to control their costs and improve their efficiency. The 1970s might in fact be seen as a period of reaction to the political and economic costs and consequences of the 1960s. The 1970s represent a period in which efforts are being made to

---

[1]In this book I use such words as "he," "his," "layman," and "craftsman" to refer to all human beings, male and female.

work out politically and economically viable ways of harnessing and controlling, and perhaps even realizing, some of the purposes and products of those changes of the previous decade. The period represents both disappointment with the performance of established service institutions, which expanded but did not change during the 1960s, and concern about finding the most effective ways of reorganizing and controlling those institutions so that they can better operate in the public interest. In health care, the pressure is to extend and consolidate public financing first undertaken in the 1960s and to ensure control of its costs.

Once the new foundation of public financing and its politically necessary requirement of accountability are established, there is little likelihood that this foundation will be changed for some time to come. The decisions to be made in the 1970s, then, are especially important. They will have fairly permanent effects on the public treasury and the taxpayer, on freedom of access to health service, on the technical quality of service, and on the human quality of service. Obviously, it is important that the decisions have a sound foundation.

But most of the debate surrounding health policy and most of the policy solutions advanced are a curious blend of the concrete and technical, on one hand, and of the abstract and vague, on the other. There is a great deal of debate about the particular financing mechanisms to be used to control costs (e.g., Eilers and Moyerman, 1971). To a lesser extent, there has also been debate about the particular administrative ways in which health care should be planned, organized, and controlled. In both cases, discussion is literal and practical, concerned with selecting one particular technique or set of techniques out of the entire range of possibilities. But it is entirely abstract and vague in its conception of the manner in which the services will be provided by the human beings who will be responsible for doing so. The fixation is on formal administrative and economic accounting devices, without serious attention to human behavior.

This fixation is very dangerous because accounting devices do not explain and therefore cannot predict behavior. As Fuchs wisely pointed out in the course of his discussion of change in the cost of health care, an accounting framework "cannot provide a behavioral explanation of cost change. That can only come through analysis of the actual behavior of patients, physicians . . . and other decision-makers" (Fuchs, 1974: 11). The same fixation on the use of easily measurable administrative and economic accounting devices has existed in the "evaluation research" upon which much policy debate is based. The results of such research may show that a program has not resulted in what was intended but rarely show "*why* the observed results occur, what processes intervene between input and outcome, what the implications are for improving the effectiveness of the program" (Weiss, 1970: 59; italics added). Obviously, no policy scheme can work much better than the actual performance of those people who are involved in carrying it out. Policy formation can be realistic only by involving understanding of how the human beings involved produce services and records of service—the process of providing care to others.

Economic and administrative data can constitute worlds of their own, real on their own terms but separate from the experiential reality they purport to measure and control. A Potemkin village, after all, can satisfy the authorities that housing is being built for the people at the same time that it can fail to house anyone at all. Ultimately, the value of a policy must be assessed in the light of the way it is carried out down at the everyday level of human action and experience: here, not in formal accounting records, is where its justification and benefit are tested. By the same token, whether or not a policy will be carried out as intended depends on its compatibility with the characteristics of those who will carry it out or on its success at changing them. There, too, policy debate is poorly informed, vague, and abstract.

DIRECT AND INDIRECT FORMS OF SOCIAL CONTROL

Central to effective social policy is the issue of *social control*. It is necessary to decide what to accomplish and how much of an investment one can make in accomplishing it. It is also necessary to set up a system by which sufficient control can be exercised over those carrying out policy to assure that they will accomplish what is intended. There are, however, a variety of methods of control, and, depending upon what it is one wishes to control and what the available resources for control are, it is likely that no one method is effective for every kind of problem. The debate about health care policy is, implicitly or explicitly, a debate about the best fiscal and administrative mechanisms for controlling the cost and the quality of care. The emphasis is on both constraints and incentives (cf. Etzioni, 1968).

No matter what the mechanism under policy debate, virtually every one emphasizes what Mannheim called *indirect* forms of social control. These consist in administrative structures that constitute a framework of limiting constraints and rewards around the possibilities for behavior. In contrast, there are *direct* forms of social control, which involve the mutual influences of human beings in everyday settings. Indirect social control "works from afar. . . . the invisible pressure in the situation itself, [while direct social control is] based on personal influence. . . and works from near at hand" (Mannheim, 1948: 274–275). It is my thesis that in being preoccupied with indirect, formal methods of control without concern for the direct methods that are used on and by those actually engaged in doing the work, policy will run the risk of at least partial, but significant, failure, for "the pathology of organizations develops from the relative incompatibility between their goals, which spring from a type of utilitarian rationality, and the means of [direct] social control, which are determined by the primary behavior and values characteristic of the cultural system of which the organizations are a part" (Crozier, 1964:8).

Ultimately, formal, indirect means of social control must be realized through the process of interaction and negotiation by which they are translated into real behavior—that is, through direct means of social control (Mannheim, 1948: 275). Thus, social policy can work out only as well as its conception of and connection with the individuals and groups toward whom it is directed. Knowledge of the nature of the direct, personal relationships and social controls operating in the health services among those responsible for providing care allows the formulation of plans that have a fair chance of anticipating how far intentions will be realized. Without empirical knowledge, one can only rely on the assumptions of formal, conceptual models.

BUREAUCRATIC AND PROFESSIONAL MODELS OF CONTROL

In recent history, two major conceptual models of the social control of human services which differ in their choice of the nature and source of control over services have been competing with each other in policy debate. It is true that it is the state that is ultimately sovereign and that it is the power of the state which underlies all other formal sources of authority. But the state, as often as not, delegates its power to other agents or grants to others the right to exercise control. Who gains that authority and how it is characteristically exercised have important influence on both the milieu in which services are provided and received and the very substance of the service itself. Both the workers who provide services and the patients who receive them are influenced in important ways by the source and organization of authority, and their reactions and interactions display the differences in the source and the exercise of authority, as I shall show in early chapters of this book.

It is the normal and traditional choice in advanced industrial society to grant the authority to exercise social control over those engaged in producing goods to the chartered corporation whose officials are responsible for directing production. Whether the institution is a government agency or a private enterprise is unimportant for determining the essential methods of control flowing from the grant of authority to administrative officials: in both cases the essential method of control lies in the creation of an administrative or managerial hierarchy. Control follows a *bureaucratic model,* the special characteristics of which were outlined in classic form by Max Weber (Weber, 1947).

"The prototype of bureaucratic control is the authority exercised through a chain of command in which superiors give orders subordinates are obligated to obey. . . . [and] the establishment of explicit regulations and procedures that govern decisions and operations" (Blau and Schoenherr, 1971: 348). In the bureaucratic model, the essential work that is responsible for attaining the productive goal of the organization—the work of producing toasters, for example, or of serving hamburgers—is performed by one group, the workers, but is formulated, directed, and coordinated by a different group, the managers and supervisors. Management attempts to exercise social control to assure that the workers will produce what it wishes. It exercises *indirect* control by creating the formal structure of the chain of command, the division of labor, and the rules and regulations as well as, on occasion, the technological devices that exercise mechanical control over the possibilities of work. It exercises *direct* control through the interaction of its supervisory officials with the workers.

In one way or another, the essential characteristics of the system of social control connected with the bureaucratic model are familiar to most readers, though often in less flattering terms than the model deserves. (For a recent, lively defense of the bureaucratic model, see

Perrow, 1970.) It is a model based on the notion that work can be specified satisfactorily by formal rules and regulations and workers controlled by hierarchical orders and supervision. There is, however, an entirely different model for the control of work which, while generally familiar to us all, is rather obscure in its details. What distinguishes it in general from the bureaucratic model is that, instead of being controlled and directed by superiors who are not trained to perform the basic, productive work, it is directed and controlled by the workers themselves. This model might be called *the professional model* (see Gilb, 1966; Moore, 1970; and especially Johnson, 1972.) Just as corporate administrators ultimately gain legitimate authority to control work from the legal status of "officer" granted by the state, so also do professionals gain their authority from the state, most clearly, but by no means exclusively, through restrictive licensing that allows them and them only to perform and control particular kinds of work.

The general parameters of the organization of the professional model are familiar enough. Given a monopoly over certain kinds of work, the profession is composed of a nominal company of equals, with internal differentiation based on specialization and prestigious skill rather than on official rank (cf. Barber, 1952; Parson, 1951). Bureaucratic hierarchy and the authority of bureaucratic office are foreign to the profession. The *indirect* forms of social control exercised over work in the case of the professional model are fairly clear—restrictive licensing, formal training and educational requirements, and the like. The *direct* forms of social control exercised over work in the professional model are less clear, but they are conventionally conceived of as self-control—individuals controlling their own behavior conscientiously by virtue of the training and dedication they gained from a long period of schooling. In interacting with one another, individuals are also presumed to exercise direct control over one another's behavior.

THE BALANCE BETWEEN THE MODELS

These two models of the organization of social control, together with elements of a third that I shall not discuss now, discriminate crucial differences in orientation for the formulation of policy. But since they are solely models—which is to say, logical constructs, aids to systematic thinking rather than descriptions—they are not embodied in pure form in any social policy or, for that matter, in any particular productive enterprise. The practical policy problem lies not in whether one or the other is to be chosen but rather in what the balance between the two is to be in reality.

In industry, as well as in finance, commerce, and the civil service, the bureaucratic model is the norm, with a fairly minor role being played by the professional model. In the human services, however, the balance is more heavily weighted toward the professional model. Even so, within the human services the balance varies markedly. Welfare workers, for example, have a comparatively small amount of discretion in doing their work, and social workers also are subject to a comparatively large amount of hierarchical supervision (cf. Ruzek, 1973; Toren, 1969). Somewhat more opportunity to control their own work seems to accrue to schoolteachers (Marcus, 1973), and considerably more freedom from administrative direction is exercised by university teachers. For physicians and lawyers there has been even greater freedom to work on a discretionary basis, administrative personnel performing only "housekeeping" and not command functions. But over the past decade, in all the human services but most strikingly in the health services, there has been a distinct increase in pressure toward strengthening administrative powers and, in fact, an effort to encourage by legislation the consolidation and formal organization of everyday medical practices that in the past have been typically organized on an individual and informal basis. The status of medicine as an almost entirely independent profession, free of all administrative authority save that which is needed for the implementation of laws establishing its monopoly and autonomy, seems to be threatened (cf. Zola and Miller, 1973). The question for policy is, what is the balance between the two sources of social control over work which will yield the best kind of human service?

The tendency today in the health services is to juxtapose the two models for control in a very special way. Bureaucratic authority is used to establish a constraining framework of administrative controls around work settings within which professional authority is then nominally free to control the actual performance of work. (For a recent discussion of such "professional bureaucracy," see Heydebrand and Noell, 1973: 294–322.) Bureaucratic management thus exercises largely *indirect* social control over work, while the workers are given the opportunity to exercise their own *direct* controls over what they do within those indirect limits. What is in the process of changing, however, is the amount and extent of indirect bureaucratic controls: in an effort to reduce costs and increase accountability, they are growing. But the day-to-day work of doctoring goes on without the exercise of *direct* administrative controls. No rules and regulations specify how doctors should work, and no administrative supervisor gives them orders. What are in the administrative domain are solely formal accounting, reporting, and disbursement devices. The concrete work of providing service remains controlled, if controlled at all, by professionals.

Ostensibly, as I have noted already, the direct controls to be found in such a situation are those ascribed by the professional model. It is characteristic for official representatives of the profession and even sociologists (cf. Blau and Schoenherr, 1971: 350-352) to assume that the direct controls actually exercised in professional settings are in fact those ascribed by the formal model, even though the model is a conceptual rather than an empirical construct. However, even the model itself, as a model, is defective in that it conceptualizes the professional modes of social control with much less precision and detail than does the bureaucratic model. There is no theoretical elaboration of the nature of the controls employed and how they work, only general reference to interaction among colleagues and to the rather bizarre assumption that the "long period of training" somehow creates autonomous paragons who are what they are no matter what the pressures under which they work.

Most important, there has been too little empirical information collected to allow one to judge the degree to which the reality of professional social controls conforms in general with the model and how and why it varies. In contrast, there have been many studies showing how particular organizations deviate from the bureaucratic model. The assumption that effective direct controls operate among professionals is thus empirically moot. If the way health workers actually control their own and each other's way of providing health services does not conform to the assumptions of policy-makers, then the thrust of policy is bound to be blunted. Thus, realistic assessment of policy options, as well as of the success of established policy, requires knowing in some detail exactly what goes on at the level of everyday work—how that work is performed and what kind of direct social control is exercised over its performance.

THE LACK OF INFORMATION

In the health services, the physician is the key worker. As Fuchs put it, "it is impossible to understand the problems of medical care without understanding the physician. And it is impossible to make significant changes in the medical field without changing physician behavior" (Fuchs, 1974: 56). If this is true, then it is all the more important to know a great deal about physicians in practice. It is particularly important to know what kind of social control they exercise over one another, how they influence the quality of one another's performance, for that social control is the critical process that mediates between formal plan and formal outcome.

Critical though it may be, such information is almost nonexistent. There are, it is true, statistics about the geographical distribution, age, sex, income, training, specialization, and test performance of physicians, and there are some limited survey data, but there is little else that is reliable. The very large literature on the doctor is constituted almost wholly of the highly personal, autobiographical reflections of unusually successful, articulate practitioners whose experience is hardly representative. The best of what are available are studies by investigative journalists, who survey the available literature and, in the empirical tradition of journalism, report observations on medical settings and interviews with selected medical workers.

Thus, it has not been on the basis of any significant body of information about practice collected from physicians themselves that policy debate and choice have gone on. Insofar as information has been a resource for policy debate, it has been information about the health of the population, the patterns of utilization of health services, the "productivity" of various kinds of health workers and institutions, and the prices paid for services. These are all accounting data rather than explanatory data. When they are used to support arguments for financing and organizing care in a particular way, they must always be buttressed by implicit and untested, merely plausible assumptions about how physicians are motivated and how they do their work. But untested assumptions hardly constitute a good guide for decision making.

Let us take prepaid group practice as a policy choice. Since the 1930s, if not before that period, many reformers have felt that the traditional form of financing medical care on a personal, fee-for-service basis and of organizing medical care around individual entrepreneurs working by themselves in their privately owned and managed consulting rooms was responsible for limited access to care, poor coordination of services, and sometimes indifferent quality of care. They have argued for financing the cost of care by the insurance principle and for paying the doctor on a capitation or salary basis. The former method would eliminate burdening the ill with the cost of care precisely when they were in need, while the latter method would eliminate tempting the physician to give service for the sake of the fee rather than the need. (For a systematic discussion of the various methods of paying the doctor, the arguments for and against them, and international evidence of experience with them, see Glaser, 1970.) Furthermore, the reformers argued for organizing medical practice into medical groups or polyclinics—places where primary practitioners and consultants would all work together, taking care of the same patients and seeing each others' work. Recent legislation designed to encourage health maintenance organizations implies that prepaid group practice is the form of practice most approved of by present policy-makers (though the legislation also permits a "foundation" organization).

Given the extraordinary paucity of studies of full-fledged practicing physicians and the complete absence of information about physicians in group practice save for the surveys I shall cite in a later chapter, the decision to encourage prepaid group practice seemed to be based far more on fiscal and ideological grounds than on grounds of empirical evidence. Why should one expect physicians in a group to perform better than isolated physicians? In industry, sociologists have documented over and over again the fact that workers are an active force in determining the character of production. They assess production norms in the light of their own conceptions of a fair day's work; they develop and seek to preserve their own methods of doing their work irrespective of the dictates of their supervisors and those who design their jobs "scientifically"; and they are often able to develop common or collective modes of managing their work which deviate from managerial expectations and to maintain them by informal but powerful processes of direct social control. The direct social control processes operating among workers can operate separately and independently of those set up by organizational officials and can even sabotage production itself. Do such processes exist among physicians doctoring together in a medical group, and do they operate with the same effect?

Those who argue for group practice claim that bringing physicians

together into a common organization to cooperate in providing health
services is likely to create different and perhaps stronger processes of
social control than exist in the case of competitive, individual practice.
The *substance* of such strengthened control processes has always been
assumed to be positive—that is, to operate to *improve* medical performance. However, there is no logical reason why improved medical performance need be the outcome. The process can work in either a positive or a negative direction. Much more information about the way
physicians conceive of and deal with their work is required in order for
one to make a reasonably well-informed guess about the direction colleague control would take in group practice.

A MODEL MEDICAL GROUP

In partial redress of that shortcoming, I shall present in this book
information about the everyday level of medical work where services are
provided. I shall be concerned less with describing the variety of proposed policy schemes than with assessing how formal schemes are likely
to be carried out in light of the way physicians make sense of their work
and its problems. I shall present a descriptive analysis of how a number
of physicians, working in a fiscal and administrative framework of the
sort that has been used as a model for policy formation, turn the requirements of the formal economic and administrative framework of
their practice into concrete services. In that sense I shall be describing
the "processes intervening between input and outcome." I shall show
how, down at the level of everyday medical work, the physician trans-
forms the intent of the formal scheme to make it compatible with his own
conceptions of need, propriety, and convenience, conceptions unrecognized by or unknown to the formal planner.

The medical group I studied was not run-of-the-mill or merely representative of the entire range of medical practice in the United States.
Rather, it was a model medical group, deliberately set up to be as close
as possible to the ideal of liberal medical reformers. It was atypical and
ideal by almost every formal administrative standard. First, rather than
being merely a partnership of three to five physicians which cannot
possibly represent the full range of specialties, as is the case for the vast
majority of American medical groups (McNamara and Todd, 1970), it
was large enough to contain a sufficiently broad range of specialties to

permit it to offer fairly comprehensive services. During the time we studied it, there were on various occasions between 52 and 56 physicians responsible for the care of about 25,000 enrolled patients. About 30—the primary practitioners—were full time, while the remainder were part time.

Second, the qualifications of the practitioners in the medical group were well above the average for the medical profession as a whole. All the physicians had the advanced training and experience that made them eligible to take specialty board examinations, and many had in fact taken the examinations and been certified as "board specialists."

Third, the physicians' basic income from the medical group did not derive from fees paid for each service provided. Rather it derived from a prepaid service contract: for each patient enrolled in an insurance program that I will call here "the Medical-Surgical Plan" (or MSP), the medical group was given a flat annual sum, or capitation fee, out of which all medical-group workers, physicians and others, were paid. In return for that capitation sum, the medical group and its physicians were obliged to provide enrolled patients with medical and surgical services inside and outside of the hospital as well as most laboratory tests, Xrays, and the like, without making any additional charge to the patient for each individual service. Thus there was no necessary relationship between the services the physicians provided to any particular individual patient and the revenue obtained from that individual. In such a situation, reason some people, the physicians have an incentive to provide preventive services. This method of financing costs and paying the doctor represents a policy position that asserts that costs should be born by all patients, sick or well, instead of by the sick person only. Furthermore, once enrolled and insured, the patient is free to seek help for his complaints early, when they are most easily cured and when complications can be avoided: he will not be constrained to delay seeking help by the necessity of paying a fee, as he might be in traditional, entrepreneurial practice.

The medical group was even atypical of all other large prepaid-service-contract medical groups in the United States in that most of these groups—such as those connected with Kaiser-Permanente on the West Coast and the Health Insurance Plan of Greater New York—are partnerships, the physicians owning the group. In the medical group we studied, the physicians were employees on salary. The net sum available for salaries was ultimately raised or lowered by the number of costly services that were provided to the patients, but given the capitation scheme, reduction or increase in services did not have the immediate and direct effect on income that is found in the practice of the individual, free-for-service entrepreneur. This, again, is an ideal arrangement according to some policy-makers, who reason that, when on salary, the physician can concentrate on doing good medical work, relieved of the pressure to provide services for the income they yield and of the necessity to be preoccupied with "business."

Fourth, it may be noted that the insurance company responsible for enrolling members and financing the care they get was not as passive as have been most nongovernmental insuring organizations. It was committed to being sensitive to consumer needs, had its own subscriber-complaint office, and actually investigated complaints and sought redress from the medical group when appropriate. Furthermore, it conformed to the ideal by having a peer-review system: it used prestigious committees of "outside" physicians to perform periodic review of the quality of care provided by the medical group. During the time of the study, one of the specialty services of the medical group was visited, and a sample of its medical records was evaluated by the visitors both for completeness as records and for what the records implied about the judgment and competence of the specialists. Such review of ambulatory care was rare in the United States at the time of the study, and it is not common even now, though it is planned that present professional standards review organizations, which initially are concentrating on hospital care, will eventually be used to review ambulatory services as well.

In sum, as a formal entity, the medical group chosen for study satisfied most, if not all, of the formal administrative criteria that present-day policy-makers have laid down as most desirable for encouraging good and efficient medical care. It was financed by the insurance principle so the cost of care could be spread among all. Its service contract was fairly comprehensive in its coverage, although it excluded dental care, continuing psychiatric care, and the cost of drugs, eyeglasses, and the like. It minimized expense to the patient and left him free of economic constraints in seeking care.

In turn, the group-practice principle centralized care for the patient, bringing together in the same place all the primary practitioners and consultants who had to cooperate in providing that care. The physicians themselves had exceptionally high qualifications for performing their work well, and the capitation principle for providing their income assured that their choice to provide services could not be based on desire for a fee. All worked together in the same setting and saw the same patients, with a central record system to which each physician would add his notes and which each physician could examine. Therefore each physician's work could be open to the examination of the others, and each could be considerably more subject to the exercise of direct social control by the others than would be the case if they all worked separately, scattered about in their individual offices.

From the abstract point of view of policy planning, then, the administrative characteristics of the medical group came close to the ideal. But what actually happens within that framework? How is work carried out? What are the problems of work, and how are they coped with? And what is the process of social control operating among the doctors? That was what the study of the group practice undertook to find out. In the next chapter I shall discuss the operating problems of the medical group. In Part II, looking at each major problem separately, I shall discuss the various ways the physicians coped with them. After discussing the significance of those varied methods of doctoring, I shall turn, in Part III, to the analysis of those elements of the physicians' conceptions and practices which underlay the process of social control in the medical group—the rules governing performance that they recognized, the information that they obtained about each others' performance, the extent to which that information circulated among them, the role of the medical recqrd in the process, and, finally, their conception of the methods by which physicians' performance can and should be controlled. In Part IV I shall describe how social control actually operated in the medical group and conclude by assessing my findings in the light of the various options for the direction of policy in the future.

2:

The Medical Group, Its Problems, and Its Rules

The medical group was located in a residential area on the outer edge of a large city, near a large teaching hospital, and within easy driving distance of the suburbs beyond the city. The residential area was primarily blue and white collar in character, but it was in the process of deterioration as inner-city residents moved deeper and deeper into it and old residents, or their children, moved out. Since the group served primarily subscribers to the Medical-Surgical Plan, however, its patients did not include the unemployed poor and elderly. Rather the patient population was composed largely of the families of blue- and white-collar workers who subscribed to the Medical-Surgical Plan through their place of employment. The patients were, then, the core of urban Middle America.

The administrative organization of the medical group was ostensibly bureaucratic and rational. The chief administrative figure was a full-time medical director who did not practice medicine and who was responsible both to the insurance company and to the medical organization that legally owned the group. He was aided by a deputy director, a physician who practiced with a reduced case load and who performed various administrative functions that only a physician was thought able to do. The day-to-day executive work, however, was performed by a full-time layman with the title of administrator.

The administrator was essentially responsible for the nonmedical operations of the group, hiring, reprimanding, firing, organizing, and reorganizing the supportive semiprofessional, clerical, and service workers. He was also responsible for the supplies needed by the physicians and for setting up and monitoring their appointment schedules and their vacation and other coverage arrangements. Insofar as he also received telephone complaints from patients who had not yet complained to the insurance company's office, he inevitably became involved in professional issues. Indeed, on an informal level he was more involved in daily issues of professional practice than were the medical director or the

18

deputy director. He was assisted by two other administrative persons, one who served as the executive secretary of his office and the other who served as the immediate supervisor of receptionists and as the first-line administrative troubleshooter for patient relations.

These five persons, the medical director, deputy director, administrator, executive secretary, and supervisor, were the key administrative personnel in positions of responsibility. Authority and responsibility varied considerably from one to another, but since there were so few and since the precise title of each provides precise identification of the person, no distinction will be made between them in identifying administrative informants providing statements used in the exposition of this book. The word "administrator" will be used for all.

The physicians in the medical group obtained tenure after a probationary period of one year. Once obtained, tenure was defined as permanent and was revocable only by the vote of two-thirds of all of the physicians in the medical group. The physicians, technically employees, were represented by an elected Executive Committee that was involved in making recommendations concerning the structure and operation of the medical group. The administration provided it with the statistical and administrative information necessary for making informed recommendations. But, as we shall see in later chapters, the Executive Committee had no real formal authority even though as a matter of principle its desires were responded to positively in most instances. And, as we shall see, it was used as a major source of formal collegial pressure on errant colleagues.

THE PROBLEMS OF THE MEDICAL GROUP

The medical group had some distinct operating problems. These may be discussed in the context of those of its special, formal features that are thought by policy-makers to make for rational, economical, and high-quality medical care. Of those features, there is first the prepaid service contract itself, which allows the patient to request service without the constraint of a fee barrier and which, as we shall see later in this chapter, may lead physicians to feel that their relationship to their patients has been changed in problematic ways. Indeed, the patients themselves also may feel that the relationship has changed (Freidson, 1961). There is, in fact, survey evidence that rather more friction between doctors and patients existed in our medical group than in the* others. (For a description of the survey, see Freidson and Rhea, 1963.)

Forty-three of the group physicians completed the survey questionnaire, in which there was a series of questions asking them to compare their patients in group practice with those they had had experience with in solo practice. Those physicians who had never been in solo practice were asked to assess the difference anyway, since we were concerned primarily with the physicians' subjective responses and were not assuming that their comparisons were necessarily objectively accurate. In Table 1 is presented a comparison of the aggregate responses of the 43 physicians of the medical group with the 774 physicians from all the groups surveyed.

In addition, the administrator of the medical group, like others in a separate survey of administrators (described in Freidson and Rhea, 1963, and Freidson and Mann, 1971), was asked to characterize the nature and the seriousness of the operating problems of his medical group. The questionnaire presented six common patient complaints and asked the administrators to "indicate their rank order of importance in [their] group by marking the most frequent, '1,' the next most frequent, '2,' and so on, for as many as apply to [their] group." The administrator of the medical group we studied intensively ranked in first place the patient complaint "that the doctor is unsympathetic, 'cold.' " Of the administrators of the other medical groups who ranked this problem as one relevant to their organization, only 2 others ranked it first; 4, second; 5, third; 14, fourth; 15, fifth; and 19, sixth. Furthermore, the administrators of all the medical groups were asked to rank some of the things about which the doctors of their groups complained. The administrator of our group marked first, as the most common complaint by the doctors of the group, "inability to get along with patients." Of the 51 other administrators who ranked that complaint as a problem, 19 ranked it first; 18, second; 11, third; and 3, fourth in rank-order importance.

In still another set of questions, the administrator was asked to indicate on a five-point scale the degree to which certain problems were important in his group. One of the items, "Physicians complain that patients are overdemanding," was ranked by the administrator right at the midpoint. Such a midpoint response does not imply seriousness of

TABLE 1

"How do you think your medical group patients compare with patients in solo practice?"

ANSWER	PERCENTAGE OF PHYSICIANS IN FIELD STUDY (N= 43)	PERCENTAGE OF PHYSICIANS IN SURVEY (N = 774)
"Consideration for the doctor, willingness to tolerate minor inconveniences and not make unreasonable demands:"		
Group patients are **less considerate**	70	20
"Gratitude for your services:"		
Group patients are **less grateful**	44	18
"General satisfaction with the medical care they get:"		
Group patients are **less satisfied**	35	9
"Willingness to follow your instructions, accept your advice:"		
Group patients are **less willing**	28	6

the problem, but when we compare our administrator's response with the responses of other administrators we find that responses were skewed toward "no problem." Ninety-three of the 124 administrators responding checked one of the two points on the side of the scale indicating that physician complaints that patients were overdemanding constituted little or no problem in their groups. Thus the midpoint response was *comparatively* serious.

In a comparative sense, then, the survey evidence we collected pointed to the existence of problems in the doctor-patient relationship at the medical group which were more serious than was the case in most of the other large medical groups surveyed at the same time, including other large prepaid medical groups.[1] Indeed, during the year in which the field study was initiated, the number of officially recorded and investigated complaints by patients about their health care increased over the year before. During the same period there was a decline in the number of housecalls recorded for the year. Whether doctor-patient difficulties were created by the patients or the physicians or any number of other factors is a moot question. But our evidence gives fairly reasonable support to the proposition that those difficulties existed and that they were greater than in the majority of large-scale group medical practices surveyed at the time.

A problem related to tension in the doctor-patient relationship is suggested by the matter of work "overload." That, too, may be connected with the existence of a service contract and a panel practice requiring the subscriber to see only physicians in the medical group serving them. The service contract does not impose a significant fee barrier, and so it leaves patients free to ask for more service than might be the case otherwise. Such increased demand for services is generally thought to be a concomitant of prepayment plans (cf. Glaser, 1970). In the case of the well-known Kaiser-Permanente prepaid-group-practice plan, one might guess that it has also experienced "unnecessary" demand from the interest expressed by its president in developing methods by which the "worried well" could be diverted away from the physician's consulting room. (Garfield, 1970. For an intelligent critical discussion of Garfield's plan, see Mechanic, 1972:72–76.)

A prepaid-service-contract plan, then, can lead to a level of demand for services which can be experienced by physicians as overload. Indeed, quite apart from patient demand, the very organization of group practice can create overload. The former director of one Kaiser-Permanente group indicated that "since physicians cannot easily be recruited in direct and immediate response to sudden increases in membership size or in membership demand, increases in demand for physician service are met initially not by increases in the number of physicians but rather by increases in the productivity of the existing types of physicians" (Saward, Blank, and Greenlick, 1968:241). That is to say,

---

[1]As an aggregate, prepaid medical groups reported more problems than did fee-for-service medical groups. The medical group we studied intensively, however, reported comparatively more serious problems than did most of the other prepaid medical groups.

when demand increases, whether because of an epidemic, increased unnecessary demand, or an increase in eligible patients, it is inevitable that the physicians will experience overload, even if only temporarily.

Overload, of course, is an arbitrary notion based on what in industry is called a "production norm." Whether or not overload exists objectively is a function of the particular production norm one accepts. A workers' complaint about overload or "speedup" represents an evaluation based on their own conception of a fair day's work. Furthermore, there is evidence that for physicians the sense of being overloaded has important relationships to morale. (For national and international evidence on physicians' responses to a large patient load, see Mechanic, 1972: 192 and Mechanic, 1974: 156.) In the medical group we studied, workload was a constant source of complaint by the physicians. The administrator recognized the problem in his answers to our survey of administrators. Asked to indicate on a five-point scale the degree to which "physicians complain that they are overloaded, have too little time," he marked the fourth point of the scale, one point short of the extreme, "a fairly serious problem." Of the 124 other administrators responding, only 20 percent checked the same end of the scale, evidence that the medical group was in a small minority of groups whose physicians were concerned with overload. The physicians themselves, in their responses to the questionnaire, also emphasized the problem: 44 percent of those responding from the medical group, compared with 21 percent of the total universe of 774 physicians, checked the item "too many patients, overloaded."

For primary practitioners, workload is created by patient requests for services. For consultants, however, workload is created by referrals from primary practitioners. And, in our medical group, the consultants complained about unnecessary referrals. In his answer to our survey, the administrator was in a small minority of 6 percent in rating as a group problem the complaint by specialists "that family doctors and pediatricians refer to them excessively." And 42 percent of the physicians from our medical group, compared with only 11 percent of the total universe, indicated that there was too much referral to specialists in the group.

It should be apparent that there were operating problems in the medical group which were comparatively more serious than problems in most other large medical groups. They were not so serious as to prevent the group from serving the vast majority of its patients without incident or to prevent the group from sustaining a reputation for providing a high quality of medical care, but their magnitude was sufficiently great to merit attention and close examination.

Such problems may all be seen as issues of social control. And issues of social control may be conceived of as issues of developing agreement about the rules by which behavior will be evaluated and ordered. The most conspicuous of such rules are those asserted by the formal agent or official of an organization that is responsible for the behavior of the organization's participants and for its relationship to the community and governmental environment upon which it depends. The administrative rules represent the organizational agent's own claims about what the work is that members of the organization will do and how they will go about doing it: they constitute the medical group's public face. (For the administrative rules of the Kaiser-Permanente plan, see Somers, ed., 1971: 106–114.)

However, the formal rules may not reflect consensus among all participants and therefore may not operate as an effective mode of social control. Essential to evaluation of formal rules are data on how the productive workers—that is, the physicians—respond to those rules and thus how likely they are to conform to them. Their perspective is not necessarily the same as that of the administration. After all, while the medical director of a group may see increased demand for services as a call for at least temporary "increases in the productivity of the existing types of physicians," the physicians may see it as creating overload, if not constituting speedup. The physicians may not be as philosophical as their medical director and may be inclined to declare much of the demand intolerable because unnecessary or "trivial" (cf. Mechanic, 1974: 161). Let us begin our analysis, then, by examining the nature of the formal rules in the medical group and by contrasting the administrative and practitioner perspectives on the areas addressed by those rules.

OFFICE HOURS AND PRODUCTION NORMS

The physicians of the medical group did not deny the legitimacy of the administration and of its authority to lay out at least some rules binding on all. At the very least, the administration was seen to serve a necessary housekeeping or supportive function, doing the dirty work that the physicians would just as soon not have to do. It was also seen as a legitimate and necessary planner and coordinator of the activities going on in the group. In the abstract, the physicians conceded that the administration had to lay down rules that were binding on all. In the concrete, however, the problem was the extent to which rules could be written at all or, if written, the degree to which they could and should be enforced. This problem existed in even so ostensibly simple an area as hours of work. Let us examine first the administrative conception of the rules and then the way physicians responded to them.

The Administrative Conception

Most rules governing hours for professional workers are superficially of such a nature as to lead laymen to feel that featherbedding and work restriction are rife: the number of contact hours per week of physicians, professors, lawyers, and even schoolteachers is usually far below that of other workers. To make matters even more difficult, those few contact hours are all that can be measured and accounted for easily, the remaining time spent by the professional at work being more a matter of assumption than of objective accountability. In the medical group, the rule was that the full-time internists were supposed to put in 25.5 office hours per week, hours easily checked by the inspection of appointment books. In addition, however, there was the assumption that they would spend an equal number of hours performing patient services for which an accounting was not required. Let us examine the administrative rationale for its method of assigning office hours and appointment schedules and its assumption about other uses of time.

[E.F.: Approximately how many hours are full-time persons supposed to spend in the office?][2] He is scheduled for 25.5 hours a week in his office. This is roughly about half the amount of time that he would be required to devote to discharging his duties. That's exclusive of his hospital visits. In other words, whatever time he has to spend in the hospital, for instance when he is on service, he has to make rounds at least four days a week and usually they make rounds seven days a week, and that takes 2 or 3 hours; so when you are on service, that extra 12 or 16 hours a week that you are putting in is not included in this. The 25.5 hours are divided up so that he has some morning, some afternoon, and some evening hours. He has to have at least two evenings a week in which he has hours after six o'clock so that working people can

---

[2]Here, as elsewhere, brackets in the text of quoted material indicate editorial clarification or an interviewer's question or comment. In the later case, "E.F." represents Eliot Freidson and "B.R." represents Buford Rhea.

come to see him without taking time off from their jobs. [E.F.: Who does the scheduling for this?] They work out their own time, as long as they are within the range. [E.F.: How do you know whether they are within the range or not?] They have to submit their schedule [to the administration]. . . . [E.F.: Do you know anything about, or is there any preoccupation with the number of patients he actually sees in an hour, whether he works slowly or fast?] Again we've worked this out in a pragmatic way over the years so that we know that something in the neighborhood of 30 percent of the patients come in for an annual physical examination. So that he has to have some time scheduled that he can put aside for doing a physical examination on people who come in to him. In addition, he has to have [office] time for people whose illness is fairly complicated and consequently requires extensive examination. We figure that a half hour is an adequate time typically, but if it is a new patient, for example, and he needs to get the history, he needs another half hour naturally. But in general he's got the record in front of him of a patient he's known five or six years and he needs half an hour for a physical. For patients who are coming back for a check on their blood pressure, a follow-up diabetes, or want to determine they have recovered from whatever it was they had, if somebody is coming back to have a scar examined or to have another injection, why two minutes may be ample. So that over the years, figuring that the man works this 50-hour week, he works 47 weeks a year because he gets vacation and time to go to medical meetings, and so on, he can't really put in more than 2,200 and some hours, and in those 2,200 hours he's got to have travel time to make housecalls and time to make rounds to see his patients [in the hospital], we figure that the average that has been worked out by the doctors over the years is roughly three patients an hour in the office. When they are scheduled at 15-minute intervals for revisits, one half hour for physical examinations, this is apparently satisfactory. (ADMINISTRATOR)

Thus, in the medical group, physicians were contracted for a certain number of hours in their office. Within that period, a certain number of patient appointments were scheduled, the number scheduled per hour determined by a conception of the average amount of time it takes to properly serve an average patient—a conception that varies considerably among the various specialties, being as little as an average of two minutes per patient in dermatology and as much as an hour per patient in psychiatry. Scheduling was intended to protect the patients' convenience by minimizing the time they waited outside the consultation room and by preventing "assembly-line" practices of cramming more and more patients into fewer and fewer hours. There was little doubt that most of the physicians in the group approved in principle of such administrative rules and their enforcement.

I think if I called up and said, "Look, I'm going to be two hours late," he may say, "Make it up." This is a little annoying. But you have a lot of people. I can see his point of view. He may say, "If five of you do this 2 hours, that's 10 hours of work. Who is going to see those patients? They have to be seen, and don't tell me they don't exist, because they do." So they have to have some sort of control, and I recognize this. (#5—PRIMARY PRACTITIONER[3])

The problem, however, is how that principle should be applied in practice.

The Practitioners' Conception

We have already seen that many of the physicians felt an overwhelming sense of being overloaded with patients in relation to the number of hours they had available to see them. In times of overload, some of which was produced by "walk-ins" who ask for unscheduled consultation in the office, the only way many physicians could cope with the work was by staying late, past scheduled hours. Probably all of the practitioners can remember at least some occasions on which they had to stay late. Unlike in conventional union work contracts, however, overtime was not paid for. None of the physicians suggested such a contract, but they did feel that because they sometimes stayed late, they should feel free to come and go as they pleased, subject only to the demands of the patient load of the day, and should be able to schedule and handle the load as they pleased.

As in their arguments supporting their desires in every area of work, in the case of their arguments for freedom to manage their own office hours and appointments schedules, the physicians relied heavily on a special conception of themselves as professionals. I shall deal with that conception in much more detail later, but its essential elements must be mentioned here if we are to make sense of the way the physicians responded to administrative schemes. One element is the dignity of the physician as a member of a very special kind of occupation that differs markedly from the blue- and white-collar worker:

---

[3]Every physician interviewed was assigned a code number in order to avoid identification by name. In this report all quotations will be identified by code number only. A number of physicians who had previously worked at the medical group but, by the time of the study, had left to practice privately were also interviewed. They will be identified here by using "L" to precede their code number.

A doctor is not a laborer, and if the doctor's patients are taken care of adequately I can conceive of no other estimations of his conscientiousness. If he comes into his office two hours late, that is his business. If it happens so frequently and the patients are so up in arms and everybody is unhappy, that's something else. But that becomes obvious. But if a guy is a little late and leaves early and his patients are taken care of, it is all that matters. (#48—CONSULTANT)

Elaboration of this idea of the physician as a special kind of person often used the image of a physician being an adult rather than (like other workers) a child.

If somebody is going to be a physician, he has enough of a sense of responsibility to see his patients when he has to and if he hasn't had this, no matter what you do you're not going to change his way of practice. I mean, you hope that they are adult enough not to need supervision. (#18—PRIMARY PRACTITIONER)

Sustaining the idea of dignity, then, was the assumption that as physicians rather than clerks and as adults rather than children, the practitioners did not need external guidance because they were committed to performing their work conscientiously and had internalized that commitment sufficiently deeply so as to be guided and controlled from within. Given the sheer mechanical difficulty of precisely arranging and meeting office hours, the only viable arbiter had to be the physicians and their conscientious judgment. It followed, therefore, that the administration should trust them.

I had one run-in with the administrator which I chose to ignore him about and I tell my secretary to do the way I say, not the way he says, and I'll be responsible. He gets mad if you tell a patient to come in half an hour or three-quarters of an hour or an hour earlier during the last hour of your schedule. But 25 percent of the time somebody doesn't show and you just have to sit there for half an hour unable to do anything worthwhile, having to wait for somebody who may or may not come. . . . On the other hand I will agree that you can push the patient back and rush and you may not give him as much time as he should have. But in this case I want to do what's more convenient for me. I expect him to rely on my basic conscientiousness as a physician. He wants to rely on some scheme so if I'm not conscientious it will come out right anyway. (#1—PRIMARY PRACTITIONER)

These firmly held ideas did not prevent physicians from recognizing the possibility of abuse on the part of colleagues. But the imposition of rules designed to prevent abuse would restrict the physicians' own independence to make their own arrangements, and this possibility disturbed them more than abuse by colleagues. Being "checked up on" was resented by some even when they conceded their violations: trust was demanded, trust that there was good and appropriate justification for violation.

> I feel after spending a good number of years in the group a doctor should be trusted as to his time allotment. If he doesn't come in there is no need to question him. When he has to leave, there is no need to question him. There shouldn't be the attitude of the time clock. (#49—CONSULTANT)

Indeed, even when the necessity of punctuality was recognized and when there was no great irritation at administrative surveillance, the tendency was to assert that administrative pressure could, in any case, not be effective in motivating the doctor. Ultimately, the argument went, punctuality was motivated by the physician's own personal conscientiousness and concern for patients, not by external rules and their administrative enforcement.

> Every time I walk in late, I always feel guilty and then my drive to come on time, which isn't too successful, is motivated by my feelings for the patient rather than for the administration or [my] feeling [that] any administration is watching me. (#42—CONSULTANT)

In general, the assumption was that when the administrative rule of keeping official hours was broken by a physician, the physician's failure was not ill-intentioned or irresponsible: his very violation of the rule was made in the light of a responsible and well-intentioned assessment of his work. The fact that his work was not defined solely by his contact hours in the office or on call of course made it possible for a physician to excuse the violation of office-hour obligations by reference to extraoffice obligations. Thus, we see that while ostensibly precise and binding rules governing contact hours could be written into the physicians' contracts and could be accepted in principle by the physicians themselves, there could be only an *effort* to enforce them in the face of strongly sustained informal norms and practices that vitiate the precise and binding qualities of the rules.

HOUSECALL AND COVERAGE RULES

The Administrative Conception

In addition to establishing rules about the hours during which physicians were to be in their offices, and the number of patients they should see in that time, the administration established rules governing the allocation of responsibility in handling cases that were not scheduled in the office during appointed hours or that were jurisdictionally ambiguous. These rules specified who was responsible for making housecalls during office hours, in the evenings, and on weekends. In the medical group we studied, as was the case in the group studied by Wolfe and Badgley (1972), the housecall was perhaps the major focus of difficulties between physician and patient, being both an inconvenience for the physician and a kind of symbol of their status to both physician and patient.

The principles for rules governing housecalls were generated by the administration in light of the terms of MSP insurance coverage, which included "necessary" home visits. The obligation to make housecalls existed under the contract, but precise rules could not be formulated. The administration could allocate responsibility for *coverage*—that is, whose responsibility it was to make housecalls—but it could not specify when housecalls had to be made by the responsible physician. A sympathetic physician described the problem succinctly.

> The administration is caught in the middle, too, with this housecall business. . . . The decision about housecalls being necessary or not is a difficult thing . . . for a physician to make and almost impossible administratively. Obviously you can't go on every one, and how can someone without medical training make such a decision on the phone? (#31—CONSULTANT)

A member of the administration analyzed the problem and its dilemmas at greater length:

> Then sometimes there are justifiable complaints where there is a conflict between a doctor and a patient. He doesn't want to make the housecall; the kid's got 104 and the mother doesn't want to bring the kid out and while we may all believe today that it doesn't do the kid any harm to bring him out here with 104° temperature, I would still accept the fact that the mother is justified. [E.F.: The doctor should have made the housecall?] Yes, with 99 or 101 even

in a kid, if you say bring them down, you aren't going to do the kid any harm. When it gets to be 104, I think the doctor is wrong. Or when the mother calls up and says, "My kid's got a rash," and there are a lot of measles going around, and he says, "Your kid's got measles." I don't buy that; you've got to see them when they have a rash. Or the kid was in and was seen for an earache and medicine was prescribed and 12 hours later the mother calls back and says the ear is no better and the kid's fever is just as high. "I gave him the medicine." He had a shot of penicillin, and the doctor says, "Well, bring him in in the morning." That's for the birds, too, because after 12 hours the penicillin should have worked and the kid should be feeling better and so on. . . . It is not an area in which there is a standard because you have to say, (a) all patients should be seen. In this, they should see every patient and make every housecall and so on. Or else you have to say, (b) there are certain circumstances under which you can prescribe over the telephone. Once you say that, you know, then it is wide open, and the guy says, "Well, this is one of those circumstances when I thought I could prescribe over the telephone." [E.F.: You do in fact say that you can prescribe over the telephone?] No, we don't, no. We don't punish them for doing it, but the rule of the group is that every patient has to be seen. [E.F.: I see.] That's the rule. I don't enforce the rule because it is unenforceable. Actually it is because the telephone is a two-way weapon, or a two-edged sword. [E.F.: Is this a written rule? Is it part of the SOP (standard operating procedure) that a doctor gets when he comes in?] No, it is not written. It ought to be, but it isn't. (ADMINISTRATOR)

Ultimately, then, all the administration could do was indicate precisely who should be on duty and responsible for providing medical services at a given hour on a given day. And while service could not be refused to a patient who walked in off the street for emergency service, a housecall could be refused without the refusal violating a definite rule. But should a patient complain and the administration feel that a housecall should have been made, it could "discuss" the incident with the physician involved and seek to exert pressure designed to discourage overready refusal.

The Practitioners' Conception

A physician's refusal of a housecall did not necessarily only deprive the patient asking for it; it could also affect the physician's colleagues. It could merely defer the patient's request to a later occasion, when it was a different colleague's responsibility, and so make trouble for colleagues. If a housecall was refused during the day by the patient's own primary practitioner and the patient continued to feel sick after his own physician's hours were over, the patient might well call in the evening, at which time the person on duty for evening coverage might have to make the housecall or at least would have to take the trouble to refuse the housecall. Under the rules, if the person covering in the evening felt that the housecall was necessary, he had to go. But since the practitioners may have had different notions of what was necessary, the "day man," for example, being "tougher" on housecalls than the "night man," the night man could come to the conclusion that the day man had refused a necessary housecall and so had "sloughed off" the housecall onto him. Since there were no precise rules governing the making of housecalls, distinct violation could not be charged. Nonetheless, physicians who had to make what they regarded as somebody else's housecalls often felt they had been taken advantage of.

It would have aided the practitioners enormously if they had had a way of controlling such sloughing off. But to do so would have required precise rules on the basis of which one could sustain a charge of violation. Irritated as they may have been about sloughing off, most of the group physicians were opposed to establishing definite rules. They were philosophical about sloughing off, in part because they felt that it all balanced out in the long run and in part because they felt that it was difficult to judge when a housecall was really necessary so that they themselves could be proven to be as guilty as those they believed had sloughed off on them.

> Occasionally when I'm on a call I'll have a patient come in who had phoned his family doctor and sometimes I'll end up making a housecall on somebody who had called earlier [during his own physician's hours], but I've never really felt this was an overwhelming burden and I felt I'm probably guilty of the same thing, if guilt is the proper term. I don't feel I would knowingly turn down a sick patient who obviously needs a housecall. (#56—PRIMARY PRACTITIONER)

Typically, the general assumption was of conscientious good intent— that a physician would never knowingly turn down a sick patient. Even in the face of conceded exceptions to that assumption, when they felt that there was deliberate sloughing off, the physicians insisted on the right of discretion and resisted the specification of a hard-and-fast administrative rule that could be invoked to label sloughing off for what it was felt to be. When, as shall be discussed in a later chapter, an administrator urged establishing a definite rule specifying when housecalls *must* be made, the physicians were unanimous in rejecting the suggestion. Their rejection was epitomized by the question, "Why can't you trust us?" And, without a rule, there was little direct means of clearing the air of diffuse resentments standing between some of the physicians on occasions of heavy demand for housecalls.

RULES FOR MEDICAL PERFORMANCE

Of all the areas of work in medical practice, the most central is that of the examination, diagnosis, and treatment of the patient—the core work of medicine. Ultimately it is that core of medical performance which justifies the very existence of medical practice. But it is precisely there that articulated and self-conscious rules were least in evidence in the medical group. This is not to say that there is no consensus in medicine about good practice: there is not, after all, wide variation in the content of textbooks in medicine. But the presumption was that if a physician was hired with a bona fide license and with the residency and practice experience making him eligible for specialty board examinations, then what was in the textbooks was in him and need not be specified in detail. Nonetheless, some administrative devices related to medical performance did exist.

The Administrative Conception

There is general agreement that there are some definite rules for many elements of "good practice," perhaps the most obvious lying in what one does in the course of a routine physical examination—what one examines and what kind of laboratory tests one orders for patients of a given age, sex, and condition. Indeed, the administration's manual given to physicians who joined the group included statements like the following:

An annual health examination includes a complete history and physical examination, routine urinalysis, hematocrit, and serology. (GROUP MANUAL FOR PHYSICIANS)

There was included in the manual and in the medical record a form for the examination on which were printed the names of the various parts of the body to be examined—e.g., fundi, pharynx, abdomen—and some of the standard characterization of findings upon examination of such parts—e.g., that the abdomen is "soft. No distention. No tenderness or rigidity. No masses or viscera felt. No hernia. No CVA tenderness." For pediatrics, a detailed immunization schedule was included, specifying the age, by the month, at which various vaccines were to be administered. The manual's amount of detail dealing with medical performance was certainly equal to if not greater than the amount of detail dealing with salary, vacation time, office hours, and the like.

Clearly specification of medical performance was possible in at least some areas of work. But it was not done as specification. The spirit of the regulations concerning medical performance was clear when the language used in memoranda from the administration to physicians which dealt with medical procedures was compared with that which dealt with office hours, vacation time, and the like. As an example of the former, a memorandum read, "The following general rules are to *guide you* in carrying out our contractual obligations for the general health examinations" (italics added). In contrast, the words "guide," "guidelines," "suggested," and the like were never used in memoranda dealing with office hours and similar issues, though tact and middle-class politeness maximized phrases such as "please make sure that" and "physicians will be sure to" and avoided the use of a phrase such as "physicians must."

The Practitioners' Conceptions

Written standards constituting routines for examinations did exist, then, but as suggestions and guidelines rather than as rules. And while most physicians were aware of the existence of such standards, there did not seem to be a very strong sense that they or their colleagues had to follow them or that failure to follow them required investigation, discussion, or whatever.

We have routine forms for immunization which recently have been changed .... We don't really know, though, whether anyone in the department follows it, and I suspect that #69 goes his own way. Every once in a while when we see his charts—we routinely do, for example, patch tests—and we

know that he very seldom does them. I don't know why. (#15—PRIMARY
PRACTITIONER)

Indeed the older practitioners, who were more prone to stress the "clinical" rather than the "scientific" approach to practice, deprecated the tendency of younger persons to follow such rules for work-ups. One specified what he felt a "standard" meant.

> There should be a systematic way of going about this in the doctor's mind. I
> don't mean to imply that the doctor should be told to do something in that
> particular order. We simply hope that in going over a person over 40, he has
> touched on the salient features of our interest in a man over 40. I don't think a
> doctor should be told, "Here's your checklist. Take it, here we go, right down
> the line." This becomes much too mechanical, and it smacks too much of the
> administration hanging over your head, looking to take your chart [and] check
> item 1, 2, 3, 4, 5, 6, 7. (#37—CONSULTANT)

It follows that if a fixed routine is inappropriately mechanical, then skipping items of such a routine on occasion can be justified. Some physicians indeed mentioned skipping such standard elements of a routine physical examination as examining the fundi and the pharynx on occasions when the demand for service was particularly great and time short.

> In order to zero in on the problem when you listen to the heart, you have to
> listen just to the apex, because you get more feel in that than at the
> base. . . . You're likely to skip the fundoscopic examination of the eye and
> not want to examine the pharynx. You're sloppier as a doctor when you deal
> with group patients because of the load that is involved. I'd much rather take
> the time to be able to do it but I don't have the time. (#17—PRIMARY PRAC
> TITIONER)

Few made such direct statements of having skipped routine elements of an examination, but many more mentioned having "been tempted to skip" elements and "almost missing" conditions. There can be no doubt that skipping took place. One cannot help but wonder whether when skipping occurred an entry nonetheless was made by the physician beside such words as "fundi" and "pharynx" on the printed routine examination form in the medical chart. If so, then a formal administrative device designed to encourage a complete examination was obeyed pro forma but was subverted in reality by the physicians' conception of their right to exercise their own discretion.

ADMINISTRATIVE RULES AND PROFESSIONAL NORMS

In this chapter I described the medical group and the areas in which there were comparatively more serious problems in that group than in other medical groups of the time. Since such problems may be seen as failures of social control, and since, in any case, an essential aspect of an organization such as the medical group is its rules, I went on to describe the way the administration specified rules governing medical work and the way the physicians responded to them.

As we saw, the medical group had a number of written rules addressed to many elements of medical work. The service contract with patients was written, specifying coverage in precise detail. So was the formal letter of understanding with physicians, specifying salary, the total number of office hours, the number of hours to be offered in the evening and, in the case of primary practitioners, the number of patients, or panel size, for which the worker would be responsible. The physicians themselves could work out coverage arrangements, but they had to be written and approved by the administration. Specific rules governing jurisdiction and responsibility in the event of functional overlap between specialties were also worked out among the parties concerned. Written routines and schedules for various facets of medical care—the annual physical examination and immunization for children being those selected for discussion—also existed. Nonetheless, it was questionable that they reflected or controlled the substance of the work performed and the manner in which it was performed. Conformity to all the formal rules related to medical work, even those dealing with the superficially simple issue of putting in a specified number of hours for a specified sum of money, was problematic.

This indecisiveness of the formal rules has been noted in much of the literature on organizations in which the prime participants are full-fledged professionals (cf. Goss, 1961, 1963; Smigel, 1964; and Scott, 1965). Weakness of administrative rules should not itself make for tension and difficulties, however, so long as other effective rules order performance. Indeed, in the case of such workers as physicians, professional norms are supposed to be that source of effective social control (cf. Parsons, 1968). However, as we shall see, professional norms did not really provide a sufficient basis for consensus about the rules governing the way one dealt with patients or, for that matter, colleagues. This was so because the professional norms seemed to be predicated on assumptions rooted in the entrepreneurial marketplace that developed historically as the institutional framework of Western medicine. The normative models for both patient and colleague relations were based on fee-for-service practice and did not equip the physicians for dealing with prepaid-service-contract group practice. Neither administrative rules nor professional norms were sufficiently effective to sustain consensus, and so the physicians chose a variety of incompatible and conflicting modes of coping with their work problems. In order to understand this situation and its consequences, let us examine the varied stances toward patients and the modes chosen to cope with the problems of work posed by the demands of patients.

Coping with Work Problems

3:
Stances Toward Demand and Supply

Ultimately, the health insurance contract had more to do with the rules governing the terms of doctor work than did the administration. The absolute income available for paying the doctors derived primarily from the MSP contract, which specified a given sum per year per insured person or family, plus additional sums computed by a complicated formula not important for present purposes. The administration of the medical group could decide how to divide up the contract income among the doctors but had to work within the absolute limits of that income. By the same token, critical aspects of the conditions of work stemmed more from the terms of the service contract than from the choice and action of the administration. For example, the most important complaint of the physicians about the conditions of work in the medical group was of overload—of having to provide more services in a given period of time than was considered reasonable. In a loose sense, such overload was a direct function of the prepaid service contract that presupposed the group, closed-panel practice.

In a more precise sense, the physicians created the very possibility of conceiving of their workload as overload by the way they made sense of their group practice. Living in a period when private practice was the taken-for-granted normal mode of organizing medical work and when human behavior was most plausibly interpreted as being motivated by economic self-interest, they constantly compared their experience with patients and colleagues in their group practice with what they would expect in solo, entrepreneurial practice, real or imagined. Their conceptions of solo, entrepreneurial practice established many of the basic parameters of what was normal and acceptable about their work and of what methods they were likely to think of and use to cope with, if not solve, their problems of work. Indeed, some could, in the light of traditional practice, see both themselves and their patients locked into an "unnatural" situation in which neither had any freedom of choice, in which both were in some sense trapped.

TRAPPED

Many physicians spoke of themselves as being helpless and exploited, using words such as "trapped," "slaves," and "servitor" to describe their position.

> Group practice is busier than a busy private practice because there is no economic barrier that confronts the patient when he wants to go see the doctor. . . . The doctor-patient relationship is disturbed because the patient has contracted for prepaid service and the doctor instead of being a consultant is becoming more or less a servitor, someone that the patient calls on when he thinks he needs it. The patient is in the driver's seat, so to speak. (L24—PRIMARY PRACTITIONER)

Since the contract was for all "necessary" services, however, it was hardly accurate to say that the physicians had to provide every service the patient asked for. They could, after all, refuse a service as unnecessary. But to do so would require a degree of interaction with patients to which the physicians were unaccustomed. The issue was the absence of a mechanism that relieved the physicians of the necessity of refusing a service, rather than the formal contract. The physicians were responding to the absence of the out-of-pocket fee that was a prerequisite for service in private practice and that was thought to lead prospective patients to restrict their demands for services.

> The easiest patient is the private patient. Look, they never call me at night except in extreme emergencies. If I tell them to bring the child to my office they'll always bring it in because there is a difference of four dollars [saved between the fee for a home and for an office visit], which means a lot. [The group patients] treat the doctor like he was a slave. "I paid you [in advance], you come here." (#25—PRIMARY PRACTITIONER)

The fee was seen as a device that forced *patients* to discriminate between the important and the unimportant, so that they would not bother the doctor by requesting an unimportant service unless they were willing to provide the physician with an immediate financial reward in the form of a direct fee. Thus, the physicians conceived of the fee as a barrier that operated before patients ever saw their doctor, thereby freeing the physicians of having to expend energy in actually refusing a service to a patient or in persuading patients to withdraw or modify their requests for service. It was not normal to have to indulge in such interaction with patients.

In addition to the way that the service contract contributed to the physicians' feeling of being trapped, the closed panel characteristic of the medical group also contributed to that feeling. Some physicians believed that the patients also may have felt trapped, since, in order to receive the benefits of their contract, they could not use any physician of their choice; they had to use the services of physicians employed by the medical group. Indeed, even within the medical group, they might have to accept someone other than the one they wanted if the latter's allotted panel were filled; when they were referred to a consultant, they were supposed to see the person with open appointment time and not an individual of their choice.

> They are more or less caught in a trap and can't go to another doctor. I know many who come in and can't stand the sight of me, and yet they still come in. Apparently they have no other choice or they're afraid to make another choice. (#26—CONSULTANT)

In contrast, entrepreneurial practice was seen (somewhat arbitrarily) as an arena for the patient's free choice, a situation that the physicians themselves considered gratifying because of their pride in having been chosen as an individual rather than as someone who happened to have had appointment time free or had an opening on his panel.

> People that come to me privately come to me because they were recommended by a friend who has been satisfied. . . . This is different from a situation where you are assigned a doctor. (#52—CONSULTANT)

Some felt a loss of the "personal prestige a doctor gets when a patient comes to him" (#42—CONSULTANT).

The closed-panel element of the group also restricted the *physician's* choice of patients, a freedom of choice thought to inhere in traditional entrepreneurial practice. Entrepreneurial practitioners were believed free to refuse services and discourage patients from returning should they choose to give up the fee or potential lay referrals.

> In private practice, if somebody is giving you a hard time, and they will, you can just stiffen your own position so that either they would accept you or they can go find themselves another doctor. (L6—PRIMARY PRACTITIONER)

The option of dropping a patient was not freely available to the group physicians, however. The reason was not to be found in a fear of loss of fees but rather in the very fact of being a participant in a cooperatively organized practice. When physicians form a closed-panel group rather than constitute an aggregate of, at best, only loosely cooperating individual practitioners in a community, they cannot act simply as individuals and drop a patient who may be troublesome to them because that patient can only transfer to a group colleague. If each person dropped his problem patients, while he might get rid of the ones he had, he would get in return the problem patients his colleagues had dropped, as his colleagues would get his. So the pressure was to "live with" such patients and to try to manage them as best one can.

> You are trapped. You can't transfer all your [patient] problems to someone else [in the medical group] because they're going to be problems to them too. (L12—PRIMARY PRACTITIONER)

Thus, the physicians were prone to see themselves as being in a situation in which the safety valves of individual, fee-for-service practice had been tied down and work pressure increased. The service contract was thought to increase patient demand for services while at the same time to prevent the physician from reducing that demand by erecting (or increasing) a fee barrier. The closed-panel arrangement restricted the patients' demands to those physicians working cooperatively in the medical group, so the physicians could not cope with the pressure by yet another traditional method, that of encouraging the patient to go elsewhere for service. Forced to remain and work within the system, trapped, both physician and patient could not avoid the necessity of negotiating with each other directly to a degree to which neither was accustomed. Demands that rarely had to be faced in traditional entrepreneurial, individual practice could not be avoided, and new, or at least more extensive, forms of interaction had to be undertaken. Traditional problems in the doctor-patient relationship required new solutions. There is no wonder, then, that there were tensions in the doctor-patient relationship.

PARADIGMATIC MODES OF COPING

The basic interpersonal paradigm of a problematic doctor-patient relationship may be seen as a conflict between perspectives and a struggle for control over services. From their perspective, patients believe they need a particular service; from theirs, the physicians seek to employ their own criteria of need and propriety. That conflict of perspectives takes place in a social and economic marketplace that provides resources to be used to reinforce the negotiation of the one or the other position. In the case of medicine in the recent past of the United States, the marketplace has been organized on a fee-for-service basis, practitioners being entrepreneurs, nominally competing with each other for the fees of prospective patients. The *merchant-customer relationship* has been emphasized.

The fee the patient is willing and able to pay together with the economic security of the physician's practice constitute the elements that are of strategic importance to entrepreneurial practice. If the physician's practice is well enough established, he can refuse service he does not want to give or does not believe necessary to give, even though he loses a fee and possibly a patient.

> In private practice of course you have problems with patients being demanding. But as I say, if you find a situation that involves a personality clash, or where you feel you don't need to make a housecall, you say, "I can't go over now," the water seeks its own level, and they get another doctor, I suppose. (L2—PRIMARY PRACTITIONER)

Conversely, if a physician wants to gain the fee and reduce the chance of losing the patient, he may give the patient the service requested even if he believes it to be unnecessary.

> I gather from my friends that . . . you need to succumb to [patients'] desires if you think that is the only way you can hold them. Often you have to . . . give up what you'd like to do in favor of what the patient expects you to do. (#9—PRIMARY PRACTITIONER)

Like merchants, physicians in private practice are concerned with maintaining or increasing their income either by forging such an invulnerable monopoly over services that patients must "take it or leave it" at whatever price the physicians ask or by giving enough patients what they want that the physicians have a secure trade at an income level they wish.

Patients can, if the marketplace is competitive enough and if they have the funds, play the customer by shopping around for practitioners whom they like and who will provide them with the services they want at a price they are willing to pay.

> In private practice [in this city] if a patient is unhappy he leaves the doctor. There must be 10 to 20 percent turnover every year. People pay for services the way you go to pay for a suit of clothes. You feel you have a free choice and if you are dissatisfied you discard the suit or discard the doctor. (#12—PRIMARY PRACTITIONER)

Before taking the trouble of looking for another practitioner, however, patient-customers may attempt to exert pressure by implying that if they do not get what they want, they will find someone else.

> Patients have the feeling in private practice that you are on a competitive basis in making money, and they threaten you with that indirectly. If you don't like to go out at night, somebody else will. (#23—PRIMARY PRACTITIONER)

Surely the pattern is familiar enough to require no further elaboration or evidence of its presence in traditional entrepreneurial practice.

In contrast to these marketplace roles, there are those most often ascribed to doctor and patient by sociologists—those of the *expert-layman relationship*. (A fairly pure elaboration of that relationship is to be found in the classic statement by Parsons, 1951.) The layman is defined as someone who has a problem or difficulty he wishes resolved but who does not have the special knowledge and skill needed to do so. He seeks out someone who does have the necessary knowledge and skill and cooperates with this person so that his difficulty can be managed, if not resolved. In dealing with the expert, the layman is supposed to suspend his own judgment and instead follow the advice of the expert, who is considered to have superior knowledge and better judgment. As I have pointed out elsewhere (Freidson, 1970a: 127–164), when there are differences of opinion of such a character that patients cannot bring themselves to cooperate, the generic response of the expert is to attempt to gain the patients' cooperation by persuading them on the basis of the evidence he produces to show that it would be in their interest to cooperate and follow the recommended course. To *order* them to comply or to gain compliance by some other form of coercion or pressure is a contradiction of the essence of expertise and its authority. Analytically, expertise gains its authority by its persuasive demonstration of special knowledge and skill relevant to particular problems requiring solution. It is the antithesis of the authority of office.

As a profession, however, medicine represents not only a full-time occupation possessed of expertise which participates in a marketplace where it sells its labor for a profit, but also, more particularly, an occupation that has gained a specially protected position in the marketplace and a set of formal prerogatives that grant it some degree of official authority. For example, the mere possession of a legal license to practice allows the physician to officially certify death or disability and to authorize pharmacists to dispense a variety of powerful and dangerous drugs. Here, albeit in rudimentary form, we find yet a third pair of roles by which to characterize the doctor-patient relationship—those of *the bureaucratic official and client*. The latter seeks a given service from the former, who has control over access to services. The client seeks to establish his need and his right, while the official seeks to establish his eligibility before providing service or access to goods or services. In theory, both are bound by a set of rules that define the rights and duties of the participants, and each makes reference to the rules in making and evaluating claims. In a rational-legal form of administration, both have a right of appeal to some higher authority that is empowered to mediate and resolve their differences. (For the classic treatment, see Weber, 1947.)

In the predominant form of practice in the present-day United States, the physician is more likely to be playing a blend of the roles of merchant and expert than the role of official, though the latter is real enough and too important to be ignored. It is, after all, his status as an official which gives the physician a protected marketplace in which to be a merchant. Nonetheless, to be a true official virtually precludes being a merchant, so that only in special instances in the United States can we find medical practice that offers the possibility of taking the role of official on an everyday rather than occasional basis and which minimizes the possibility of playing the merchant role.

The medical group we studied was just such a special instance, for it eliminated the fee and discouraged the profit motive, while setting up its physicians as official gatekeepers to services specified in a formal contract with patients by an insurance agency with supervisory powers of its own. The contract laid down the basic set of rights and obligations and established the position of the physician as an official gatekeeper to services. Under the rules, primary practitioners authorized the provision of a whole array of services—not only their own but also those of consultants who, even though covered in the contract, could not see a patient without an official referral, and the services of laboratories, which could not provide covered tests without an official group physician signature.

However, the situation that created the option for the physicians of being more officials and less merchants than was traditional also created the option for patients of being more bureaucratic clients and less shoppers or customers. Just as inability to function like a free merchant created discomfort for some of the physicians, so did the untraditional problems of management created by the patient who could not "take his business elsewhere" and who instead acted like a bureaucratic client who could demand service on the basis of his rights under the formal terms of his contract, for which he had already paid. The physicians were confronted with a style of demand for which they were not prepared; indeed, they were confronted by a new kind of demanding patient.

PATIENT STANCES TOWARD DEMAND

In the physicians' own conversations, they did not talk to each other or to the interviewers about their routines. They talked about their crises. They did not talk about slow days, but about those days when the work pressure seemed overwhelming. They rarely talked about "good" patients unless they received some unusual letter of thanks, card, or gift of which they were proud; they talked incessantly about the problems they had with patients. They almost never talked about routine diagnoses and their routine management, but they talked often about the anomaly, the interesting case, or one of their goofs. It was by the problematic that they symbolized their work, and it was in terms of the problematic, even when it constituted a small proportion of their work, that they evaluated their practice. Thus, it should be understood that while the number of demanding patients was statistically small, and work in the medical group was largely routine and unproblematic, the physicians tended to evaluate the satisfactions of their work on the basis of that small proportion that was problematic. Indeed, many who left the medical group explained their decision by referring to the kind of demanding patient they had to deal with in the group, even while conceding that the number of such patients was small. What was the "demanding patient"?

Obviously, a patient can demand a service in a number of ways and with a variety of supportive resources. And while they were not precise in their discriminations, the physicians did seem to recognize differences among those patients they considered to be demanding—that is, those whose requests for service were, in their eyes, excessive and undesirable. Their criteria were based largely on the stance the patient took toward asking for service and on the medical character of his presenting complaints. By these criteria, they were prone to discriminate two basic types of demanding patients—one dictatorial and the other supplicant.

> There are people who . . . make a diagnosis and call up and demand that we be there. They don't call asking for advice, in other words. They have the attitude . . . "I have decided this is necessary, and you come." Another type of demanding patient would be someone filled with anxiety and asks for many calls for minor things because they are anxious. (#2—PRIMARY PRACTITIONER)

Of the two, one should be familiar to the informed reader as the ambulatory, community-practice version of what is called a "crock" by medical students and house staff working in medical-school clinics and teaching hospitals. (For example, see Becker et al., 1961.) This kind of patient adopts the stance of the *layman* and treats the physician respectfully as the expert, but he asks for services that the physician does not feel equipped to give. The good patient who adopts the layman stance is one who seeks service only when it is necessary and appropriate—that is, he seeks service only when his complaint is considered by the physician to be important rather than trivial and only when it refers to a condition that the physician feels he can treat effectively. If the physician designates the patient's complaint as something unimportant or something for which nothing can be done, the good patient accepts the physician's word and does not bother him again for the same complaint.

The demanding patient, in contrast, presented complaints that the physicians regarded as trivial and which they believed to be untreatable because their cause was psychological rather than medical. All the physicians had to use on the patient were what they considered to be palliative forms of treatment rather than cure. They were irritated by such patients because they required the time to be babied, rather than being able to be treated instrumentally, and because they believed them

to be "well, or have the same kind of anxieties we all have" (#1—
PRIMARY PRACTITIONER). Furthermore, such a patient confronted the
doctor with failure; he or she "can never be reassured. You know you
are not getting anywhere with him and you just have to listen to him, the
same chronic minor complaints and the same business" (#2—PRIMARY
PRACTITIONER). "I'm just not satisfied with my results, and the patient
just keeps coming back, worse than ever" (#11—PRIMARY PRAC-
TITIONER). Finally, some physicians worried about the possibility of
overlooking something real among the diverse imaginary complaints of
such a patient.

> The greatest difficulty is that people with any sort of psychosomatic complaint
> are just as likely to come down with organic illness as anybody else, and
> because they keep complaining all the time an organic illness is easily over-
> looked. . . . One was almost overlooked because she was psychoneurotic.
> She had a CA of the uterus for which I sent her to the gynecologist. I sent her
> because she had some unexplained bleeding, and he, knowing her too, tended
> to brush it aside, and she had to see him two or three times because he decided
> it was just the usual [psychosomatic] complaint. I sent her back twice.
> (#24—PRIMARY PRACTITIONER)

But while these psychologically demanding patients filled some of the
physicians with irritation and even despair, they did not fill them with
shock and outrage. After all, they begged for service and did not directly
question the physician's status as expert. The institutional framework in
which services were offered was irrelevant to the stance these
psychologically demanding patients assumed in requesting service except insofar as it might make their requests less frequent because of a fee
barrier or more frequent because of a prepaid service contract. In contrast, it was those patients who made deliberate and aggressive use of
the possibility of pressure on the doctor offered by the institutional
framework of practice—whether their complaints were trivial or serious,
psychosomatic or organic—who constituted the other kind of demanding
patient. And that kind of patient filled the physicians with shock and
outrage.

One manifestation of this type, met within entrepreneurial practice,
assumed the stance of the aggressive *customer:*

> There is no respect for the doctor even in private practice. A patient was
> nasty to me because I was rather late in making the housecall. The patient
> said, "If I tell a doctor to come at eleven, you have to be here at eleven." I

came at quarter past eleven. Describing this to other doctors, one of them said, "You made a mistake. Medicine is like any business, you've got to please your client. You've got to apologize and try better the next time." I was shocked at the lack of respect shown the doctor. (#25—PRIMARY PRAC-TITIONER)

By and large, however, the freedom of the physician with a secure practice, and the mobility and lack of contractual commitment on the part of the financially competent patient, in the context of a comparatively competitive urban-practice setting, made such stories of patients playing the demanding-customer role rare. The impression was given that in fee-for-service, entrepreneurial practice, aggressive confrontations were rare because the patient withdrew instead to shop around among other practitioners.

The physicians felt that confrontation was far more likely in prepaid group practice than in entrepreneurial practice.

People who can pay will demand the same thing on the outside, too, from their paid doctor. If they don't get the service, they'll call somebody else, that's all. But they are not going to call him a so-and-so because they don't make out. . . . "All right, I'll get somebody else," and that's the end of it. But here, they must get my service because they've paid for it, you see. It would be nice if they didn't have to make the trip [to the medical group], and they have comprehensive medical care, so they say, "Why don't *you* come over [on a housecall instead]?" There are very few such people, but all you need is one every once in a while. (#5—PRIMARY PRACTITIONER)

Many of the physicians discussed this kind of patient as if he were a demanding customer in a competitive market, and their reports of such patients' own terminology in making demands—using such phrases as "you're paid," or "I'm paid"—support such an interpretation. However, I am inclined to feel that the emphasis is mainly one based on the settled habit of both physicians and patients to see medical care in terms of interaction in the marketplace even when prepaid group practice in effect precluded the possibility for everyday interaction to go on in monetary, fee-for-service terms. The medical group entailed periodic negotiation of terms, it is true, but on an everyday basis it entailed a stable contractual arrangement that specified rights to demand and obligations to supply services of specified kinds. Negotiation took place not in cash terms but in bureaucratic, contractual terms. To be demanding in such circumstances was to adopt the stance of an aggressive *bureau-*

cratic client, not that of a customer. Clients did not, like customers, threaten to take their business elsewhere; they demanded their rights under their contract and threatened bureaucratic trouble. A long-time, highly respected member of the medical group described how difficult it was for many physicians to accept demands phrased in such terms.

> It's one of the hardest things for a new man to take—the feeling that the patient can call you and insist that unless you want to go through a great deal of unpleasantness you are obligated to go and see him if he feels honestly that he deserves to be seen and is anxious. The feeling that the patient has this power under his contract to insist and demand that you come to see him, even if you don't think it is medically justified, is a hard thing for some men to swallow. (#21—PRIMARY PRACTITIONER)

The power of the contract implied correctly that such patients, aggressively playing the role of bureaucratic clients, quite naturally and appropriately to the role threatened to employ or actually employed devices for redress made available to them by the institutional framework of the group practice. They could complain to the administration of the medical group or to the office established by the insuring organization to receive and investigate complaints. And on occasion they could make claims for compensation for expenses incurred out of pocket during the course of obtaining justified medical care outside the medical group after they were refused service by a group practitioner. While the contract assured only necessary care, neither did it define it nor would the physicians allow a definition. Such ambiguity in a bureaucratic context contained the potential for much controversy of a sort that most of the physicians would rather have avoided.

It follows that, just as effective customer behavior in the market requires the special characteristics possessing the wherewithal along with the intellectual and social capacities required for calculating advantage and bargaining, so does effective aggressiveness in a bureaucracy have its personal prerequisites. The more familiar with bureaucratic procedures; the more able to read, use, and understand the language of contracts; the more verbal; and the more respectable the status, the more likely it is that a patient can be an effectively aggressive bureaucratic client. The 17 physicians who did generalize about the social characteristics of demanding patients yielded, in sum, a caricature of the demanding patient as a female schoolteacher, well enough educated to be capable of articulate and critical questioning and letter-writing, experienced with bureaucratic procedures, of high enough social status to be sensitive to slight and to gain attention when making a complaint, and, in the physicians' eyes, neurotically motivated to be demanding in the first place. If we add political connections to this—connections as a trade union official, friendship with a local political figure, and the like—we complete the basic portrait of the social characteristics of the kind of demanding patient who was generic to the prepaid-service-contract practice of the medical group.

PHYSICIAN STANCES TOWARD SUPPLY

Just as we can delineate various stances of patients in demanding services, so can we delineate the stances available to physicians in supplying these services—more particularly, the way they value, direct, evaluate, and thus supply their services. There is the stance of the *expert*, in which neither personal gain nor administratively defined efficiency is an essential element (cf. Hughes, 1971; Parsons, 1968; and Veblen, 1964). The central focus of his work is the work itself, the ends of which he seeks to both define and determine himself. His goal is to perform his work well, as "well" is defined by the colleague group. Thus his focus is on the intrinsic quality of the work as such, and his preoccupation is with the problems posed to performance by the characteristics of the object of work—that is, by the raw materials, whether physical or human, with which he must work and by the circumstances surrounding the work. Work is evaluated by its intrinsic interest, its special challenge to workmanship. The amount of work that gets done, in the sense of the number of products or items, and the cost of that work in light of the income from it, are subsidiary issues. The emphasis is not on standardizing work units or products but on the peculiarities of individual cases, on the essentially unstandardizable, esoteric complexity of the work and its challenges. Supply of goods or services is carried out on the basis of judgment about the intrinsic character of the work implied by the source of demand and not on the basis of either standard rules or market gain.

In the case of the *merchant*, or entrepreneur, the essential purpose of undertaking such an activity as providing a service is profit in the form of personal gain (Smith, 1970). Both quantity and quality of work are a function of such gain, within the practical limits to assessing gain posed by the competitive situation and prevailing ideas of a reasonable, or at least not outrageous and criminal, profit. Thus, the merchant's supply of services expands and contracts in quantity and quality as the possibility of gain, and his personal interest in gain, increases or decreases. Problems of work tend to get reduced to monetary issues and to be evaluated in monetary terms.

Finally, we may say that the bureaucratic *official* is oriented toward efficiency gained by conformity with enforceable rules (Weber, 1947). He provides services on a basis in which, ideally, personal monetary profit plays no part. The framework of effectively enforced rules and the work resources he has available provide the practical limits of what he can do. The pressure of his striving for rationalization leads him to reduce issues of quality of work to standardized quantities, given the assumption that a minimum standard of quality is guaranteed by the substance of the rules that establish both the qualifications prerequisite for holding office and at least the broad parameters of the tasks involved. Through the official's working in concert with fellow officials, collective work norms arise independently of the formal rules, and the fellow officials, too, by their notions of a fair day's work, a good or reasonable job, press for a standardized level and direction of effort.

Every one of those stances toward work was a possibility for physicians, though under given circumstances some are more difficult to assume than others. The merchant stance was rather difficult to assume in the medical group and so, to a lesser degree, was the expert stance. The easiest stance to assume was, as we shall see, that of the official, but such a stance was by no means inevitable. And while in some cases the sheer complexity of the empirical considerations involved precluded making precise reference to these stances, it may be useful to keep them in mind as we turn to examine the empirical descriptions of how the physicians responded to the patients' demands for services, what services they chose to restrict the supply of, and what they chose to supply freely.

4:

Creating Supply for Demand

Of all the services supplied by the medical group under the terms of the contract, the housecall was the most problematic. This appeared to be the case because by virtually no available criteria could the legitimacy of demand be satisfactorily evaluated in advance. As a subscriber, the patient was entitled to housecalls without additional payment, but only at the discretion of the physician: no automatic bureaucratic criteria could be used. Medical need was the ostensible criterion of legitimacy, but all the physicians had as evidence by which to evaluate such need was a layman's description of complaints over the telephone; and often, when they were on duty at night, all the information they had was a description of complaints over the telephone by a layman who was not their patient and thus whose judgment was unfamiliar to them.

The problem was intensified by the fact that the housecall represented a largely unwanted expenditure of time and energy on the part of the physician. It was, therefore, no wonder that housecalls were a problem and that the physicians of the medical group were constantly complaining about patients' demands for housecalls. The anecdotes they told each other, as Blau, 1955, showed in an entirely different context, functioned to gain mutual support of their disinclination to make such housecalls but also revealed their evaluation of them.

The anecdotes often emphasized the trivial and "inconsiderate" character of the demand.

> In one case they called three or four times insisting I get there right away to climb five flights of stairs. In one case, when I got there, they said, "Well, the baby is sleeping. We don't want to wake him up. Go away." (#28—PRIMARY PRACTITIONER)

Indeed, the trivial must be emphasized to justify refusal to make housecalls because making housecalls was clearly required in the case of a true emergency—an unanticipated, sudden onset of life-threatening symptoms. The physicians refused to justify housecalls simply because they were convenient for the patient; they were *in*convenient for the physician and thus could have been justified only by serious medical need that prevented the patient from traveling to see the physician in the office.

> I told her I would no more think of calling someone for insomnia to come out [on a housecall] when it is zero degrees out to give a shot of barbiturate than I would think of jumping off the [local] Bridge. And of course I didn't go. (#7—PRIMARY PRACTITIONER)

Furthermore, the demand for a housecall was considered to demean the physicians and point to their own lack of status. The patient would not expect anyone really important, such as a true specialist, to make a housecall.

> A surgeon won't go out to a house to see an acute appendicitis with 103°. . . . Yet if a pediatrician told them, "Bring the child in so I can take a look at him," "Oh, no, he's got a temperature, I can't take the child out." (#12— PRIMARY PRACTITIONER)

Finally, there was the purely instrumental problem of diagnosing, let alone treating, an ailment in the home rather than in a setting where a variety of both diagnostic and therapeutic resources was available.

> It was . . . a youngster they were having difficulty with, and he wasn't coherent and they told me he was a diabetic . . . and there was a question of whether he was in insulin shock, a diabetic coma, or whether this was unrelated, or epilepsy. . . . They refused to bring the kid into the Emergency Room and demanded a housecall, which I finally made. When I got there, it was impossible to tell whether he would be in insulin shock or whether he was an epileptic. I told them we should have had that kid in the Emergency Room so we could draw a blood sugar and find out. . . . I said the only thing I could do [at home] was to treat him for insulin shock. "I'll give him some sugar because if he has that, we've got to treat it. If he is an epileptic, well, the seizure is over. . . . "We started giving him some glucose in water, about 50 cc. After I had given about 5 cc, she let go his arm and she said, "You've given him enough." So she pulled the needle out, and at this point I was furious and told the parents that the youngster didn't get good care because they were afraid to cooperate and meet me at the Emergency Room. (#7— PRIMARY PRACTITIONER)

All the physicians in the medical group probably would have agreed that some symptoms reported on the telephone were serious enough to require a housecall. As one put it, "Certainly nobody would argue about making a housecall for a patient who has chest pains and can't breathe. I mean, this is too elementary" (#4—PRIMARY PRACTITIONER). However, the same practitioner went on to say, "But feeling weak and dizzy and having a temperature of 99.5 and a little nausea, most doctors would say in the group, 'Well, just don't eat anything for a couple of days and call me back if you don't feel better,' " and they would refuse a housecall. But while everyone would make a housecall in the former situation because of its clear medical seriousness, some would also make a house-call in the latter situation based on entirely different grounds.

Let us reexamine the medical criteria. Chest pain, turning blue, and difficulty in breathing are clear signals of a serious, life-threatening situation, referring to an organic condition. At the same time as such symptoms exist, patients and those around them also manifest fear and anxiety. But when the physician rushes over, it is not the fear and anxiety so much as the probable physical condition of the patient which draws him there. Some physicians, however, felt that anxiety itself, even if surrounding no life-threatening condition, warranted attention on medical grounds. The same physician who drew the distinction between the two extremes of symptoms and who, in fact, made more housecalls than virtually all others in the medical group, went on to say about the patient with such trivial symptoms as weakness, nausea, and a low fever: "If the patient is too anxious, I'm afraid we will have to go. . . . The patient with anxiety great enough deserves a housecall. Many doctors in the group don't feel that way. They feel they're a nuisance when this happens, and they react to the patient accordingly." (#4—PRIMARY PRACTITIONER). Differences in medical philosophy, then, underlay some of the differences in evaluating the request for housecalls, evaluations critical to the understanding of when and why housecalls were ever made.

Some physicians were inclined to adopt the stance of the *official* by referring to the nature of the service contract, the rights of the patients, and their resignation to both the contractual obligation and the inevitability of patient harrassment should one not go immediately. Comparatively little attention was paid to the state of mind of the patient as someone needing help, on whatever the misguided basis. Rather, the patient was attended to as a bureaucratic troublemaker.

I'm more likely to go on a housecall to a group patient. They have the feeling they have already paid for this, whereas in private practice I just won't go. It's simpler to make a housecall than to argue with them, or to have them call every hour on the hour at night. (#55—PRIMARY PRACTITIONER)

A few of the physicians, however, reversed their emphasis, insisting on their right, under the terms of the contract, to be the arbiters, and adopting an extremely hard line toward the patient and making rather few housecalls.

Those who adopted the stance of the *expert*, however, could differ on the criteria by which they would evaluate the justification for a request for a housecall, but the central emphasis was on treating the patient. While those who were new to practice often were inclined to make a housecall for fear of missing something in the telephone description, others in practice long enough to feel sufficiently secure and justified in their decision refused what they considered to be inappropriate demands and were fully prepared to risk the bureaucratic threat of formal complaints and the possibility of having to defend their decisions.

I think I've gotten more tough because I have more assurance in dealing with the patient. They are not going to frighten me, and if they want to call somebody up or something [and complain] about it, this doesn't concern me because I feel I'm doing my job properly. I'm more secure about my status as a physician. I will very often volunteer to go on a housecall when a patient doesn't feel it necessary if I think it is. (#8—PRIMARY PRACTITIONER)

Finally, it seems appropriate to mention those physicians whose stance emphasized the necessity of educating the patient to the group-coverage situation and to the nature of housecalls as the practitioner saw them. Such a stance did not involve "giving in" to patients because of their willingness to pay for an unnecessary service, because of their prepayment, or because of their capacity to make bureaucratic trouble. In some cases it could involve providing them with a medically unnecessary service as a method of establishing socially necessary trust so that they could be persuaded that future housecalls might not be necessary.

I first had a lot of trouble in the group with patients, but now I realize it is silly. They were really anxious and ignorant, and we weren't getting anywhere fighting about making a housecall, so [later] I would go. I would say, "Well, I see nothing and I don't think there is anything wrong. I'm not going to give penicillin because that's wrong. But what I'll do is come back tomorrow if you want me to, and I'll keep coming back until you are clear in your mind that there isn't anything wrong and you really don't need a housecall." I feel if I show my good faith this way, after a while they won't expect me to come. This way I educate them. (#2—PRIMARY PRACTITIONER)

A well-established, highly respected senior practitioner reported differ-ent techniques, techniques apparently responsible for his being both popular with patients and one of those who made fewer housecalls than the average of the group.

When virus is going around, you try to explain there is no specific treatment except bed rest and that there are many other people with much higher tem-peratures who really need [housecalls]. But you stress the fact that what they should do is keep in touch so that in case things do get serious we'll be able to go out. . . . Usually I can anticipate what the patient is going to say. I already have a bit of information from the [telephone] operator and before they give me all their symptoms I say, "You have this and that and so-and-so and so-and-so." I proceed to tell them how they feel and . . . I explain about treatment and that penicillin has no relation to the illness and is even danger-ous. But if there is apprehension in the patient's voice you don't push it too far. (#20—PRIMARY PRACTITIONER)

The expert does not stand on his official status or economic position in the marketplace, but undertakes to persuade the layman of the propriety of his opinion. Indeed, the expert must teach the patient how to adopt the stance of layman when he has been accustomed of being a bureau-cratic client or a customer.

SUPPLYING OFFICE SERVICES

Simple and uniform patterns in the supply of housecalls were difficult to discern, perhaps because there was no formal framework of any sig-nificance constraining either demand or supply. Many variables—the patient's and doctor's personalities, their conceptions of symptoms and complaint, their conceptions of rights and obligations, and the like—were in free interaction in a rather thoroughly discretionary milieu. Easier to perceive was the patterning of the supply of other kinds of services.

Organizing the supply of office services was rather diferent from or-ganizing the supply of housecalls because in the former case the physicians had to have a certain number of office hours every week, and their receptionists were instructed by the administration to schedule any patient who called for an appointment. There was no discretion entailed: if a patient called for an appointment, he got one. Only if he wished an immediate, emergency appointment was the request evaluated; otherwise an appointment was made automatically, and the time period allotted to the appointment was set by administrative rules. Thus, by and large, office services were scheduled on demand, and it was the physicians' job to supply them. The problem was how they supplied them and what they supplied, particularly during periods of heavy demand, when people walked in for emergency visits without appointments.

The problem was the human as well as the technical quality of the service, a distinction that the physicians themselves made. Most, in fact, believed that when they were overloaded with work, the human quality of care tended to deteriorate.

> In a private office you take 10, maybe 15 minutes [for a routine revisit in my specialty]. In a clinic I might see a patient in 2 minutes. In the group I compromise for 5 minutes. Sometimes when I'm really rushed I can't see them that long, so what happens in group practice is that if there is anything organically wrong, they are well taken care of. But if any supportive therapy is needed, you don't have time. And I think a lot of the group patients need supportive therapy. (#33—CONSULTANT)

Under circumstances perceived as overload, the care they gave was often impersonal, lacking amenities, and, on occasion, virtually mechanized. An efficient physician described how the consultation could be organized when time was short.

> I sit and write when a patient is getting dressed. I sit and talk on the phone while writing, and I'm checking off lists and working on all those things. I don't let a patient relax. I keep him going. It's tense, that's all, and it's true, if I have a day where I get a couple of cancellations I enjoy myself tremendously. (#1—PRIMARY PRACTITIONER)

This impersonalization was not seen by all as the absence of a mere amenity: a number felt that the personal quality of care was essential to high technical quality.

> The problems I have adjusting to is with time and with myself. I'm continually irritated at the lack of time, that I don't have enough time to do the kind of

work that I want to do. I like to talk to people and I don't have the time to do that unless I cut corners. [BR: How do you cut corners?] I cut corners by cutting out talking and cutting out the social history, and the social history, for an internist, at least, gives him a key to at least half his diagnoses. (#13—PRIMARY PRACTITIONER)

Thus, by some standards, the technical quality of the care the physicians could give suffered in the face of the number of patients that they had to deal with in the time available in their office hours. We have already seen in Chapter 2 how even some of the purely technical standards for the physical examination were lost in corner-cutting.

Not all the pressure was relieved solely by cutting corners. At least some physicians manipulated the bureaucratic system itself in order to gain more time to deal with each patient. In one reported case, appointments were invented in order to leave longer time periods for each real appointment.

By changing the scheduling plan you get a lot more time for patients. You can do a better job. We do it. [BR: By subterfuge, squeezing in, stretching out?] Right. And a good secretary will write in a few extra names at key points on occasion . . . [though] you can't usually anticipate when you are going to be in a jam. (#13—PRIMARY PRACTITIONER)

But rather more often was it reported, paradoxically, that physicians relieved pressure by *increasing* the supply of *future* medical or non-physician services. A number of the physicians indicated that in times of overload they often gave a perfunctory, "screening" examination and then asked the patient to return for another visit at some future date when, presumably, they hoped they would have a more leisurely schedule.

Other services—namely, X rays and laboratory tests—were also increased in an effort to cope with demands for office consultation.

Dealing with a large volume of patients, one way of doing it . . . is to simply get the patients started on lab work and get them out of the office . . . and have him make an appointment to see you again the next day. (#21—PRIMARY PRACTITIONER)

Thus some proportion of the rather large number of laboratory and X-ray services used in the medical group were generated by the physicians themselves in the course of trying to cope with their office work-

load. There is some evidence that such a tendency to order a comparatively large number of laboratory services exists in other prepaid-group
contexts—in the Kaiser-Permanente group described by Saward, Blank,
and Greenlick, 1968: 239–240, in which such services were described as
"functional substitutes for physician and hospital services," and in the
national sample of group practitioners studied by Mechanic (1972: 153).
To cope with daily pressures, the physicians in our group cut the visiting
time of patients either by referring them out for tests and the services of
consultants or by providing only a partial service and asking them to
return. The measured administrative unit of the office service was preserved intact, but its content was contracted and, to compensate, the
number of office services provided was increased.

This was also the case for the consultants. As we shall see, referrals to
consultants constituted yet another way of cutting short an office visit.
Having no similar safety valve, the consultants could only themselves
restrict their services or at least, like those primary practitioners who
encouraged the patient to return on some other occasion, delay the
supply of optional or borderline procedures.

> So when you say, "Doesn't this contribute in some sense to neglecting
> surgery which isn't too terribly essential?" the answer is, "Yes, it certainly
> does. . . ." You know, it's just borderline. We'll wait and see what happens
> [instead of scheduling surgery right away]. (#52—Consultant)

One might suspect that while deferring or resisting surgery may contract
the supply of services in one sense, it may also increase it by increasing
the number of times a patient will visit a consultant to be reexamined in
advance of any ultimate surgery. In a curious way, by the *administrative
measures* of the supply of service, there was an increased supply in
answer to demand, but the supply of service as the physicians conceived
of it actually remained fairly constant: the total time was simply redistrib-
uted among an increased number of shorter office visits and substitute
services.

DEMAND AND SUPPLY IN X RAYS
AND LABORATORY TESTS

Patients demanded housecalls and office services first and foremost.
But in the course of their interaction with the physicians, once they get

to see them, they would demand also X rays and, more particularly, laboratory tests, services with special analytical interest for the circumstances of our medical group. Laboratory tests and X rays are similar to prescriptions for drugs in that, in ordering them, the physician acts as an official in a controlled system, a gatekeeper whose signed approval is necessary before patients can receive what they ask for. In the medical group the physician was such an official in a double sense not found in entrepreneurial practice. Like all licensed physicians, he signed an order before patients could obtain prescription drugs, tests, and X rays. But *unlike* entrepreneurial physicians, he was also an official in the unusual sense that, in order for patients to obtain lab tests as a benefit of their service contract without out-of-pocket cost, they had to obtain the signed order of a group physician and not just any licensed physician.

This circumstance led to an analytically interesting situation. On occasion, some patients chose to use the services of outside physicians who were not members of the medical group and who had to be paid fees out of pocket. Knowing their contractual rights, however, the patients obtained orders for tests and X rays from their outside physicians and tried to get the orders authorized by group physicians so they would not have to pay for them. [This seems to have been dealt with in the British National Health Service by the denial of benefit rights to patients of private doctors (see Mencher, 1968: 34).] This circumstance puts the group physician in a virtually pure role as official gatekeeper. On grounds of recognition of the bona fide medical status of the outside physician, as well as on the grounds of the patients' contractual rights, the group physician could simply approve the order automatically and transmit the results of the tests to the outside physician.

Facilitating the adoption of the stance of an *official* was the fact that, while tests and X rays were diagnostic tools, most had no direct influence on the patient's illness or health. There was usually no real issue of harm to the patient from such orders. Thus, tests and X rays could be considered to be mere commodities provided by the medical group under the terms of the contract, irrelevant to the issue of using expert judgment to determine therapy. Thus, when patients asked group physicians to order a test, many agreed without serious resistance.

> About lab tests, if a patient asks for one . . . I'd just as soon have it done. If somebody is really upset about their obesity and wanted a basal, well, what do I care? I let him have a basal. (#9—PRIMARY PRACTITIONER)

This response was essentially that of a bureaucratic official, expressing commitment to rights under the rules rather than commitment to one's own expert opinion. However, while some physicians explained their giving in by reference to being so tired and overworked as to lack the energy to attempt to persuade the patients that the tests they asked for were unnecessary, most justified their action by the therapeutic effect of the test in relieving the patients' worry. That way, their official action became converted into a therapeutic action, making it seem that they were still in charge as experts.

> Sometimes I send a kid for a test because somebody told the mother something and she'll never rest. She'll worry without the test. I use the test to reassure the mother. (#25—PRIMARY PRACTITIONER)

This is not to say that the physicians were wholly passive. There was, after all, the argument that "by giving in, you are just feeding the patient's anxiety" (#2—PRIMARY PRACTITIONER), and most who were inclined to accede to the patient's demand were prone to distinguish between minor, inexpensive, infrequent, and reasonable tests, which they might order on patient request, and major, expensive, frequent, and irrelevant tests, which they would resist ordering. In resisting them, they stressed professional reasons.

> Sometimes a patient might request a test which in my mind is completely unreasonable, has nothing to do with the case. I explain I don't feel it is indicated. I could tell him tests he never heard of which maybe he should request. "I'm not an attendant in a grocery store who takes an order for a box of Wheaties and a bottle of milk and is expected to serve it up to them. I'm a doctor. Let me be the doctor. . . ." Most people sheepishly accept it at that point. (#20—PRIMARY PRACTITIONER)

The issues changed markedly when the demand for a test was supported by the request of an outside physician. There, the doctor could not refuse because he was the doctor and the patient was a layman, since it was a physician who had ordered the test. Furthermore, to refuse could also (and on occasion did) make for a professionally embarrassing situation that violated colleague etiquette. In these circumstances, some of the group physicians saw their role as completely official in character, the responsibility for the patient and the order passing out of their hands.

He has chosen to go outside, and we have this contractual obligation to provide tests. This then becomes a matter of courtesy. . . . The test is automatic, mechanical. I would just order it. Then I serve not as a physician but as a representative of the group. (#21—PRIMARY PRACTITIONER)

A few refused to assume such an official role and insisted on examining the patient themselves before writing out the order. But, by and large, most physicians simply approved such requests.

I have already referred to some evidence that the comparatively generous use of laboratory tests and X rays may be a special characteristic of prepaid group practice as such, and not an idiosyncrasy of the medical group we studied. Here and in my previous discussion of the supply of office services, I have tried to show some of the elements of the process by which such increased supply took place. Some proportion of the total supply was provided in answer to demand for the entirely different commodity of personal consultation and was generated by the physicians themselves as a way of reducing the time they spent with individual patients on a given busy workday. An additional portion was provided in fairly mechanical answer to patients' demand on the grounds of their contractual rights. And yet another portion was provided as a function of the physicians' considered judgment of what would be appropriate to order as a diagnostic aid to their work. Each form of supply could be seen as rather different in origin and function, though the same service was supplied in every case. And while the formal, contractual, administrative framework of the work in the group obviously provided the possibility for some forms of supply, and indeed may have encouraged official stances toward supply, the practitioners themselves were active in evaluating the nature of the demand and choosing the stances they adopted toward it. So, too, was it for another operating problem of the medical group—the supply of consultant services.

DEMAND AND SUPPLY IN CONSULTANT SERVICES

The use of consultants, like the use of laboratory tests and X rays, required the primary practitioners to act as official gatekeepers. In the medical group, patients generally could not get an appointment with a consultant without referral from their internist or pediatrician. The primary practitioners perceived a serious problem of management in dealing with patients inclined to demand such referrals, while, as we saw, the consultants complained of excessive referrals from the primary practitioners.

As did tests and X rays, referral to a consultant constituted a device by which harried physicians would reduce the pressure of the stream of appointments during their office hours. On hearing a complaint, they could save a great deal of time if they referred the patient to a consultant without examining the patient further.

> If you are seeing patients at the rate of one every seven or eight minutes, and it takes three or four to ask them how they feel and get them undressed, you look for as many shortcuts as possible. One of the ways—I'm sure I do this myself—is to give the work to somebody else. If [they] have a backache, send them to physiotherapy. That gets them off your back. . . . They come back and say it doesn't work, and they try to accuse you. You look at them and say, "I did my best. I sent you to a specialist." You shrug your shoulders. The load is so great that the buck is passed. (#9—PRIMARY PRACTITIONER)

Other physicians adopted something resembling the stance of the official less on the ground of time pressure than on the rather more purely bureaucratic ground of the patients' contractual right to see a consultant if they wanted to see one.

But the dilemma was that if the primary practitioners dealt with their patients solely by referring them without making a definitive diagnosis and providing effective therapeutic advice, they ceased to play the role of a consulting *expert* and became primarily referring agents, *officials* who wrote a referral slip without which the patient could not see a consultant. The primary practitioners—themselves all board-eligible specialists—were well aware of this threat to their status, and many were deeply concerned about it.

> Because of the ease of referral here, the patients want a special doctor for every part of their body. This tends to relegate me, an internist, to the job of a physician who simply refers, and you only take care of what's left after they see the specialists. This is a sore point. I usually try not to refer a patient to the specialist unless it is something I feel needs him or something I want an opinion on. (#18—PRIMARY PRACTITIONER)

Efforts to maintain one's function as an expert, then, tended to take the form of resisting ready referrals. But even that stance contained its own inherent contradiction, for insofar as the expert relies for his influence upon his capacity to persuade the patient of the proper course of action, unlike the official, who can assert his authoritarian prerogatives under the rules, he must leave open to the patient the right to seek another opinion, the right to consult another expert. Honestly held to, the stance of the expert surely must be capable of bending in the face of persistent patient wishes: the physician could first attempt to persuade the patient to accept his recommendations, but he must give in after a time if the patient remains unpersuaded.

> Many times I'll say to a patient, "I'm not sure I can cure this, but let's try. If it doesn't work out, then we'll send you to the dermatologist," or whatever it is. (#16—PRIMARY PRACTITIONER)

Indeed, virtually all the physicians conceded that they would give in in the face of repeated requests for referral. Only one suggested that, if a patient persisted in the desire for a referral against his judgment, he would ask him to transfer to the panel of another doctor.

THE ELASTICITY OF UNITS OF SUPPLY

In this chapter I have attempted to discuss most of the activities in the medical group which got concretized into health services, or "utilization," by administrative schemes. Interaction with the patient over the telephone might possibly have been described in the medical record, but it was not counted as a service. Only when a housecall was actually made, an office visit scheduled, or a test ordered was a health service registered from which utilization statistics could be made up. The units of measurement—the housecall, the office visit, the test, the referral, the consultant visit and procedure—constituted arbitrarily chosen slices of the total set of activities that medical work, in or out of the medical group, entailed. They were chosen more because they were amenable to separation out as measurable units than because they were necessarily the most important or desirable indicators of the essential substance of medical work. They were chosen, in short, for their administrative convenience and relevance, and they typically became quantities whose qualities and contexts came to be either ignored or considered inconsequential. It was in response to those qualities and contexts, however, that the physicians created the patterns of supply that, in turn, changed the measurable quantities of services.

Indeed, what was measured as a definite and fixed unit of service was in fact quite elastic in both its content and its function. This was most clearly and instructively the case in the medical group for the primary practitioner's office visit, the laboratory test, and the consultant service. We saw how the duration and substance of the primary-practitioner office visit were subject to contraction as the contingencies of the work-day changed. The office visit could be very brief, involving the most superficial examination followed by orders for diagnostic testing and an additional office visit. The same function could have been accomplished in many instances by an office visit of longer duration, an order for tests, and a subsequent telephone consultation about the outcome of the tests were the system for scheduling appointments and dealing with walk-ins different and were the physicians to change their conception of their duties.

The inherent elasticity of the content and function of the office consultation was nowhere more in evidence than in those instances in which referral to other colleagues was possible, for there, unlike in the case of ordering diagnostic tests, it was possible to at least temporarily shift the responsibility for the patient to someone else. And variation in the point at which such responsibility was shifted was accompanied by changes both in the content of the work and in the jurisdictional boundaries of the various specialties in the division of labor. The very meaning and substance of specialization can change. Let us examine the interrelations of the physicians of the group now and see how changes in referral practice lead to changes in the substance of the various specialties.

5:
Renegotiating Specialty Boundaries by Referrals

The primary practitioners were the ones who first saw patients, whether in the home or in the office. Furthermore, they were the gatekeepers to most other services in the medical group, particularly those of the consultants. But as gatekeepers they did not function as a receptionist would, simply transmitting those making inquiry to the proper office or person and never seeing the questioners again. The primary practitioners, even when they did transmit patients almost as automatically as would a receptionist, nonetheless, at the very least, had to see the patients again after they had gotten their tests or consultant services and assessed the results. The primary practitioners were supposed to be responsible for their referrals in the sense that they were supposed to be interpreting, coordinating, and managing all the services that the patient had received from other sources. This, in fact, is what a multispecialty medical group is supposed to entail—it is supposed to be a venture in which a variety of specialized practitioners work together in a single organization so as to provide a broad range of *coordinated* care for their patients. While the same range of services is available to patients in most urban communities, coordination is not guaranteed by solo, fee-for-service practice or by ambulatory hospital facilities and public clinics.

The social mechanism by which cooperation among physicians around an individual case is instituted lies in the *referral*. (For a recent study of referrals among practitioners in solo practice, see Shortell, n.d.) At some point in his work with a patient, the practitioner concludes, for a variety of possible reasons, that it is necessary to send that patient to a colleague for examination and perhaps treatment. At that point, each physician comes to play a specialized role in a professionally organized division of labor. One becomes the consultant to the other. One does work that the other has chosen not to do or at the very least one provides advice and opinion to the other: something is added to the work of one by the other. The point in the course of their work at which the primary practitioners make their referrals tends to establish the boundaries of both their and the consultants' jurisdiction, though, as we shall see, the consultants may claim different boundaries than the referral itself implies. That boundary defines the limits of the work the primary practitioners do—the content of their work—and establishes what kind of work they seek to have the consultants do.

The issue of jurisdictional boundaries lies at the analytic core of referral relations between colleagues. This issue is often overlooked in the course of interpreting such facts as I have already cited in Chapter 2 about tensions both in our medical group and in others between primary practitioners and consultants. The fact that in salaried medical groups consultants complained of excessive referrals while in fee-for-service groups the complaint was either absent or precisely the reverse—that primary practitioners did not refer enough—can be interpreted, with some justice, in vulgar economic terms. But at bottom there is much more to it than personal economic advantage.

The physicians we studied, true children of their time, were prone to interpret the motive for making and welcoming referrals as economic self-interest. Like the physician quoted below, they were inclined to evaluate behavior by comparing it with what they felt it would be under fee-for-service circumstances:

> One day I had a kid walk into my group office with acute appendicitis. You know, they have surgeons on emergency call, and I got on the phone and called him and he was at a party someplace. So I got him on the phone and said, "I'm going to give you an acute AP." This was about eight o'clock at night, and he started cursing over the phone. He's a young guy. He just finished his residency maybe a year or two before. A young surgeon—if this was a private case he would have kissed my ass. He would have given me a present, he would have been so happy. (L21—CONSULTANT; FORMER PRIMARY PRACTITIONER)

But, in using vulgar economic interpretations of the behavior of their colleagues, they were implicitly assuming that referrals were simply quantitative units, without qualitative elements of importance. If one has nothing to gain, one sloughs off work; if one gains a fee, one welcomes work. The substance of the work remains unchanged; it is only the number of units of work that changes. The fact of the matter is, however, that much more than merely amount of work and income were involved in the tensions surrounding referrals in the medical group. Excessive referral involved the use of criteria for referral which changed the jurisdictional boundaries to which the physicians were accustomed.

What was referred, the amount of referral, and the way referrals took place constituted a de facto renegotiation of customary jurisdictional boundaries usually taken for granted as right and proper by most of the participants, boundaries upon which a great deal of their self-esteem depended. Not solely quantitative production norms but also the very substance of production—the nature and content of the work that each physician in the division of labor performed—were the issue.

SUBSTANTIVE AND NORMATIVE SPECIALIZATION

The physicians' preconceptions about what the practice of medicine was could not help but be influenced by the historically dominant framework in which practice has taken place. They were in fact accustomed to thinking of the jurisdictional boundaries among the specialties and, more particularly, between the primary practitioner, or referrer, and the consultant in terms of the institutional framework of entrepreneurial, fee-for-service practice. Indeed, it can be argued that there is no consistent logic guiding the delineation of the content of specialized practice which is based solely on the content area or technical substance of some form of medical work. I would, in fact, argue that in medicine, if not in all areas of human work, the substance of specialization as it is actually practiced always reflects conventional institutional distinctions that have grown up out of the way in which specialization happened to have developed in a particular marketplace, organized in a historically specific way. In the United States, as in Western Europe, the historically dominant mode of organizing the marketplace has been entrepreneurial.

Conceptions ordering specialization may be seen as both *substantive,* or categorical, and *normative,* or symbolic. That is, specialization is not delineated solely by the limitation of work to a particular organ, technique, procedure, or whatever; it is also delineated by the limitation of work to tasks that have been evaluated normatively as appropriate to the person involved. Furthermore, both substantive and normative criteria of specialization are embedded in the social organization of the way the work is performed, including the career of the worker himself, a social organization obviously connected with the marketplace in which work is carried out.

In the entrepreneurial marketplace surrounding our medical group, the division of labor was organized into broad categorical specialities. Young physicians entered the marketplace as general specialists and aspired to limit their work further as they built up their practice— sometimes aspiring to a recognized subspecialty. Their success at "specialized specialization" was understood to be a career contingency, something to be gained during the course of a successful career. Young neurologist-psychiatrists, for example, had to expect initially to have to practice psychiatry, no matter what their preference to concentrate on neurology, because the demand for psychiatric services was considerably greater than that for neurological services. They hoped to be able to build up their neurological referrals sufficiently over time so as to be able finally to refuse psychiatric referrals and work with neurological cases only. Similarly, young surgeons had to expect to start out practice by performing whatever general surgery they could get and hope to be able to gradually come to the point of limiting the cases they would accept to the specialized surgery to which they aspired. Given the well-known emphasis of American medicine (and medical education) on increased specialization, it is not difficult to imagine the degree to which physicians measured career success by their attainment of subspecialty, superspecialty, or even just pure specialty practice. Specialized training thus gives a very broad categorical emphasis, while career aspiration narrows that emphasis. Career failure lies in remaining a general specialist and never being able to become a specialized specialist.

That substantive limitation due to jurisdictional boundaries or to practice in a division of labor is bound up with notions of success indicates that there is another very important element involved in defining the substance of specialization, an element that is social and normative rather than technical and substantive. Criteria of status in professions run parallel to criteria of work substance in being career contingencies rather than givens. Indeed, the boundaries of specialization in medicine or in any other professionalized division of labor in fact cannot be explained on grounds of substantive or categorical limitations of task. Even general practitioners' work cannot be defined by reference to the "general" substance of their work because they do not deal with every conceivable human complaint. There is a large corpus of everyday complaints that are managed by patients themselves using their own "medical" remedies without recourse to a physician. Genuine as they may be as complaints, they are not considered important enough to take to a general practitioner. And if they are taken to one, the general practitioner is likely to consider them trivial and his or her services unnecessary. By the same token, a physician whose practice is "limited to the eye" does not in fact deal with every conceivable complaint about the eye—he deals with only some, and what he does deal with cannot be defined adequately on technical grounds alone. The prime criteria for discriminating what is in his jurisdiction within the entire substantive universe of possible complaints about the eye are normative. These normative criteria emphasize the important rather than the trivial, the major rather than the minor, the esoteric rather than the common, and the interesting rather than the routine.

Some normative limitations on jurisdictional boundaries are implicitly given in a broad way by the general status relations between primary practitioners and consultants. Just as patients have explained their limited utilization of primary practitioners by claiming, deferentially, that they did not want to bother the doctor (Freidson, 1961), so we heard some primary practitioners in the medical group say that they did not want to bother the specialists with minor complaints. Other normative limitations are given in a very broad way by general conceptions of what the various specialties are. Still others, perhaps the most important for our present purposes because they are more fluid and negotiable, are considered by specialists to be contingencies of a successful career in the medical marketplace—those limitations that are both the unfolding rights of a process of gaining success and at the same time the display or mark of such success. As he becomes successful, the consultant can restrict his work to what is important, major, esoteric, and interesting. A mark of his success is his capability to do so.

Clearly, jurisdictional boundaries are neither simply drawn nor stable throughout the individual career. Furthermore, they are contingent upon the institutional framework within which practice goes on. In solo, entrepreneurial practice, they are loosely limited by little more than state medical licensing laws (Derbyshire, 1969) and quite variable standards for granting "hospital privileges" to physicians. Thus the range of career possibilities for individual physicians is quite wide, with marked contrasts between the young, just-started aspirant and the elderly success. The fee-for-service mode of paying the physician in entrepreneurial practice also influences jurisdictional boundaries, since, just as a fee-barrier stands between the prospective patient and his use of primary practitioner, so does it constrain referrals by the primary practitioner because it means an additional fee to the patient, who may be reluctant to incur the cost. Thus, in the entrepreneurial marketplace, the number of all possible specialist services provided to patients is likely to be limited by the barrier of the out-of-pocket fee; so also is the *type* of specialist service. The out-of-pocket fee thus *broadens* the range of services and the jurisdictional boundaries of the primary practitioner and *narrows* the range of services and jurisdictional boundaries of the consultant.

The substance of specialization, therefore, was in part an artifact of the institutional framework of practice. Furthermore, that framework reinforced the specialist's aspiration to deal with only the important and interesting cases, and thus it contributed to the development of conventional understandings about what it is a specialist *properly* does in his work, and what it is he resists as inappropriate, even demeaning. Trouble arose in our medical group, however, because, first of all, there was greater homogeneity in training and aspiration among all the group physicians than would be found in the greater variety of physicians in community practice. Let us recall that all the physicians, including the primary practitioners, were board-eligible specialists, and they had the aspiration and self-concept historically associated with such training. Furthermore, let us recall that there was no fee barrier. The outcome was that, contrary to the thrust of traditional entrepreneurial practice, the prepaid-medical-group practice tended to encourage *narrowing* the range of services of the primary practitioners and *broadening* that of the consultants. Those whose conceptions of career success and of specialization were formed in the customary terms of entrepreneurial practice could not help but be unhappy with the referrals they made or with the referrals they received. It was thus no wonder that referrals to consultants constituted one of the prime focuses for tension and conflict in the medical group. Let us take a more detailed look at the physicians' responses to the problem of referrals.

THE VARIED GROUNDS FOR REFERRAL

I have been arguing that specialty boundaries and, more particularly, the boundaries between primary practitioner and consultant in the medical division of labor are not given by some stable technological necessity' but rather reflect social conventions and institutional arrangements given in a particular time and place and negotiated by the participants. If this is the case, then it follows that one must expect, as a *natural* consequence, not an anomaly, that new institutional arrangements for practice will create the possibilities of new criteria for referrals and new jurisdictional boundaries for specialization even though skills and technologies have not changed. And since the initial criteria used to evaluate behavior are almost of necessity the preexisting institutional arrangements with their customary practices, tension and conflict are almost inevitable. Such was certainly the case in our medical group.

The official rationale for the position and function of the primary practitioner in the medical group was familiar to most of the physicians and was disagreed with by none. Patients were not to seek out specialist consultation on their own initiative. They could see a consultant only through referral by the primary practitioner, so that their care could be controlled and coordinated by professional standards. The primary practitioner's task was essentially one of technical evaluation and was not considered to be especially problematic in most cases. So it was that the rationale could be simply and reasonably stated by a number of practitioners:

> The family doctor is the hub of the wheel. In order to eliminate the possibility of nose and throat surgery, the consultations go through him so that he knows what's going on and who they've seen and why, and he has his finger on the whole record. So he's in a better position to act as the master of ceremonies. He has control of his patients, and oftentimes a consultation requested [by the patient] may not be necessary or even advisable. . . . But if a consultation is really [needed], he will give them the authorization to go see the particular specialty requested. (#46—CONSULTANT)

But, from what I have already noted in prior chapters about the social and economic context of practice in the medical group, it is virtually impossible to believe that the decision to refer could be made on purely technical grounds of medical necessity or advisability. In Chapter 4, I already touched on the roles of overload, of the lack of a discouraging fee barrier to temper patients' requests for referrals, and of the presence of nominal contractual and ethical rights to such referrals in creating pressure to refer to consultants more often in the group than on the outside. Some of the greater number of referrals stemmed from these

factors: no matter how hard the primary practitioners might try to dis-
suade a patient determined to see a consultant, ultimately they would
have to give in on both contractual and moral grounds.

> Let's say there is a patient with a backache who wants to see the orthopedist,
> and I know damned well the orthopedist isn't going to do anything for it. Most
> patients I can discourage. . . . [I say that] if I found indications of a disc, by
> all means I'd refer them immediately. But there are patients who won't accept
> *not* seeing an orthopedist, and I don't know how else to handle them except
> by referring them. Once you see they feel they must see them, or they must
> see the psychiatrist, I usually give in. (#20—PRIMARY PRACTITIONER)

Furthermore, prepayment allowed the primary practitioners themselves
to make referrals that advanced their own management purposes, purposes that involved no purely technical medical necessity. Such referrals
were essentially rhetorical or persuasive in nature and might very well
not have been made were fees necessary for the patient.

> I refer to specialists to allay fear. . . . One lady who may still have residual
> cancer I referred several times back to the surgeon and radiotherapy so that
> she especially will feel she is being given adequate care. She felt everybody
> was interested in her, everybody was trying to do the best for her. So she is
> easier to handle. (#13—PRIMARY PRACTITIONER)

The new framework also allowed referrals to be made so as to establish
the fact that the primary practitioner's judgment was sustained by a
more authoritative consultant.

> There are many times I have the opportunity to see many children's feet and I
> know many of these feet get better by themselves. On the other hand the
> feeling is, "Well, if something can be done we should do it now." And it is
> remarkable how much pressure there is from patients, and lay shoe salesmen
> and things like that. They'd say, "Well, if you had handled this when you
> were young, it would be all right." So you pretty much want an orthopedic
> consultation on record (#12—PRIMARY PRACTITIONER)

Such "covering" consultations could also be requested by physicians
fearful of possible malpractice suits who were seeking to have a consultation on the record to protect themselves. All such referrals could be
made more easily in the institutional framework of practice found in the

medical group, where a fee barrier did not exist to make at least some patients reluctant to accept a referral.

In considering the elements entering into referrals, it is important to note that only some referrals were initiated by the patient and made against the physicians' better judgment. Just as the physicians were active agents in increasing office visits and the use of laboratory tests, so they were active agents in making referrals. The lack of a fee barrier did encourage some patients to demand referrals, but it also removed a source of patient resistance to referrals that the primary practitioners wished to make for their own medical, legal, management, or scheduling reasons. The lack of a fee barrier freed the physicians to be able to use the referral in sometimes new ways or, in any case, in ways not readily available to them in entrepreneurial practice. It also allowed some to redefine their own specialized roles, thereby helping resolve some of their own problems in conceiving of themselves as specialists.

The most prominent specialists in the medical group—because of their number and their organizational role—were the internists serving as primary practitioners. All were eligible for certification as bona fide specialists in internal medicine, and they were jealous of their specialist status. But they served in the same functional role as general practitioners in that they were the first to whom patients took complaints and so were confronted with many ordinary and routine disorders. One primary practitioner who left the group claimed to have done so because he saw that generalist role as an undesirable lifetime career.

My image of an internist or a consultant was somebody that wasn't a GP. He doesn't go seeing people with sore throats and backaches. He does this at the beginning, when he is young, in the first years of practice. He'd go and look at babies and see colds . . . but when he got 10 or 15 or 20 years of practice he is not seeing colds and sore throats primarily. . . . I felt in the group I'd always be a family physician, doing all these little things, you know. It's one thing when you get sick and you have to have a little menial thing done, it becomes very important [to the sick person]. But from a doctor's standpoint, this isn't their main aim in life, they want to be consultants, specialists, super-specialists. . . . I went through a three-year residency. I took another year's training. I know all about the esoteric diseases and I wanted a chance to use all my esoteric knowledge. I felt [in the medical group] all I'd be doing were common little problems. Of course the patient has to be taken care of, but I didn't feel I wanted to do this forever. You can have nurses seeing all the bruises. (L21—CONSULTANT; FORMER PRIMARY PRACTITIONER)

A highly respected, senior primary practitioner who stayed in the medical group seemed to agree with that evaluation by expressing his rather resigned acceptance of the trivia.

> I think early in the game all of us who became internists had to accept the fact that we weren't going to be consultants who waited for physicians to refer to them. The internist was already an anomaly when I started practice. It was hard to tell a patient what you were except by exclusion. You have to be a family doctor and deal with all of the patients, that is to say, all the problems they bring to you. You couldn't say, "This isn't serious, don't bother me with trivia." To rebel against this is self-defeat. Unless you go into a pure specialty today, like psychiatry or ENT, you have to accept it, and it seems unlikely that it will ever change. (#21—PRIMARY PRACTITIONER)

Nonetheless there is evidence that in the medical group at least some of the primary practitioners did, on grounds of specialized training, drop some of the trivia by referring it out. They did so even though they admitted that "any joker could do it" and that referral to a consultant was not really necessary.

> There is a good deal of orthopedic stuff that I send down that I can do myself, but I do very few injections. Even though I'm capable of doing it I don't feel I should. It is an orthopedic procedure, and one of the virtues of the group is that we can keep the stuff we can handle and send the stuff out that we are not trained to do. This is a fringe area and any joker could do it, but still, we aren't really trained in the orthopod's problems. If orthopedics were really crowded and I had more time, I could do some of it myself. So too with physiotherapy. (#7—PRIMARY PRACTITIONER)

The boundaries of specialized competence were therefore rather elastic. Indeed, the same narrowing of jurisdictional boundaries could be observed even among some of the consultants in the medical group. A number said that they handled minor complications connected with their specialized practice outside if they had to, but would rather not do so. The medical group gave them the opportunity to refer such cases out to other consultants.

> In my solo practice . . . I feel obliged to handle minor complications like hemorrhoids instead of calling in a proctologist, in order to avoid another bill to the patient. But I don't enjoy taking care of that sort of thing . . . and I'd rather leave that to [another] specialist. (#30—CONSULTANT)

This inclination to refer to consultants what on the outside would be conceived of as inappropriate trivia was quite evident to the consultants of the medical group, who commented on the unaccustomed characteristics of their case load.

I see a lot of things [in the medical group] that I never see in my private office—things that I really *shouldn't* be seeing, a lot of minor things. Family doctors are much too anxious to rush patients down to see me and the other specialists. I never see, for example, shortness of breath in my private office. I can only think that the family doctors are just too busy or just want to get rid of patients by sending them down here. (#29—CONSULTANT)

Needless to say, the consultants' inclination to evaluate referrals on the basis of what are normal jurisdictional boundaries in solo, entrepreneurial practice did not lead them to accept them graciously. At best they could think only that the referrers were overworked. But more important was the fact that the different institutional organization of practice allowed both patients and primary practitioners to express desires and norms that previously were discouraged. The sense of overload, the necessity of coping with it, and well-schooled conceptions of specialized competence and status interacted in both primary practitioners and consultants to produce the new referral pattern. More would be referred than was likely in entrepreneurial practice. The consequence was that referrers were, in effect, making themselves more specialized, with narrower jurisdictional boundaries than in entrepreneurial practice, and that consultants were finding themselves with a less specialized practice, with broader jurisdictional boundaries, than would have been the case in a successful entrepreneurial career. And what is essential to understand is that much of this referral was *not* forced and reluctant. It represented to the referrers an opportunity to get from consultants help of a sort that they could not expect in traditional, entrepreneurial practice and also an opportunity for themselves to be more like the specialists they were trained to be.

MAKING THE REFERRAL

Since the institutional arrangements in the medical group permitted referrals that were far less likely to occur on the outside, differences in conceptions of what was and what was not necessary or appropriate were bound to exist. They were particularly likely because all of the consultants had outside entrepreneurial practices against which to compare their group referrals. Under such circumstances, the nature of the interaction that went on between referrer and consultant must have been very important in establishing the kind of relationship that existed between them. How, then, were referrals made? Did the referrer communicate to the consultant the reasons for his referral, particularly when the case being referred was not one that commonly was referred to a consultant in private practice?

Only in unusual cases was there much effort at communicating to the consultant the reasons for a referral. When primary practitioners consciously made referrals because they were unable to manage a demanding patient, some took pains to convey their difficulty to the consultant so that he would at once forgive them for making a nominally unnecessary referral and also would respond appropriately to the patient.

> The chronic types [of demanding patient] you just don't refer. . . . If they persist, I'll give in and write a note on the chart [to the consultant] that I tried to persuade them there was nothing there, but they insisted on seeing the specialist. Then the specialist can say, "Your doctor told you this is nothing and it is nothing, goodbye." They get the bum's rush. (#15—PRIMARY PRACTITIONER)

Similarly, primary practitioners would request back-up when a patient would not accept their diagnosis. They would refer to a consultant while asking him to confirm the original recommendation. This situation seemed to be particularly common in pediatrics, in which patients pressed for tonsillectomies that their physicians were reluctant to recommend. In such an instance, referrers carefully selected the consultant so as to be sure he had the same reluctance to perform tonsillectomies as they had, and a note often was written to him which attempted to gain his cooperation in supporting the referrer's position.

In especially difficult, complex, or serious cases, direct and sometimes extensive discussions were held with the consultant before the patient was sent to him. And when immediate or emergency care for and attention to a patient was desired, the primary practitioner tended to contact the consultant personally in order to discuss the nature of the problem directly and to assure the cooperation of the consultant.

By and large, when special communication to the consultant was undertaken by the primary practitioner, rather few problems of coordination and cooperation in the care of the patient were reported. It was in the routine referrals, even for surgery, that problems were likely to arise because in ordinary referrals in the medical group communication was quite brief and because it was precisely those referrals that most often seemed, by outside standards, unnecessary. Routine referrals took place by means of a referral slip written by the practitioner and sometimes (but apparently not always) a note written on the patient's chart describing the complaint, the referrer's findings, and the reason for the referral. For routine referrals, communication was almost wholly written, truncated, and formal, without direct contact with the consultant. Those routine referrals were both the most common ones and the ones serving as a problematic focus for the periodic flare-ups between consultants and primary practitioners. Let us look at how the consultants responded to them.

CONSULTANT RESPONSES TO ROUTINE REFERRALS

In considering consultants' responses to referrals, we must remember that all primary practitioners were not the same in their stances toward referrals. Both primary practitioners and consultants were aware of this situation, though the latter differed greatly in the amount of sympathy and understanding they could feel for the former. In a long but precisely articulated comment, one consultant analyzed the various sources of what he believed to be medically unnecessary referrals, designating some as "pardonable" and some as even desirable.

I would say close to 80 percent of my referrals are unnecessary, because every headache is referred to me, every backache, every numbness in the middle finger—things which all may be of sinister significance if made by a layman. But I expect a physician to use some discrimination. [Behind some of] these overreferrals is a tremendous feeling of insecurity. Some of them come out of hospital practice very young and feel inadequate. But furthermore, there are men already in the group for a long time who have personal problems with respect to having a certain amount of self-assurance and belief in their own capacity. Both of these groups, when I get their patients I have an attitude of, "Well, nothing again." However, when I get referrals by another group of physicians, I take it very seriously and study it thoroughly because I know those men. If he sends them over to me he must have some good reasons, some well-founded suspicion. Even if nothing turns up, his reasoning was good. Occasionally you run into a situation where a man is overworked. He doesn't have the time to evaluate them thoroughly, and he may refer like a traffic cop. This is pardonable. Also on occasion I've encouraged a family doctor to send patients who have no organic . . . disease. It's a question of, let's say, family pressure where the family outright asks the family doctor whether the husband or the son or the wife shouldn't see [me] and I tell the family doctor, "Look, it's much better you send them over even though you may feel there is nothing the matter with them, than to be judged as a stubborn man who feels his ego would be hurt. This is part of good public relations. You just have to do it whether you like it or not." (#34—CONSULTANT)

Clear and logical as the above analysis of overreferral seems, it nonetheless contains within it some unanalyzed assumptions about the division of labor and the roles of both consultant and primary practitioner. It draws a jurisdictional line between those complaints, symptoms, and signs that the primary practitioners should deal with themselves and not refer and those that they can properly refer. Where the line should be drawn is, it should be clear by now, a matter of opinion and perspective and is by no means stable. But taking the drawn line as a given, the analysis did sum up many consultants' views of the sources of overreferral.

One kind of referral was of special interest both because it especially angered the consultants and because it represented a virtually pure bureaucratic response to work. I refer to referrals that were made without a thorough physical examination of the patient (a work-up), referrals sometimes made without the primary practitioner having even seen the patient.

All the referrals in the group use physiotherapy as a way of passing the buck. They're too busy, and they realize maybe the complaint of the patient may be in a number of areas, but rather than examine the patient, which is time-consuming, they'd rather refer him right out. Often there is no work-up. . . . We get a one-line note like "back pain," you know. (#39—CONSULTANT)

That kind of "passing the buck," by referring on the basis of the categorical area of complaint alone, in essence passed on to the consultant the task of true discrimination and subsequent referral. By foregoing the function of expert in favor of that of the official, the primary practitioner in making such a referral in essence pushed over on to the consultants the task of being, within the broad systemic or anatomical limits of their specialties, the primary practitioners who dealt with all manner of complaints, including the trivial complaints that they had attempted to escape by becoming specialists in the first place. *Anything* having to do with the eye or the ear, for example, got referred, without screening for the trivial; in short, solely substantive criteria were used, without reference to normative criteria. Such referral in essence narrowed the jurisdiction of the primary practitioners' responsibility and expanded that of the consultants.

Not all consultants responded to such referrals in the same way. Some were outraged at having oversimple but substantively appropriate problems referred to them. They did not want to expand their normative jurisdiction and were sardonic about the "professors" who felt too important to deal with the trivia themselves.

Family doctors were sending patients down to ENT for taking wax out of ears. . . . We put a stop to it. None of the professors upstairs can wash wax? If they can't wash wax, then the nurses are perfectly capable and trained to do so. Let the nurse do it. Don't [ship] wax down to us when we already have an overloaded schedule. (#51—CONSULTANT)

Others, however, were perfectly willing to take jurisdiction over complaints with which they would not normally have the opportunity of working in an entrepreneurial setting.

I have no complaint about overreferral at all. I feel that out in private practice fewer things are referred because the men in private practice tend to do a lot of minor surgery themselves [without referring to surgeons]. In the group practice the internists are more willing to refer it out to the other person. For example, I feel I should treat ingrown toenails myself. For an internist to handle it is *artificial*. I do lots of bumps and lumps, taking out sebaceous cysts. (#41—CONSULTANT; ITALICS MINE)

Similar differences existed in response to referrals that were not preceded by the work-up necessary for "efficient" specialized work. Some consultants refused to do the examination themselves or at least protested when they had to do their work without benefit of the findings of such an examination recorded in the chart by the primary practitioner. A few had even refused to accept patients who had not been examined, thereby restricting their jurisdiction to highly focused, specialized work that presupposed background work. Others, however, were perfectly willing themselves to take over the general, evaluative function of the primary practitioners so long as they remained within the general substantive boundaries of their particular jurisdiction. Indeed, such consultants were inclined to feel that the primary practitioners were not really well enough trained or experienced to be able to perform such a function adequately.

> Internists get all upset when it comes to doing vaginal examinations. They are not used to it. It is embarrassing. It involves all this rigamarole of the patient getting undressed, with the nurse coming in there and so on. So they don't want to do it, and I don't really blame them. They just don't do it well. . . . And how could they work up a patient for me? I'd expect to give the patient a complete physical myself. (L16—CONSULTANT)

Such variability in willingness to accept a broader jurisdiction and thus to accept the redefinition of specialty practice created by excessive referrals by primary practitioners no doubt stems from a variety of factors, including the relative security of the specialty in the marketplace, the philosophy of the consultant himself and of the segment of the specialty (cf. Bucher and Strauss, 1961) to which he belongs, and his own interest in increasing the amount of time he works at the medical group.

THE ELASTICITY OF SPECIALIZATION

In this chapter I have addressed myself to several facets of a practical problem of the medical group which would be expressed very crudely as tension over referrals between primary practitioners and consultants, referrals that were characterized as excessive. Superficially, that problem could be defined in the quantitative terms of workload and cost: given the large number of patients they saw, and given the lack of economic incentive to provide them with all services, the primary practitioners eased their patient burden by referring some to consultants, thereby creating a heavier workload for the consultants. Since the consultants also had no economic incentive to deal with a larger volume of cases within their prescribed hours, they protested about excessive referral.

But both in referrals and in protests there was a selectivity that could not be discriminated on simple quantitative or economic grounds. Not all cases were referred, and not all referrals were protested. The type or quality of referral was an issue of equal if not greater importance than the number of referrals in delineating the source of conflict. Furthermore, by examining what was chosen for referral and how that influenced the tasks that consultants were accustomed to perform, it was possible to show that not merely the quantitative workload but also the very substance of specialization in the division of labor, the very nature of the work by which specialized services were defined, was at issue. The unit of specialized service which was used for accounting remained the same administrative unit, but its substance had changed. Thus specialization itself proved to be elastic in character, with the sources of stress and resistance stemming from the physicians' conceptions of their dignity and career success—their very identities as physicians—rather than from impersonal technical imperatives given by work itself.

6:

The Organization and Control of Work

In my discussion of medical work in the group, I attempted to show that in the organization, presentation, and performance of doctoring there were genuine problems that were important enough to be worthy of extended description and analysis. These problems had quite direct bearing on the satisfaction of patients in the medical group and on the satisfaction and morale of the physicians themselves. The problems of ordering diagnostic tests and referring to consultants also had quite direct bearing on the cost of operating the medical group. Furthermore, it was possible that these problems of work had bearing on the technical quality of care, for occasional skipping of elements of medical routine may have led to missing conditions at an early stage, when their treatment might have been easier and surer.

However, our primary purpose was not to do an evaluation of the quality of care or the efficiency of the medical group so much as to determine how and why it operated as it did. We were not so much concerned with measuring results as we were with analyzing the nature of the social processes that create these results. Given the unavoidable economy of research effort and emphasis, the almost total absence of systematically collected empirical information about these processes led us to believe that their description and analysis took precedence over correlating inputs with outputs without knowing what lay between them. By describing and analyzing in detail how the doctors perceived their work, their patients, their colleagues, and the administrative framework of their group and how they coped with the problems posed to their work by each of these elements, we can create an informed foundation for interpreting and explaining outcome data in something other than almost wholly speculative terms, as has been the case for most policy discussions.

Some of the emphasis of the past few chapters has been on what was common to most of the physicians—the norm. But in particular cases the emphasis has been on variety. It can in fact be argued that the strength of an intensive study of a single organization lies more in its coherent delineation of the variety to be found within it than of the norm, because the chances are greater for at least segments of the variety to be found in other groups than for the norm to be duplicated. Thus, in the past few chapters, inductive analysis of the variety of responses that the physicians made to the prepaid service contract governing some of the terms and conditions of their salaried work, bearing on their patients' methods of seeking services and on their colleagues' methods of providing, withholding, and ordering services led to a typology of stances toward work problems rather than to the delineation of a norm, or an average. Since most of those interviewed were at least in part engaged also in solo, fee-for-service practice, the typology could be constructed on a more comprehensive basis than might be implied by the rather rare and unusual salaried practice we studied.

THREE STANCES TOWARD WORK

The variety of individual responses I reviewed could be organized and clarified without undue distortion by reducing them to three distinct stances toward the contingencies of work. The stances were delineated essentially by reference to the kind of decision-rule guiding the course of coping with problems of work and the value or norm used to justify such choices. Two stances have been current in self-conscious, abstract thought for some time—one at least since the time of Adam Smith and the other at least since the time of Max Weber. They may be summed up parsimoniously as "the individualistic pursuit of gain" and "disciplined conformity to legitimate rules." The third stance has been developed conceptually more recently and can be summed up as "commitment to an organized craft."

We saw the threads of those stances running through the way the physicians made sense of and coped with a variety of work issues. Indeed, the difficulties some had in coping seemed to stem from their utilization of a stance appropriate to one kind of practice but inappropriate to another. For virtually all of the physicians, to some degree, but for some more than for others, aspects of the entrepreneurial stance were present even though the work situation was not organized on an entrepreneurial basis. After all, they were the middle-class children of a capitalist civilization.

It is possible to elaborate those stances by the empirical terms in which they were practiced. The stance of the *physician-merchant*, or entrepreneur, guided primarily by desire for personal material gain, involved a tendency to provide service only when a fee was attached to it, qualified by technical criteria of medical necessity or responsibility. In the case of demand for housecalls and office visits, the entrepreneur's response was to supply them on the ground of the patient's willingness to pay, which establishes the importance of his need. This rationale justified even the provision of medically unnecessary services: As one physician put it, "The patient pays for his anxiety." Receiving a fee rewards the practitioner for providing unnecessary service.

It must not be thought that this tendency was invariant, however, since the entrepreneur's position in the marketplace and the degree of his interest in material gain can vary. When materially secure, with a satisfactorily high and steady flow of income assured, the entrepreneur may very well refuse some demands for service on the ground that they are unnecessary, inconvenient, or inappropriate. Conversely, if the entrepreneur's practice is economically insecure in a highly competitive market, he may provide services not only for the fees they entail but also to avoid losing his customer to a competitor. Thus, in his therapeutic decisions, he might administer tranquilizers, vitamin B_{12} injections, or antibiotics; prescribe other popular drugs; or even perform surgical procedures such as tonsillectomies if these were what patients demanded. Furthermore, both to avoid losing a customer to a competitor and to avoid alienating the customer by incurring the additional expense of a referral to a more specialized practitioner, the entrepreneur may be inclined to stretch thinly his armamentarium of skills by, instead of referral to a specialist, diagnosing and treating complaints for which he has not had extensive training.

In the medical group, physicians with a strong entrepreneurial stance were likely to trim, reduce, or refuse services simply *because* no material gain was attached to each service unit of work. Some physicians were accused of doing this by others. In contrast, the *physician-official* was in an entirely different position, and if he restricted services, it was for a different reason. The continuous need for monetary gain from a fluid, fee-for-service marketplace was supplanted by basic economic security in the form of a salary and a stable organizational career in the medical group. The aim of the physician-official was to work within a set of contractual rules defining his duties and obligations and minimizing his discretion. As we saw, the service contract of the medical group specified rights on the discretionary basis of medical necessity and so actually deviated considerably from Weber's ideal-typical bureaucracy. But discretion remained a critical element insofar as the physician who wished to exercise it had to risk paying the price of possible bureaucratic trouble that could be created by patients demanding services to which they had nominal contractual rights.

The physician-official's stance was to avoid trouble by minimizing discretion and, wherever convenient, providing patients what they were nominally entitled to, whatever the medical necessity. Thus, the thrust of the official stance was to supply fairly automatically all contractually covered services save those—such as the housecall—which seriously inconvenienced the physician. The conscientious official did not stand on pride in professional status, but conveyed the client's contractual rights to him without demur. The official practiced discretion to the extent of shaving the personal and technical substance of his services where necessary in order to be able to perform them within the limits of time and workload specified by his work contract. In the course of minimizing discretion, he was inclined to refer to consultants categorically, without himself extensively evaluating the case. That narrowed the range of what he was responsible for and broadened the range of jurisdiction and responsibility for the consultant.

Finally, there was *the physician-craftsman*, or expert, a stance that was rather more shadowy than the others but undeniably present. Its focus was not on gain, or on rules, but rather on the skillful and conscientious performance of work as it is evaluated by fellow workers, or the collegium. His reward lay in the satisfaction he obtained from performing his work well, in the trust of patients, and in the respect of colleagues for the quality of his performance. Discretion was a necessary and valued part of work. For the physician-craftsman, the focus of effort was on judging the *functional* propriety of particular services in particular cases. The ground for decision was an expert assessment rather than a formal rule or gain. Thus a request for a housecall was judged by its medical urgency without reference to rule or fee. In addition, since the authority of the physician-craftsman was based on persuasion and the evidence rather than on market position or official status, a request by a patient would be responded to as a problem of discussing the evidence and so persuading the patient to cooperate with the recommendation.

To such physicians in the medical group, an unnecessary request was taken to be an occasion to educate the patient about the circumstances in which a service would be beneficial or harmful in order to cultivate a cooperative relationship that could facilitate future work interactions. Unlike the official, the craftsman insisted on making full use of discretion, but he used discretion in the light of the perceived requisites of good work rather than as a means to cut services down to match the gain they would yield. The decision to make a housecall, to order diagnostic tests, and to refer to consultants, therefore, was made in the light of commitment to the knowledge and skill connected with medical work. The wellspring of that knowledge and skill and the ultimate arbiter of the decision rules involved in its application was the community of fellow workers, the collegium.

The three stances I have delineated can, as I have shown, be matched with three stances taken by patients toward seeking services. In fact, some problems of work were created by some patients' suspicion that physicians were refusing service because they were not being paid a fee and were behaving accordingly, while other work problems were created by the anger that physicians felt when patients behaved like bureaucratic clients. Each stance represents a different way of performing what are usually treated as "the" roles of the doctor and the patient. And of the three, it is apparent that the stance of the physician-expert is usually considered to be the ideal—is what the physician is *expected* to be (cf. Parsons, 1958). Indeed, social policy has thus far left much discretion to physicians partly because of its assumption that they are *not* motivated primarily by the possibility of gain or by the desire to avoid inconvenience and bureaucratic trouble. But, as we saw, the physician-craftsman stance was not easy to sustain in the medical group.

THREE PRINCIPLES FOR ORGANIZATION AND CONTROL

The stances I have described are very difficult to assume when the social and economic organization of work does not provide them with the resources they need. It is difficult to act like an official when there are no systematic rules and regulations; it is difficult to act like a merchant when there is no system of exchange based on money; it is difficult to act like a craftsman when there is no organized, supportive collegium. While it was possible to observe the elements of all three stances in the medical group, it should be apparent that its administrative organization and its mode of financing made the stance of the official far more possible to assume than would be the case in the organizing and financing of ordinary entrepreneurial practice. To more clearly delineate such facilitating circumstances, it is useful to specify logically consistent principles of collective organization and control which parallel each of the stances.

Constituting the ideological and structural support of the stance of the merchant is the principle of organization of the classical free market, in which there are only nominal restraints on free, individual competition.[1] In the free market, productive work is motivated fundamentally by the desire for material gain. What work people do, how they do it, what they produce from their work, and how they assign value to it are essentially functions of market demand. Workers would be seriously handicapped should they be personally committed to the performance of any particular kind of work, since they should be prepared to work on anything that yields a high wage. Thus, in the free market, the worker is expected to be physically, psychologically, socially, and legally free to shift from one kind of work to another as demand (or supply in the light of demand) shifts.

Essentially calculative of advantage, the worker competes with all others for the limited gainful work available in the marketplace. Demand sets the tone: the worker supplies what is demanded because that is the route to gain. The worker's personal judgment of the quality of his product is essentially irrelevant to the process, since it is the market and demand that set value and money that measures it. He may cooperate with other workers who perform related tasks in a division of labor, but he does so only because it is to his material advantage and does not (or should not) develop any sense of solidarity with others or any real collective organization.

The free-market model also makes certain assumptions about the consumer of the production of the worker—the customer. If anyone is the controlling agent, it is the customer. In order for this to be plausible, the model must assume that the consumer is capable of judging the value of the product reasonably accurately and of calculating his own material advantage, so that he is both inclined and able to choose intelligently and

---

[1]Most of the work of contemporary academic economics has little bearing on this sketch, since it restricts itself to elements of exchange such as productivity, consumer demand, and capital investment. I am concerned with the social and psychological assumptions that underly such analysis and with their implications for the organization, evaluation, and creation of work. Such assumptions are most clearly evident in the less technical literature, particularly in the work of the great Adam Smith.

parsimoniously among competing products in the marketplace. By calculating relations among cost, quality of product, and his own needs, he
and his fellow consumers will contribute to an aggregate market demand
that eschews work products that are either of high cost or of low quality
or both. Such a selective, calculating demand is assumed to encourage
workers to produce goods at a low cost. In consequence, more products
will be available to all consumers, and the standard of living will rise to
everyone's benefit. Society will thus reach, as Adam Smith put it, "universal opulence," composed of a large variety of goods and services that
are within almost everyone's means.

The free market gains its coherence by the *unplanned* compatibility of
the aggregate of material interests of producers and consumers engaged
in exchange in the marketplace on the basis of rational calculation of
advantage. In contrast, the coherence of the rational-legal bureaucracy
stems from the *deliberate* planning and control of work on the part of a
limited, elite group, whether government officials or managers of particular productive enterprises.[2] What workers do and how they do it are
a function of the systematically drawn-up plans and rules both created
and enforced by the administration, which is, itself, in theory controlled
by rules specifying the limits of its powers.

Different tasks are deliberately created with some stated productive
end in mind and are arranged into jobs coordinated by special hierarchical offices, which are themselves defined and specified as jobs. Since
the aim is predictability of production, the thrust of rationalization is
toward the standardization of tasks and work roles. For both productive
workers and officials, the assumption is that the material security and
predictable career prospects provided by the plan (Stinchcombe, 1974),
in conjunction with the legitimacy ascribed to the plan and its

---

[2]Max Weber's analysis of the types of authority and their sustaining administrative apparatus (1947) constitutes my major source here. But it is important to note that I am
concerned more with a *principle* for organizing work than with bureaucratic institutions.
Thus the principle of rationalized control and planning, which is in logical opposition to the
free-market principle, can nonetheless be adopted by industrial managers of particular
enterprises in capitalist nations. Indeed, the principle has been perfected more by
capitalist industrialists seeking greater efficiency and profits than by socialist planning
administrations. "Scientific management" in business administration and Taylorism in the
design of productive tasks—both developed under capitalism—are better illustrations of
Weberian rationalization than are the civil service bureaucracies Weber seemed to have
had in mind when he wrote or the planning authorities created by contemporary communist or socialist governments. It may be remembered how enthusiastic Lenin was about
Taylorism and how much the planning and managerial principles used in the Soviet Union
resemble those in the West.

functionaries, will lead them to perform in accordance with the rules and produce predictably. This is to say, it is assumed that their performance will be disciplined by the rules. It is further assumed that the requisite tasks for gaining a given productive end can be reduced to rules and that only minimal individual calculation of personal advantage, or discretion, need operate. Where the task involves the direct provision of service to a clientele, it is assumed that the clients can both learn and understand their rights under the rules, and thus that they can and will seek and gain their just rights. The workers, not being competitors in a free labor market, are bound together by the formal rules defining their secure positions, legitimate functions, and career prospects. Should they evince solidarity beyond that defined by the rules, it is likely to be a "status" solidarity among all those on a given supervisory level, though functional "situs" or "departmental" solidarity may also exist.

Whereas the thrust of work in the free market is toward a *gainful* product, and the thrust of work in a disciplined organization is toward a *standardized* product, the thrust of work in the collegium, or organization of fellow craftsmen, is toward a *qualitative* product.[3] The intrinsic value of the product can be legitimately judged only by the collegium, not by the customer or the manager, for it is claimed that only the collegium possesses sufficient knowledge and skill to do so. Insofar as the work is produced by only one kind of worker, without specialization, relations among workers are based upon occupational solidarity. Where a division of labor is required, the work is coordinated by the workers themselves, using functional criteria mediated by the authority of expertise and its qualities of persuasive demonstration.

Neither market advantage nor the authority of office is granted legitimacy in coordinating and directing effort in the professional model. Influence and status are based on superior skill and knowledge rather than on money or official position. Consistent with that criterion, the

---

[3]My sources here lie partially in the well-known analyses of professions by Parsons (e.g., 1968), Goode (e.g., 1969), Moore (1970), and others. I myself have criticized such analyses as being empirically inaccurate (Freidson, 1970a, 1970b), and I do not mean to retract that criticism here. Such work may best be seen as struggling toward recognizing and delineating an abstract collegial principle for organizing and controlling skilled work which is quite distinct from that of the free market and of rationalizing managerial authority and which has pertinence to such historical institutions as guilds, crafts, and professions. (See my paper on the "occupational principle" for the organization and control of work—Freidson, 1973.) On the nature and consequences of commitment to special skill and technique, see Veblen (1964) and Ellul (1964). On the social psychology of social identity and work, see Becker (1970), Hughes (1971), and Bensman and Lilienfeld (1973).

relation of workers to each other and to their clientele is one based on the persuasive demonstration of the value of the skill or knowledge embodied in the work. The clientele are led to use the products or services of the craftsman or expert because they have gained faith in their value, not because the products or services are cheap or an official entitlement. But since the claim is that the workers' skill and knowledge are sufficiently complex or esoteric to be unstandardizable, then it follows that laymen cannot assess its quality sufficiently well to be their own guides. In the professional model, therefore, the client is conceived of as being unable to judge the product and as being without any formal rights to control it. The worker must assume responsibility for the welfare of the client as well as for the public good: neither equity adjudicated by a set of legitimate rules nor a favorable position in the marketplace can adequately protect the client.

THE TRANSFORMATIONS OF MEDICAL WORK

These three different principles for organizing and controlling work presuppose differences in the conception, measurement, and evaluation of work and work products. *The way work is organized and controlled influences the nature of work itself.* As we saw empirically in prior chapters, the substance of particular tasks, such as making a housecall or a referral, was not stable and invariant, a function of some irrevocable technological imperative. Rather, particular tasks were transformed by the worker's stance or by the stance of colleagues in the division of labor who referred work. Insofar as such varied stances may be seen to be encouraged selectively by the social organization of the work setting in which they are assumed, we should expect the transformations of each to flourish more in one form of organization than in others.

Essentially, I should expect variation in the social organization of work to lead work effort to focus on attaining different work outcomes or measures. In the free market, since the prime criteria of value are high gain for the producer (or his employer) and low cost to the consumer, we should expect work to be oriented to producing as many salable units as possible of a sort that would attract and hold the demand of customers, for so is gain generated. Tasks would multiply to supply available demand, their worth justified by the gain they generate. In the free market, *cost* and *gain* are the prime criteria of work. In an administered social organization, however, work is a function of deliberate rules seeking to assure some predictable outcome determined by management. In order for work to yield a predictable outcome, it must be in some sense standardized by criteria that can be laid out in advance by means of rules that minimize variability and discretion. Work thus gets transformed into something mechanical enough to produce a *standardized* result—either a standard product or a standard measure or record of a product. In order to become standardized and predictable, work must become automatic and categorical either in its substance or in the way it is measured or accounted for. Qualities are anathema. In a collegium of workers, work tends to undergo constant refinement and specialization independent of client demand. Commitment to skill, knowledge, or technique for its own sake leads to the generation of new applications and pressure toward extending its application beyond traditional occupational boundaries: commitment to it inevitably leads to occupational imperialism. Under such circumstances, work tends to be the antithesis of standardization and, if unconstrained by external realities, indifferent to criteria of cost. The collegium attempts to gain the acceptance (and support) of the lay world by emphasizing those values of its work which are priceless: it emphasizes values that transcend money and quantitative measurement, and it stresses the creative and the dynamic. Thus the work of doctoring can assume significantly different guises as it is controlled and organized in different ways; the same service in accounting terms can, under the facade of the record, be markedly different.

THE WORLDLY STATUS OF THE MODELS

The logical models of different ways of organizing work do not correspond to any historical reality. Indeed, while they may have some plausible relationship to contemporary reality, they were not sketched out with the intent of portraying reality so much as with the intent of separating out on analytical grounds the various images juxtaposed and confused all together in the world. But while each model is merely an analytical construct here, each has, in fact, also served as part of distinctly different political-economic ideologies. Each has served as a plan advanced by the committed participants of a social movement and as an ideology by which to persuade those in power or with potential power to initiate the practical political and economic steps necessary to reorganize the world in its image.

Each is constantly invoked today in the debates on public policy and concrete legislation. Each serves as a model on the basis of which public policy can be formulated by those in power, though the reality of politics in the United States virtually precludes a policy based exclusively on only one of them. As I have already noted in Chapter 1, present-day policy combines elements of both the professional and the bureaucratic model. It also includes some of the assumptions of the free-market model in its use of fee-for-service modes of paying the doctor and of economic incentives to encourage greater efficiency.

But while the models are abstract, the policies are formal and, in health care if not elsewhere, rely almost entirely on *indirect* methods of social control. They rely on creating a constraining framework around the possibilities for behavior without at the same time creating methods of direct control to ensure that the desired behavior is supported. That characteristic is in part a necessity, for only a virtual revolution would make it politically feasible to nationalize the profession and create a state-controlled, bureaucratic medical service. That characteristic, however, is also one chosen willingly on the basis of the assumption that what the indirect formal constraints did not control the profession itself would control by its own direct methods.

The medical group we studied has been taken as a topical test case of that assumption, for it operated within a kind of framework of indirect administrative controls toward which national policy has been moving, and its physicians were free of the direct administrative controls that exist, for example, in industry or in most civil service agencies. No supervisors attempted to exercise direct control over the medical worker's performance. How can we assess the effectiveness of that choice to nest the professional model inside a bureaucratic framework? First, we can say that if an organized and purposive system of direct social control exists in an organization, we would expect comparative homogeneity to exist among the workers in their outlook on and performance of work. Second, we can say that if a policy of organizational control is effective, we should expect that the workers' performance and outlook would be compatible with that policy. What was the case for the prepaid-service-contract medical group?

The administrative plan did in effect successfully abolish the fee barrier and the fee for service, but it did not, in and of itself, impose any further conditions on the physicians. By and large, I think it can be said that the problems of the medical group described in Chapter 2 indicated that, from the point of view of the intent underlying its fiscal and administrative organization, something less than optimal performance took place. The constant struggles over housecalls, the ordering of diagnostic tests, and referrals to consultants displayed the nature of those problems and suggested that the indirect social controls of the workers were not effective and did not sustain the intent of the administrative plan. This may *not* be taken as reason to reject the value of such an administrative and fiscal arrangement, however, because it relied on professional control for its implementation; the nature of the internal-control processes not the plan, may have at fault. If these internal-control processes are critical, tinkering with elements of the administrative framework by reinstituting fee barriers, fee-for-service payment, and the like may not improve performance very much at all, or if it does it may do so for the wrong reasons. Obviously, the internal process of direct social control is critical, but it has the status of a black box, an unknown. Unknown, it mediates the production of output from input.

What can we guess about the nature of the direct social controls of the collegium of physicians in the medical group from what we have learned already? If the physicians' conceptions of their work and performance were homogeneous and uniform from one to another, we could assume that there was some effective selection and/or social-control process operating in the medical group. But there was, in fact, wide variation both in orientation or stance toward work and in performance. Apart from what I have already described, I might note that, in the administratively collated monthly service statistics of the medical group, there was a very wide range of variation among individuals in the number of housecalls they made and in the diagnostic tests they ordered. Furthermore, consultants referred to a wide range of variation among individual primary practitioners in the making of unnecessary referrals. Thus, we can say that, whatever the nature of the process of direct social control among the group physicians, it neither followed the intent of administrative policy nor developed its own homogeneity in orientation and performance. Patently this must lead us to conclude that the nature of the process of direct social control exercised among the physicians of the medical group was not something to be merely assumed and taken for granted but rather something to be considered problematic, something to be investigated. The remainder of this book will be addressed to its analysis.

THE ELEMENTS OF SOCIAL CONTROL

How does one go about analyzing a process of social control? What issues must one address in order to be reasonably complete in one's analysis, and what elements must one describe and isolate? As a term and as a concept, "social control" is rather vague. Some of the discussions in the sociological literature limit themselves to an examination of the formal system of legal control and its agents (cf. Gibbs, 1972). Other discussions are addressed to the concept in a very broad way, concerned with the dominant social values guiding the delineation of deviance and its management (cf. Pitts, 1968). Even Mannheim (1948), who was deeply concerned with precisely the policy issues addressed here, remained distressingly vague about the various elements of the process of social control.

In the more limited context of the social control of work in formal organizations—particularly manufacturing organizations—there is a great deal of information available on the operation of informal controls and on many of the facets of the influence exercised by foremen and supervisors, but no real analytic framework has grown out of those studies which could guide us here. Perhaps because so much of the research has gone on in formal organizations that are structured by strong, legitimate managerial authority, a great deal of the process is taken for granted and more attention is focused on, for example, the degree to which various participants exercise control rather than on the nature and substance of the process itself (e.g., Tannenbaum, 1968). Since our interest is in professional rather than bureaucratic control, however, there is no authority or hierarchy to organize and exercise it, so we must be concerned with isolating and analyzing as many of the essential elements of the process as possible, minimizing what we take for granted.

Recently, Dornbusch and Scott (1975) have attempted both to conceptualize the issues involved in social control in organizations and to collect comparative data testing some of their conceptions. A number of their distinctions prove useful to the present task of analysis. First, central to the issue of social control is the matter of who has the right to attempt to exercise control over another—who has the authority to attempt to influence another's behavior by the exercise of rewards or sanctions. As we saw in Chapter 2, the physicians recognized the essential legitimacy, or validity, of the administration's right to exercise control over the assignment of workloads and scheduling, but it was not at all clear that they approved of it or recognized its propriety. As Dornbusch and Scott summarize the distinction,

> Subordinates may believe certain norms governing power relations to be *valid* in the sense that they do acknowledge that the norms do exist, and subordinates may view certain norms governing the power relationships of the *proper* in that they believe that these norms are as they should be. (DORNBUSCH AND SCOTT, 1975: 41; ITALICS ADDED)

Throughout my analysis in subsequent chapters, we shall see physicians contesting the propriety, if not the validity, of various norms, techniques of surveillance, and sanctions.

A second distinction connected with the exercise of control and related to that between validity and propriety refers to the legitimacy of the exercise of social control by a particular person. As we shall see in Chapter 7, the physicians did concede that they were indeed employees and that the medical director was *authorized* by the officials of the organization that owned the medical group to exercise control. Nonetheless, they themselves were not inclined to *endorse* the exercise of that power as legitimate (Dornbusch and Scott, 1975: 42). Given the primacy of direct professional control in the medical group, we should expect that administrative authority would not be endorsed by the physicians and that they would instead emphasize the legitimacy of their own authority.

Central to the issue of control, of course, are the *rules* that establish what is expected of those who perform work in a particular setting or, more commonly, that specify what is undesirable, below minimum standards, or otherwise deviant. Such norms or rules must be addressed in comprehensive terms to be understood adequately. They cannot be represented as only a set of mere don'ts: to be usable, they must also embody definitions of the persons who have the authority to define deviance, judge it, and sanction it; definitions of the kind of person to whom particular rules apply; and definitions of the circumstances in which particular kinds of performance may be properly judged as deviant. Once we know how the physicians of the medical group conceived of the work they did and what criteria they used to define adequate performance, we can understand at least part of the reason for the way they exercised social control. We have already seen in Chapter 2 how they responded to administrative attempts to establish rules and control deviations from them. In Chapter 8 I shall explore the nature of the rules the physicians themselves recognized and emphasize in particular the way they delineated mistakes as deviations from acceptable performance which could be said to warrant reproach and efforts at control.

Rules setting the criteria for work performance are obviously a necessary element of any process of social control, but they are not sufficient by themselves. Control would not take place if there were no rules, but, by the same token, control could not take place if there were no system of *surveillance* by which performance could be observed. One could not know that rules were violated without some method of collecting information about performance. Furthermore, for purposes of control, that information about performance must be actively *evaluated* in the light of the rules in order for those judging performance to be able to conclude that it was satisfactory or unsatisfactory.

> To arrive at a performance evaluation requires the identification of the value attained on one or more selected properties of the task. The identification of such a performance value requires that information be gathered on the task performance which is to be evaluated. The decision concerning which information will be used in order to arrive at a performance evaluation is termed the "sampling decision." (DORNBUSCH AND SCOTT, 1975: 140)

Additional elements of a system of social control, therefore, are to be found in the bases for *evaluating* performance, in the opportunities for *observing* performance, in the method of *collecting information* about performance, and in the *disposition of information* about performance. In Chapter 9 I shall describe how the group physicians addressed the problem of evaluating the competence of their colleagues and what criteria they regarded to be most important. Then, in Chapter 10, I shall describe how surveillance took place, what evaluative information on performance was collected and by whom, and, finally, how that information about performance was circulated or distributed through the colleague group.

The emphasis on the circulation of information about performance is especially important for the analysis of the process of social control in a collegium because there is no recognized hierarchical authority whose duty it is to supervise and collect such information. In a collegium, the essential issue lies in the degree to which *all* members have access to evaluative information and take action on it. The issue is not, as in a hierarchy, the degree to which responsible supervisors have such information. Without broad distribution of evaluative information about performance, social control cannot be a collective function of the collegium. In the practical terms of social policy addressed by this study, without a system of surveillance in which all members of the medical group observe and evaluate each other's performance and a system by which they share their information and evaluations, it is difficult to see how the medical group could, as is commonly assumed, contain a process of social control which is much different than that to be found among solo practitioners scattered in their individual offices throughout a locality.

After consideration in Chapter 11 of the physicians' views of the medical record as a special source of evaluative information, I shall turn finally to discussion of the selection and use of *sanctions* by which control may be exercised. In Chapter 12 I shall discuss the selection of sanctions by analyzing the physicians' conceptions of the propriety of applying particular sanctions to colleagues as well as their conceptions of the effectiveness of those sanctions. Finally, bringing my analysis to a close, I shall describe, in Chapters 13 and 14, the sanctions the physicians used and the occasions on which they used them.

Having thus described the *rules* employed by the group physicians to *evaluate* performance, the system of *surveillance* over performance, the *distribution* of evaluative information, and the choice and application of *sanctions* to control errant behavior, I shall be in a position to evaluate the nature of the process of professional social control in the medical group and thus be able to suggest an explanation of the variation in performance found among its members.

The Foundation for Social Control

7:

The Neutralization of Formal Authority

A number of elements form the foundation for social control. The most conspicuous among them revolve around the formal authority of those whose official position is one of responsibility for the performance of others and of the legitimate right to give them orders and exercise corrective measures in the event of deviance. Such formal status is manifested in the form of a hierarchy of titles and offices, lower units being accountable to higher units and appropriate authority being assigned to each unit. But the formal elements of official offices, hierarchies, and ascribed authority do not actually constitute a foundation for social control if their ascribed prerogatives are not exercised. And the exercise of these prerogatives depends on the willingness and capacity of officeholders to do so, as well as on the willingness of their subordinates to grant their authority legitimacy and thus to obey. Without that, the formal order is simply "mock bureaucracy" (cf. Gouldner, 1954); to understand the real nature of social control, one must look beyond the formal order.

On balance, the medical group could be said to be more of a mock bureaucracy than a functioning bureaucracy, because the ascribed powers of various hierarchical positions were exercised and honored far less often than one might expect. This is not to say that formal authority was not exercised at all, for we have already seen evidence of attempts at laying down rules and enforcing them, and in a later chapter we shall see how the administration came, by default, to serve an ultimately critical role in the social-control process. Nonetheless, I shall try to show how much of the formal authority in the medical group was neutralized by the reluctance of its holders to employ it and, perhaps most importantly, by the unwillingness of the working physicians to grant it legitimacy. Indeed, whenever an effort was made to employ formal authority to order their work, the group physicians resisted it in no uncertain terms. The medical group was a classic case of "bureaucratic-professional conflict." (Cf. Benson, 1973, for a critical review of the literature on such conflict and a restatement of the analytical issues.)

Illustrative of the effective power of the collegium was the response to an administrative attempt to develop rules governing housecalls. The following is an account of that attempt, constructed from my handwritten notes taken at two successive meetings of the Executive Committee.

ADMINISTRATOR: I'd like to make a rule that any person with rash and fever should be seen by the doctor. Some doctors are not seeing them, diagnosing measles, chicken pox, allergy on the phone, saying, "I'll call the druggist." Second, should they be seen at the group rather than in the home if they're infectious?

#23: Such a rule would not be fair. An enormous number of housecalls would be made for the second child who comes down with the disease later.

#20: The vast majority of them have a history of exposure to someone with the disease.

#47: Why did this come up?

ADMINISTRATOR: I discovered it reviewing some records. They were all children's records that I saw, some family doctors and some pediatricians doing it. Now we can make the rule, qualifying it by, "unless the first child was seen and the second reports rash and fever."

#23: Why don't you trust us? We've been handling it for years.

ADMINISTRATOR: If discretion is not adequate, we must make a rule. Do you bring the children to the group rather than make a housecall?

#23: Yes. Every time this happens we've kept track and it doesn't matter much as far as it means exposing other children to them in the waiting room.

ADMINISTRATOR: Could you show me the statistics?

#23: I don't know if we can find them, but we've kept track and it doesn't matter.

#20: We're exposed all the time, and we're not quarantined.

#51: I went from the top floor of the building and down again after I opened the ear of a kid with scarlet fever. I didn't wash thoroughly. Sometimes I don't even wash my hands.

ADMINISTRATOR: Semmelweiss is revolving in his grave. . . .

#20: [*To the Administrator*] It's your field; what's the incidence of congenital anomalies in women infected by measles?

ADMINISTRATOR: There are few, but our responsibility differs when we ask the child to come in to the group, compared to when a mother brings one in on her own. If we say in the first case, "Bring the child in," rather than make a housecall, we assume responsibility. It's not good medical practice.

#23: We're so rarely mistaken.

ADMINISTRATOR: I wish I had your confidence.

#23: In 99 percent of the cases it's chicken pox.

ADMINISTRATOR: On the phone you say, "It's just a rash." When pustules are reported, "Tell the kid to stop scratching." When there are scabs, "Well, the kid had chicken pox."

#20: Let's table this. I make a motion.

#1: [*Laughing*] I second it. . . .

#20: I don't know anyone who asks someone with rash and 104° to come in rather than making a housecall.

ADMINISTRATOR: I'll change your mind.

ADMINISTRATOR #2: It's tabled.

ADMINISTRATOR: Okay, we'll bring it up again next week.

[*Executive Committee Meeting, one week later.*]

ADMINISTRATOR: The rule about rash and fever was tabled last week. What do you want done?

#47: #23 feels that the chances of cross infection in the waiting room are small.

ADMINISTRATOR: That's common sense, but the opposite view is common sense too. There's no data or evidence. . . .

#20: Why did you bring it up?

ADMINISTRATOR: I told you last week.

#20: No, you didn't.

ADMINISTRATOR: A patient of #12 complained. I checked the [insurance service record] forms [which indicate the diagnosis and where the service is performed] and found that this is done often. I felt this was a bad practice.

#4: [*Garbled statement, apparently neutral on the topic.*]

ADMINISTRATOR: Only housecalls, then? [*Silence.*] Not acceptable.

#51: We should leave it to individual judgment.

ADMINISTRATOR: Well, we'll see.

Clearly, there was little support for a rule specifying when housecalls must be made. Such a rule could have been promulgated in theory, but, as the administrator stated a year earlier, it would have been difficult, if not impossible, to enforce it. The physicians did not grant legitimacy to such a rule and, characteristically, felt the issue should be left to discretion. The physicians were dubious of both the legitimacy of orders that might have emanated from officeholders and, indeed, any authority that might have been imputed to formal office. As we shall see, while formal office existed in the medical group, the legitimacy and the power of hierarchical authority were in fact neutralized, leaving to the informal organization of the medical group—the collegium—the responsibility for stimulating and guiding the performance of its members.

THE AUTHORITY OF THE ADMINISTRATION

The formal administrative hierarchy clearly provided the organizational prerequisite for the bureaucratic control of all work in the group. Most of the physicians recognized the formal legitimacy of the authority of the director of the medical group, but their recognition was tinged with ambivalence and even, sometimes, disfigured by denial. Indeed, one senior man deplored his colleagues' tendency to gloss over the authority of the administration, but he himself did so by the qualification "in a measure."

> We've always claimed we have some degree of autonomy. But I think some of the men don't understand that the director is in a measure our chief. And on occasion he will sometimes rightly make decisions, even though he might be willing to discuss things. Some of the men think we're like a partnership. (#47—CONSULTANT)

The issue essentially seemed to be the difference between what was recognized to be legitimate by *official* standards of authority and what was accepted as legitimate by *professional* standards. It in fact seemed to lead to contradictions in the physicians' responses to questions about what the administration was for. A number of physicians differentiated between functions that were proper or legitimate for the administration and those that were not. Several, for example, distinguished what they called the legitimate function of seeing that physicians were doing their job properly and maintaining the quality of medical work from the improper function of controlling practice or "professional decisions," though how the former could be separated from the latter was not clear.

> The only thing they shouldn't control is your method of practicing medicine and the actual treatment of the patient. . . . But the administration should be able to control the doctor and his obligations to the patient. (#26—CONSULTANT)

Apart from those few who allowed no legitimate role at all for the administration beyond record-keeping and other forms of housekeeping, in general the physicians tended to at once concede and deny legitimacy to administrative authority over most facets of the doctor's work. (Similar findings were made by Goss, 1959, 1961, 1963.) It was in discussing particular issues of work that some clarification of this contradiction was gained.

One function that all physicians conceded to be both legitimate and desirable for the administration was housekeeping. Indeed, being relieved of housekeeping duties was one of the major virtues of the group practice argued by its proponents. But what does housekeeping include? Equipping and maintaining consultation rooms, hiring, training, supervising, and paying receptionists, nurses, aides, and clerks, and maintaining the building are all elements of housekeeping which are accepted without question as contributing to the smooth running of the group. So also did the scheduling and supervising of office-appointment hours, but, as we have already seen, the legitimacy of such activities was not accepted by all physicians.

Superficially, it would not seem inappropriate for the administration to see that the hours of office-appointment time for which it had contracted with a physician were fulfilled. A number of physicians in fact felt it was perfectly appropriate that the administration check on hours so as to assure itself that scheduled patients were seen. Some also felt that it was perfectly appropriate for the administration to reprimand physicians for not conforming to the requirements of their contract. However, the matter was not so simple. While the obligation to have a certain number of office hours a week was contractual, as was, for primary practitioners, the obligation to care for the medical needs of a panel composed of a certain number of patients, a strong segment of physician opinion insisted nonetheless on the impropriety of a bureaucratic approach to evaluating that obligation. We have already noted that many asserted that the individual practitioner himself should be his own judge as to the way he managed his time. He was treated like a laborer, a child, a clerk when he was evaluated by clock time and when he was subjected to reprimand or question about clock time. These critics emphasized their status as independent professionals who should be their own bosses, and, as we have already seen, they questioned the logic of administrative accounting that dealt solely with time missed in regular hours and not with extra time put in past regular hours. It is important to understand, however, that they were not arguing for more precise accounting of work time so as to get bureaucratic "credit" for overtime; rather, they were arguing that they did overtime for which they did not expect credit as a way of showing that they were responsible enough to be free to use their own judgment about their regular working hours.

While there was some difference of opinion surrounding the issue of administrative control over office hours and professional time in general, there was considerably more controversy surrounding the issue of ad-

ministrative involvement in circumstances in which patients were dis-
satisfied with their physicians. Indeed, there were highly contradictory
viewpoints. Some physicians felt that if their patients had complaints,
they should speak to their own physicians, and not to a third party
administrator, about them. In essence, they did not want the administration involved at all in handling patient complaints, feeling that it in some
way demeaned them or undermined their relationship with their patients. Other physicians felt that all patient complaints should receive
attention from someone beyond the physician involved. Some asserted
ethical grounds, others felt it was an important way by which patients
could ventilate their feelings harmlessly, and still others simply did not
want to be bothered with dealing with the patients themselves.

Given the de facto channel for complaints that could not be avoided or
dismantled, there was general consensus among the physicians that the
administration should deal with complaints in such a way as to protect
the doctors.

Right or wrong, the administration should back the doctor (#58—PRIMARY
PRACTITIONER)

But whatever the strategy of the administration in managing patient
complaints, the very fact of such management remained to rankle some
if not most of the physicians in one way or another. What seemed to be
at issue was accountability of the individual physician to a third party
who had some sort of authority over him. Such accountability was seen
as a diminution of professional status and was often compared to being
in the position of a schoolchild or a salesperson in a department store.

Backing the physician has not been as powerful as it might be. When a man or
woman can complain about a physician on a trivial nonsensical level exactly
as they can to an owner of a department store about a salesgirl, and they're
not told in no uncertain terms that this is trivial nonsense and we won't
tolerate such complaints, when the complaint is given too much credence and
the patient is reassured, the assumption is, even if it hasn't happened, that the
doctor was called on the carpet and the patient has this kind of power over
him. In my opinion you are destroying an element of the practice of medicine
and more important you are undermining the morale of your physician.
(#43—CONSULTANT)

In essence, the view seemed to be that the administration should not serve as an independent third agent but rather should serve as an agent of the physicians in problems of patient management. Any other role constituted illegitimate interference with the doctor's practice. And the exercise of administrative authority on behalf of the patient was bitterly resented.

Finally, we can examine the physicians' responses to the use of administrative authority in coping with a problem they all recognized—the ordering of laboratory tests and X rays. These orders cost the medical group a considerable sum of money: indeed, a great many felt it was an excessive sum. Nonetheless, they were unanimous in insisting on their corporate right to control the use of such services. Those who felt that some control should be exercised phrased that control in the context of professional consultation and persuasion rather than in terms of administrative quotas or regulations (though quotas and guidelines set up by the municipal department of health for the use of scarce flu vaccine during an epidemic were not really opposed by anyone). As the following remark indicated in answer to the interviewer's leading question about administrative regulation, individual judgment was stressed.

It wouldn't be proper for the administration to regulate the use of X rays such as reducing them by 10 percent. If they started to cut like that, it gets foolish. An X ray should be made when it is medically indicated. Use your best judgment. You have to take X rays at the drop of a hat when there is any suspicion. You are better off. You pick up a lot of things like that. (L17—CONSULTANT)

Nonetheless, since expenditures on tests and X rays reduced the sum available to pay the doctors, their use influenced physician income. A number of physicians felt that a committee might be used to reduce the utilization of tests and X rays. If the physicians were sufficiently aroused (and administrative initiative in collating and publicizing statistics and costs was considered a legitimate method of arousing them), they would influence one another's judgment so as to be sensitive to cost when they considered ordering tests or X rays.

There should be some sort of control over tests and X rays, done in committee. If one doctor spoke to another, he might come around saying, "You ordered so many GI series, do you think that should be the first part of the

work-up, or do you think it could wait a while? Or do you think you ought to
see the patient two or three times before ordering it?" (#11—PRIMARY PRAC-
TITIONER)

Similarly, education and persuasion were suggested as modes of reducing unnecessary referrals. But this was a colleague matter and not one in
which the exertion of administrative authority was acceptable. Some
years before we studied the medical group, an administrative directive
attempting to limit the ordering of tests and X rays was almost unani-
mously and very strongly opposed.

The import of this review of the physicians' evaluation of the legitimacy of the formal authority of the administration should be clear: while
the ultimate legality of the administration's authority to hire physicians,
determine their office hours, and receive and investigate patient complaints was unquestioned, the propriety of such authority was questioned by at least some physicians in all areas of work. Given such
evaluations of the legitimacy of administrative authority, it is not difficult to understand why it was rarely exercised in a direct fashion as a
formal order. Rather, neutralized by physicians' resistance, it was at-
tenuated into influence, somewhat reinforced by the fact that a formal
system of officeholders did exist, but personal and informal nonetheless.
And, as we shall see, the officeholder, for conscious ideological reasons
and perhaps for unconscious reasons of prudence, abdicated some of the
responsibilities of the office to the physicians. The social form that this
abdication took was precisely that form which many physicians in the
medical group felt would be a more appropriate alternative to an administrative hierarchy—a governing committee composed of representatives of the physicians themselves. The Executive Committee of the
medical group was the chosen instrument answering that common professional yearning for self-government.

THE AUTHORITY OF THE EXECUTIVE COMMITTEE

The bylaws of the medical group contained some very carefully written passages on the Executive Committee:

The Group shall be directed by a medical director appointed by the Board of
Trustees [of the employing organization]. He will be *assisted* by an executive

committee. . . . Functions of the executive committee: to act as a comitia minora for subjects referred by the Group. To act as an *advisory* committee to the medical director on subjects for which consultation is sought. . . . The executive committee will present the *opinion* of the Group and the medical director on matters of policy. They will act as an arbitration committee in any major conflict between any two members or between a member and the medical director. (ITALICS ADDED.)

In the light of such care in formulating the functions of the Executive Committee without specifying any formal authority, it should be no surprise that the medical director, in an interview, should have said the following:

In an official sense, the Executive Committee does not exist. It has no . . . status whatsoever [before the Board of Trustees]. It has no legal standing or rights. And the Executive Committee of this group cannot bear the burden of any act or lack of action that happens. Whatever happens in this group is my responsibility. (ADMINISTRATOR)

In the light of the vagueness of its mandate, it is understandable that the physicians were unclear about the functions of the Executive Committee. There were great differences of opinion and knowledge about it. Ten doctors who had been members of the group for at least one year expressed complete ignorance about the functions of the Executive Committee; some were not even aware that it existed. Others in the group expressed rather general puzzlement about its functions. Some saw it as mere "window dressing," and others saw it as merely a symbol. A very large number—17—explicitly stated that the Executive Committee had no significant governing functions, and that the "owners" of the group and employers of the physicians made all important decisions. Only eight of the physicians took a positive position by claiming that the Executive Committee performed governing functions. One specified that the role of the Executive Committee was to screen physicians applying for open positions and thereby uphold the quality of care. Another claimed that it served an important function by organizing the expression of physician opinion.

The Executive Committee serves an important function because a doctor should have some place to assert his voice. The front office doesn't see the group from the doctor's point of view, and there should be something to express it, if only in an advisory capacity. I don't think it has much power. But if something came up and it was considered important and all the family doctors were against it, I think the director would have to sit down and listen to us. (#18—PRIMARY PRACTITIONER)

Clearly, even positive evaluations of the rule of the Executive Committee in governing the group were modest. And when asked how that role could be expanded and strengthened, few members of the group had any recommendations. One felt that the Executive Committee should be a body separate from the administration, presumably without administrative officials included in its deliberations. Others felt, in rather general terms, that it should have more independence and power. By and large, a diffuse discontent, with a vague, even if sometimes strong, feeling that it should be a more powerful body was expressed about the role of the Executive Committee. As the physicians perceived it, it was obviously in no position to serve in any significant capacity that required formal authority or power.

But while the physicians assigned the Executive Committee little role beyond being a sounding board for their opinions, perhaps even a "cat's-paw" for the administration, the medical director at once asserted its lack of official authority, as we have already seen, but at the same time asserted his own abdication of decision-making power to it. Furthermore, if we bear in mind his predecessor's failure to establish a rule governing circumstances in which housecalls must be made and his mention in the following interview passage of having to succumb reluctantly to persistent Executive Committee proposals to buy night coverage from others after midnight, we can understand such abdication as being as necessary as it was principled.

The Executive Committee was set up in order to apply [Board of Trustee] policy to group practice, and the Executive Committee will work in two different ways. In the first place they will take proposals that I make and discuss them and decide whether they should be carried out in the way in which I make the proposal or in some modified way. Or they may create subcommittees to discuss them, analyze them, and suggest how they should be carried out. That's when I initiate something. The Executive Committee may also propose to me. They may say, "We don't want to work after midnight. We want you to hire doctors to work for us after midnight," and I fight this for five years and then succumb. But you can't say that I delegate authority to them. Actually, we are part of the same instrument. I have willingly and deliberately abdicated my sole responsibility. [But] I [remain] responsible to the [employing organization] for whatever happens. (ADMINISTRATOR)

On balance, the material available to our study suggested that, while the Executive Committee had no formal authority of any kind, it did have rather more influence than might be presumed from its lack of formal authority. The influence of the Executive Committee stemmed from its capacity to portray itself as representative of all the practitioners in the medical group. Insofar as it was representative of the medical group, it reflected the kind of resistance the physicians would mount in the face of attempts to impose, by formal authority, particular rules for work in the medical group—resistance to which a prudent administrator must pay heed. Conversely, as in the case of hiring physicians to "cover" after midnight, the Executive Committee represented the kind of demand on the part of the physicians of the medical group which was persistent and strong enough to virtually require recognition and, finally, implementation by the administration in spite of its reservations. Thus, while the Executive Committee had virtually no formal authority, it had a great deal of influence on administrative decisions affecting the physicians of the medical group.

THE AUTHORITY OF THE CHIEFS

The last source of potential formal authority to be explored as a source of social control over the performance of the group physicians lay in the office of the "chief." In the medical group it happened that in each of at least the major specialized areas of practice—internal medicine, pediatrics, surgery, obstetrics-gynecology—a senior person held a special position sometimes designated as "chief." As a more experienced, senior professional, his qualification to supervise the performance of his colleagues could not be seriously faulted, as could the qualifications of full-time administrators. As a practicing member of a specialty, his competence to evaluate the details of specialized work could not be impugned. The problem was, however, that the role of the chief was as ambiguous as the other formal roles in the group, though the exact substance of that role varied from one specialty to the next.

Most of the chiefs disclaimed serving in any formal supervisory func-

tion, though, in the course of describing what they did, it was apparent
that they considered themselves to have somewhat more responsibility
than did the average practitioner for the performance of their colleagues
in the same specialty, if only because they were notified of patient complaints about physicians in the department and also served as a formal
channel of communication to and from the administration when the
physician did not wish to deal directly with the administration. One chief
rather clearly outlined his self-imposed restrictions placed on the supervisory role, alternately denying the desire to supervise and expressing
frustration at the impossibility of doing so effectively.

> Officially I am the chief of the department, but I do not meddle into treatment.
> I'm very reluctant to talk to a colleague unless it is something absolutely
> obvious. We have excellent people, and there are not many mistakes, really.
> If there is a mistake in the human relations area I always discuss it: somebody
> that should have gone on a call that did not, let's say, and the patients are
> upset and I get the complaint. I always talk about that. Now it can happen that
> I will notice a mistake on a chart. I do not go through the charts. It's not
> defined as one of my duties. The idea was to the contrary. *I felt it was not my
> duty to have control over what people are doing.* Everybody practices his own
> medicine. . . . If I get the chart of the patient by coincidence because the
> person is on vacation or wasn't present, I may see what I think is negligence,
> or the doctor should have done this or that, and I put a note into the chart and
> tell the doctor that. Usually the same thing will happen and I will find the
> same mistake [from the same person]. It is almost impossible to retrain a
> person. But we are very lucky as I say. There are not any really gross mis-
> takes. (#23—PRIMARY PRACTITIONER; ITALICS ADDED)

Another, in contrasting the role of chief in the medical group with that of
chief in a teaching hospital, explicitly denied the possibility of assuming
the strong supervisory role of the latter, largely because of the volume of
material in the medical group. He minimized the formal qualities of the
role in the medical group in order to avoid assuming the kind of responsibility for performance which is expected of the chief of a department in
a teaching hospital.

All the chiefs were involved in working out coverage arrangements,
improvements in routine communications (the design of referral slips,
the filling out of the medical record, and the like), and other administrative issues dealing with the logistics of care. But of the seven chiefs from
whom data were available, only two claimed to lay down guidelines for

therapeutic practices in their departments. The inclination of most chiefs was to minimize the formal prerogatives of the office in medical affairs and emphasize its administrative character and, in medical affairs, its advisory or consultative character (cf. Goss, 1963).

The subordinates of the chiefs were even more insistent on the lack of bureaucratic and even, in some cases, professional authority of their superordinates. As we shall see, a complaint about a physician in *another* specialty might be taken to one's chief for discussion, particularly if the offender were senior to and unacquainted with the complainant. So might the psychological handling of a problem patient be discussed and advice sought. But almost all such consultation involved the initiative of the subordinate; unsolicited advice was resented. Not all felt the need for advice, and of those, not all saw their chief as the authoritative source of advice for their specialty. When age and seniority were similar between staff and chief, there was little inclination for staff members to consider their chief to be authoritative. The personal qualities of the incumbent, far more than his status as chief, seemed to be the decisive variable.

My chief is a well-known man, but I feel I'm a colleague rather than an inferior. We are more or less partners, and it wouldn't necessarily be true in any other areas. I may have come in as a tyro, but I didn't. I came in as an experienced man. I do almost anything I want to by myself without any overseeing kind of chief at all. (#45—CONSULTANT)

In all, it seems that the office of the chief, if indeed it was an office in the medical group, lay, in reality, somewhere closer to a mere title that justified assigning an individual additional perquisites, including slightly more salary, than to a true formal office that possessed workable authority independent of the characteristics of the incumbent. Except in surgery, where as a specialty there was a strong tradition of close supervision, and where the individual who was chief had the respect and liking of most members of the medical group, there was little evidence that chiefs, as superordinates, engaged in systematic attempts to both supervise and guide the performance of their colleagues in the various specialty departments. Most denied that this was part of their task; many asserted that, even when they wished to exercise influence over the performance of the members of their department, they could not do so by virtue of the resistance of their subordinates. Thus, insofar as it was a formal office at all, the office of the chief was largely empty of formal authority and could not be used to explain the level of performance that held among the physicians in the medical group or even the differences between specialties.

THE RESTRICTION OF AUTHORITY TO INFORMAL INFLUENCE

Formal authority might be defined as the capacity and inclination of an individual to use his incumbency in a formal office or position in an organization to systematically and deliberately direct the behavior of others defined as subordinate by their formal position. I tried to show that in some sense the authority of the administration was absolute, resting on a direct mandate from and responsibility to the Board of Trustees of the owning organization. Nonetheless, the subordinates of the medical group, the working physicians, were inclined to concede legitimacy to the exercise of administrative authority in only extremely limited areas of their work. There was no real issue of recognizing the *formal* legitimacy of such authority. The issue was, rather, willingness to accept the systematic and regular exercise of that authority over the whole range of their work. In essence, the physicians resisted the use of formal authority on the part of administrative officials. In turn, the administration minimized its reliance on formal authority to govern work behavior.

The issue did not center solely on the legitimacy of formal *administrative* authority, however, for the chiefs of specialist units in the medical group were working physicians, and they too were not accepted as possessing the right to give orders. Even unsolicited *advice* was resented. At bottom, the issue seemed to revolve around the idea of formal authority itself. The office of the chief, thus, was exercised in much the same way as were the offices of the administration—loosely, charitably, and without insistence on obedience or conformity in all but those areas connected with the service contract for patients and the employment contract for the physicians. And even there, in the only areas ordered by systematic, formal rules specifying office hours, coverage schedules, and the like, the implementation of the rules was not formal or bureaucratic. They were not enforced systematically or mechanically, as they would be, for example, were the physicians required to punch a time clock and accept payment only for hours (and minutes) in attendance. Discretion was the rule rather than the exception, and individual judgment was the guide to discretion. Both by virtue of the willing abdication of those in formal positions and by virtue of the physicians' resistance to the use of formal authority, the dominant source of rules by which one evaluated performance lay in the collegium rather than in the administration.

8:
The Rule of the Collegium

If we conceive of social control in formal administrative terms, we can specify the structure of legitimate formal authority, the rules or laws it promulgates and administers, the nature and amount of feedback available to it about performance which allows it to become aware of infractions of the rules, and the steps it takes to deal with infractions it has discovered. Since I have shown that much of the formal authority of the medical group was essentially neutralized, so that the collegium was left to govern itself, it is therefore necessary to conceive of the foundation for social control in the medical group in informal collegial rather than formal administrative terms.

Informal social control poses rather more of a problem to discovery and analysis than does formal social control because it is not consciously and deliberately created and specified. Nowhere codified and promulgated as announced law or regulation, its agents of control undistinguished by uniform, title, or office, its system of surveillance and detection an unexceptionable part of everyday activity, informal social control is difficult to grapple with. Even if we focus on only the target of social control—the deviant—the informality and diffuseness of everyday settings are such that rather little conceptualization of deviance in these settings has been developed, focus instead having been on deviance from formal, civil-legal rules and from ceremonial rules (cf. Denzin, 1970). Even more difficult to conceptualize than deviance are the elements that create the label for it, collect selective information about it, and transmit and take action on information about it. All these elements must be described and analyzed, however, if we are to understand how the collegium of the medical group constituted a social-control system and why the system operated as it did to allow or encourage the physicians to cope with their work problems the way they did.

Its very unselfconsciousness, its very lack of deliberate formulation, makes informal control something unlikely to be divisible into tidy analytical units that are distinct and mutually consistent. While we can make our own analytical distinctions between rules (the law), detection

120

and apprehension of deviance (law enforcement), and management of deviance (the judicial and corrections systems), they do not find clear and definite empirical support in an informal system such as that of the medical group because there is no division of labor among the participants: everyone can participate in and shape every element of the process. Empirically, the analytical elements overlap, merge, and blur. However, in order to describe such a system in a sufficiently orderly way that its essential character can be grasped, one must structure the report of the data in ways that are more artificial than the ways one must structure the report of the data about a formal system, which can often be described by use of its own terms and distinctions. Thus, in this chapter I shall use the term "rules" to hold in loose kinship a number of related, normative, and performative ideas that may seem to have little relationship to rule as we think of it in the context of formal laws and regulations. However, I shall try to show the relevance of all these ideas to the problem of understanding how and why some forms of behavior and work performance and not others are considered to require control of some kind.

THE CHARACTER OF PHYSICIANS

Any set of rules, prescriptive as well as proscriptive, is based on a set of assumptions about the persons involved—assumptions about their mental and physical capacities, their moral inclinations, their essential motivation to perform and conform, their capacity for change, and the like. The law, for example, is predicated upon an image of conscious, calculating, knowledgeable persons whose behavior may be influenced by the deterrence of known penalties for apprehension and conviction. In its treatment of offenses by those judged insane (cf. Szasz, 1963), juvenile (cf. Platt, 1969), physically handicapped (cf. ten Broek, 1966: 590–593), or otherwise not normal persons, the law makes specific exceptions predicated on its assumptions about the character of these excepted persons. As in the law, so it was in the informal rules and regulations of the medical group. The physicians in the medical group seemed to share a very special conception of themselves. They assumed that the physicians were essentially ethical, conscientious, and competent, these qualities being organized into an individually expressed but stable pattern of behavior. From this followed the fundamental rule that one owed one's colleagues (and was owed by them) respect, trust, and protection unless overwhelming evidence pointed to the contrary.

The physician was seen as a person whose work behavior had been laid down at some time in the past. Part of such behavior was an immutable function of personality. Such behavior could not be changed in any significant way and could be only accepted and lived with.

> Apparently this colleague of mine's behavior with respect to family doctors has quieted down. I haven't gotten as many complaints about him as I used to get the first year. And it is not for me to say what his problems are, I'm not a psychiatrist. I can guess that he hasn't really grown up yet. So this is a question of personality, which to me is something you live with. (#40—CONSULTANT)

Personality manifested itself in the way a physician managed his patients and also in such elements of work as the ostensibly technical matter of ordering laboratory tests.

> As to those even who have been out of school for a long time who order a lot of tests, nothing can be done about them. You cannot change the individual. Some people want to have all kinds of tests, even if the chances of their revealing something are quite remote. And others are more apt to go without them. (#24—PRIMARY PRACTITIONER)

Such elements of work style as the ordering of laboratory tests were also seen as a matter of taste, which relied on the idea that each individual exercised his free judgment and was essentially incomparable to any other in his choices. The pure individualism of the physicians, an individualism that was not a mere difference so much as an assertion of autonomy stemming from their work, was stressed.

> Physicians are individualists basically in their work whether they work for a group or not. You are working as an individual with your patient, and this is your day-to-day work. Whatever your natural reactions are, whether you are on salary or in solo practice, you are still an individualist. (#56—PRIMARY PRACTITIONER)

THE RULE OF TRUST

This notion of a highly individualistic person who neither could change very much from what he was nor would submit to the ordinary procedures of organizational control was the foundation of the essential tenet that the physician must be trusted. In my earlier discussion of doctors' relation to their patients, I mentioned the doctors' sense of insult when they were treated as persons accountable to the patients or to an employer rather than being trusted, autonomous, and accountable only to themselves. The physicians believed that they should be trusted by their patients. While they might have been disturbed by their patients' seeking another opinion about some difficulty because such an action reflected on their competence, they were even more disturbed by a patient's doing so without their knowledge, "behind their backs," because it implied that their patients did not trust them, that it is a "break [sic] of trust." (#4—PRIMARY PRACTITIONER)

By the same token, as we saw already, many physicians felt that the way they allocated their office hours should not have been checked up on by the administration. If the physician were not on time, it should have been presumed that he had good reasons for not being there and would manage nonetheless to fulfill his responsibilities adequately by the use of his own initiative as a conscientious physician. Not to be trusted constituted a slur on one's essential conscientiousness, and when there was such an implication of distrust in the medical group, deeply emotional responses followed. If conscientiousness was not assumed, one's very status as a professional was demeaned.

Trust was justified by the assumption of special personal characteristics. Over and over again the physicians used words referring to maturity and adulthood to suggest what it was that must be assumed of them as persons and, conversely, what must not be implied about them. They must not be treated as if they were naughty children or schoolchildren.

It makes me feel like a little baby to have administrators checking up on me for the lack of punctuality. (#43—CONSULTANT)

As we saw in statements in earlier chapters, it might be appropriate to check up on children and on lesser mortals in lower-status occupations, but it was not appropriate to do this to physicians. Indeed, checking up on a physician was in some way insulting, even immoral.

> The chief of the service had the receptionist check up by clocking L30 in and clocking him out. I felt very badly, and at the time I felt pretty disgusted with the chief. It's like being a traitor, and this is one of the things that upset me. (#2—PRIMARY PRACTITIONER)

Checking up was associated with "kindergarten teaching," "dossiers," and even "gestapo" and "Big Brother." In short, the basic assumption that the physicians made about themselves was that they were essentially mature persons who would work in their own individually chosen ways to perform their special tasks in the best possible way. Given that assumption, it follows that they should be granted trust by patient, administration, and colleague so that they would be free to do their tasks in the way they felt was proper. "Thou shalt trust physicians" was the basic commandment, justified by a particular conception of physicians as special people especially deserving of trust.

ETHICS

Given this image of the physician as someone deserving trust, what rules guide his trustworthy performance? Central to the rules guiding human behavior is the issue of right and wrong, ethical and unethical. And, in fact, among professionals the claim is of a special degree of probity that lesser occuptions are not supposed to have. What were the ethical principles of medical performance? Curiously enough, we could raise rather little interest among the physicians by interview questions about the problems of ethics in medical work.[1] Ethics seemed to be unproblematic to them and rather less related to being a doctor than to being a properly brought up (middle-class) human being. Ethicality was "pretty much common sense" (#11), was learned "when you are

---

[1]Since this study was carried out, there has been enormous growth in national interest in issues of ethics in medicine—particularly in ethics in medical research and experimentation and in treating the dying patient (see Katz, 1972). Perhaps a study of present-day physicians would uncover more interest in the issue, but it must be remembered that the physicians discussed here are community doctors, concerned primarily with ambulatory care and little involved in research. The findings of Babbie (1970) imply that community practitioners are rather less concerned with ethical issues than are medical scientists.

brought up by your mother" (#17). To most of the physicians the word seemed to refer to the norms of decency and honesty that were expected of all proper middle-class people and that had not and need not have been taught to students in medical school. There was nothing about the principles of ethicality guiding the doctor which was esoteric, known only to the professionally trained.

This is not to say that it was always easy to find agreement on whether an act or not was proper. Clearly illegal acts, particularly those involving money or claims of money, posed no problem.

> Sometimes patients asked to put down six visits instead of two on an insurance form. We all get requests like that, but nobody in his right mind would do anything but refuse it. . . . It's an illegal thing, you know, when you falsify a record. I don't think you have to be taught. Nobody teaches you not to rob a bank. (#38—CONSULTANT)

Conversely, similar issues of fraud or perjury where no concrete economic gain was at issue yielded ambiguity and controversy about propriety. On an occasion when schoolteachers went out on strike, and many were afraid to stay home and appear to be striking but were afraid to go to work and appear to be strike-breaking, there was great pressure on the group physicians to resolve the dilemma by signing certificates of illness that would allow the teachers to stay home without appearing to be on strike. A lively controversy arose among some of the physicians about the ethical and professional issues involved. In that instance, of course, what was at issue was not solely a simple matter of fraud but also a matter of consciously behaving on the basis of one's political convictions rather than on the basis of one's medical judgment, a matter of weighing ethical priorities and establishing precedents.

ETIQUETTE

Interview questions about what was ethical and what was not received answers that were singularly without substance except when colleague relations were involved. In attempting to answer our questions, many physicians were led from issues connected with patients or the law to those connected with colleagues—issues that are sometimes called "problems of etiquette" in the medical literature. In general, the rule seemed to be that priority was given to the avoidance of any cooperation with a patient insofar as it would give a colleague offense and to the protection of colleagues. Critics of professions have all commented on this basic rule of colleague solidarity, some using G. B. Shaw's phrase "conspiracy against the laity." The rule was that one should not criticize colleagues—either in public or in private. One might, if one wished to pay the potential interpersonal cost, privately criticize a colleague to his face, but one had to exercise the greatest of care in public not to damage the individual's reputation and career.

The problem of applying and articulating this rule was of course compounded when a patient was being shared by two practitioners and served as a kind of go-between. When it appeared that two practitioners disagreed on diagnosis, treatment, or whatever, a certain amount of tact was essential for the protection of each.

> The only really important ethical problem is tied up with how much you should tell a patient and also occasionally how far you can twist the truth to cover a colleague without actually lying to a patient. (#27—CONSULTANT)

In some cases one restrained oneself from commenting to the patient on the behavior of other colleagues partly because of recognition that the other practitioner might have had a good, but not immediately apparent, reason for what he was reported to have said or done and partly because of a tendency to discount the adequacy of the patient as an informant.

> Part of what you learn about ethics or propriety is what you read in journals. Some have sections on what you are suable for. But then, there is a certain basic common sense that you learn not to criticize. You just don't pass off-hand remarks about people, you know, that he is doing something wrong. It took me maybe a half a year to learn that you can't believe what a patient tells you about what a doctor said because he may be misinterpreting it or he doesn't understand. (#9—PRIMARY PRACTITIONER)

Restraint in comment was the rule, therefore, sustained by the belief that one had to discount the patient or any other layman as an informant and trust one's colleague.

The rule was that a disagreement between colleagues should be dealt with in a spirit of caution and with a conciliatory, noncommital rhetoric. Talking noncommittally to patients in order to avoid difficulties with or for a colleague extended even to instances in which a practitioner had reliable information on the basis of which he disagreed so absolutely with a colleague that he could not define the difference as one of mere opinion. This disagreement was most difficult to handle in a referral relationship, since the relationship could not be severed to avoid controversy but had to be brought to a conclusion around a common case.

A patient will be sent to me as an acute AP. He's already been told he needs an operation—that he is going to have one—and I find he doesn't have appendicitis. I think to myself, "The doctor's a fool." On the other hand, how am I going to tell the family and the doctor, without making too much about it? That I'm not going to operate. That there isn't anything there. This happened a couple of times. I tell the patient that there are indications that he may have this, and it should be watched, and I try to make it so that the doctor doesn't appear incompetent. You know, "You should watch this, there is a question. . . ." I say to the referring doctor, "Well, you've got reasons for suspicions, I can see why you are suspicious, but I feel this will subside and I think it is preferably an enteritis." (#48—CONSULTANT)

As we shall see, in some cases it has seemed necessary for one to contradict a colleague, however tactfully, in order to preserve the integrity of one's own work with a particular patient. But the rule of trust and the obligation to be protective of colleagues because of that trust were primary.

TYPES OF MISTAKES

In theory, it would seem that in medical work, as in other kinds of work, there must be technical rights and wrongs that, if violated, would justify the breech of the rule of trust by imputing deviance to the performer. Not everything in medicine is a matter of opinion. Separate from general ethics, distinct from etiquette, are the rules of good medical practice, the technical care of medical work. These rules could be discussed positively, as medical textbooks and clinical instructors discuss them, but for our present purposes it seems more useful to define them negatively, by lapse or violation. The layman uses the word "mistake" to designate in a general way violation of the rules of good medical care (cf. Hughes, 1971:316). Significantly, it is a word that does not necessarily reflect on the performer's motivation or integrity and so may not threaten the physicians' views of their special trustworthiness. It does, however, threaten their view of their special competence, and it was a word that not all were inclined to use (cf. Stelling and Bucher, 1973:664–666). Nonetheless, in probing lapse or violation of technical rules of performance, we used the word "mistake" in our interviews and allowed the physicians to correct our usage if they chose. Let us turn now to their ways of making sense of mistakes, keeping in mind the fact that we are seeking understanding of the criteria they used to discriminate between good and poor work performance, between conformity and deviance.

In attempting to determine the nature of deviance from medical standards as the group physicians perceived and coped with it, we found it rather difficult to obtain a very clear picture in part because of semantics, for the physicians were not agreed on terminology; in part because of the technical differences between specialties that emphasize different processes, problems, and outcomes; and in part because of the complexity or vagueness of the criteria that appeared to be operating. Nonetheless, it is possible to say with great confidence that most physicians agreed that everyone makes mistakes simply by virtue of the fact of working. Insofar as it is a human being rather than a machine performing some function, "mistakes will happen," as the common saying goes. Being human, the physician could not be perfect. In this sense, some number or proportion of mistakes was excusable and did not constitute deviation from a technical rule. Some physicians would not even call this group mistakes, and few were ashamed of them. They were *normal mistakes*. In contrast, there were mistakes that were in some sense inexcusable, of which the individual was ashamed. These were *deviant mistakes*.

Several individuals' statements displayed the rough distinctions involved and allow us to begin to understand the issues surrounding the rules of good practice. The first statement, by a pediatrician, showed the ambiguity of the word "mistake" in that "mistake" referred both to the choice of the technical process of diagnosis and treatment and to the seriousness of the outcome of the process, which reflected on the adequacy of the diagnosis and treatment employed. Mistaken diagnoses as well as mistaken modes of treatment were freely admitted to, but they were qualified as not "badly" or "seriously" mistaken and were treated matter of factly in the interview. It was recognized that there might be enough ambiguity in the available evidence to lead to doubt about what diagnosis or treatment to employ. In that circumstance, a mistaken choice of diagnosis and treatment could occur and would not itself reflect on the physician. It would be a *normal mistake*. However, a definite and generally accepted rule governing choice of treatment—namely, to treat the more serious of the suspected ailments—exists in medicine, and if choice is not made by that rule, a quite different kind of mistake is committed: When a clear rule is violated, this violation is a *deviant mistake*. Contrary to Stelling and Bucher's finding (1973:665), furthermore, the rationale of the decision rule revolves around anticipating the *outcome* of a choice: to minimize the possibility of a serious or life-threatening outcome, the rule is that, when one is in doubt, one should assume the more serious of the possible disorders and treat it so as to avoid the possibility of the more serious results.

> [BR: Have you ever had a mistake?] I don't know. I've never killed anybody. [BR: Have you ever misdiagnosed something?] Sure. [BR: Ever misdosed somebody?] Yes, but not badly, you know. [BR: What happens when you do something like that?] I rectify it. If you give somebody a little too much medicine and the mother calls back and tells me the child is drowsy, then I cut down the dosage. . . . The case of scarlet fever I was talking about, this man made seven calls in five days, and then he asked me for a consult and he kept telling the mother it was German measles. But if it is German measles, why make so many housecalls? If you are in doubt, and this is possible, the accepted practice is to treat the serious disease. . . . I told the offending physician he made a mistake. (#55—PRIMARY PRACTITIONER)

The word "mistake" was used, but it was used less in the sense of a mistaken diagnosis, which could happen to anyone, than in the sense of a violation of an accepted rule to treat the more serious of two illnesses in the face of legitimate doubt as to which illness was involved.

An incorrect choice of diagnosis or treatment, then, need not have been more than a normal mistake that could happen to anyone. As a choice, it was reasonable at the time of choice, but later, when one observed the response to treatment or other results or outcomes, one might discover it to be incorrect. Another practitioner's comments allow us to elaborate further on the difference between normal and deviant mistakes: he distinguished between *glaring mistakes*, which resulted from carelessness or simple ignorance on the part of the practitioner, and *understandable mistakes*, which resulted from the unusual nature of a case which one could not have been expected to have known in advance and thus for the outcome of which one was not responsible (Stelling and Bucher, 1973: 667). The former, in contrast to the latter, were not excusable. The contingencies of work and the state of the art by themselves were thought to cause the understandable mistakes, and there was no reflection on competence or conscientiousness; glaring mistakes, however, implied either *ignorance* due to poor training, thus reflecting on competence, or *neglect* due to poor attention, thus reflecting on conscientiousness.

> Basically there are two kinds of mistakes. One, basically, [since] there is a tremendous dividing line [between the two]. One is where you make a mistake where it is very easy to see. It's an error in judgment where, well, all right, in retrospect you shouldn't have done it. But it is not a glaring mistake from the point of view of lack of knowledge or from the point of view of being very careless. . . . The other is when you do something really very poor. (#57—PRIMARY PRACTITIONER)

Finally, there was an element that most physicians emphasized continually in their discussions of mistakes—the element of judgment (cf. Burkett and Knafl, 1974). The term "judgment" was often used to delineate the process by which one used one's knowledge to decide on a diagnosis and plan of treatment. The process of choice and evaluation itself, dependent on but separate from knowledge and skill as such, might be defined as judgment. A consultant discussed mistakes from the point of view of the kind of judgment employed in decisions.

> One must remember that a mistake may be looked at from a layman's point of view and from the doctor's. The layman's view is that everything you see involves fresh thought and judgment, which is not true. When a thing falls into a certain field of behavior and a diagnosis is clearly established, obviously it doesn't require fresh judgment. Let me give you an example. If I'm treating a certain type of small, limited carcinoma of the skin, that's a routinized treatment therapeutically. It doesn't require fresh judgment. It would involve a little judgment depending upon the location of the lesion. But should that lesion be a larger one and its behavior much more malignant, then it requires fresh judgment, so that's the difference. A great deal of work starts off by falling into a pretty clear category. Fresh judgment involves the exception. When would be the greater error? An error where fresh judgment isn't involved or an error where fresh judgment is? I would say where fresh judgment is involved, there is no error. We are not talking about the technique. There is no error because such cases are *not* true to form. It's where fresh judgment would be involved but was not exercised [and routine followed instead]. That would be the greatest error. (#36—CONSULTANT)

Thus, what I call "deviant mistakes" may be said to have occurred in instances in which routine judgment was exercised while fresh judgment should instead have been exercised. Where no routine knowledge and technique exist, and fresh judgment instead is required, mistaken choice of diagnosis and treatment can be determined only retrospectively, by the outcome. Where fresh judgment is required, the outcome uncertain, and error itself determined retrospectively, the error is normal, excusable, and in some sense not an error at all.

"Normal," excusable mistakes, then, are those that every physician could conceive of making because of lack of information, the uncertainty of medical knowledge, the limitation of available techniques, and the uniqueness of the case. Many physicians would not even call these "mistakes"; in the interviews some called them "so-called mistakes." Such normal mistakes are less mistakes than they are unavoidable events; they are not so much committed by the doctor as they are suffered or risked. They do not reflect on the physician's competence so much as on his luck. Thus, one should not judge or criticize a colleague's apparent mistakes because "there but for the grace of God go I."

In contrast to normal mistakes are deviant mistakes. Essentially, deviant mistakes seemed to be those that are thought to be due to a practitioner's negligence, ignorance, or ineptitude, reflecting upon his lack of basic or reasonable competence, ethicality, conscientiousness, and judgment. They consist in failures to follow the widely agreed-on rules of good practice. These are the mistakes that are frequently called "blatant" or "gross," "serious" being an adjective more often used to delineate the consequences of a mistake rather than its analytical character (cf. Stelling and Bucher, 1973:665).

RULES AND ROUTINES IN GOOD PRACTICE

Critical to the distinction between normal and deviant mistakes is a conception of rules and routines to be followed in good practice—what every competent physician should be able to recognize, should know, and should be able to do successfully. It is the conception of the *limits* of rule and routine which distinguishes the physicians' conception of mistake from that of laymen. Laymen are inclined to expect more knowledge, skill, and predictable performance from medical work than are physicians and so are unlikely to subscribe to the notion of normal, excusable mistakes. And, after all, since it is they or those they care for who suffer the consequences of a mistake, laymen are hardly inclined to be as detached as physicians. In contrast, physicians excepted many things that laymen would include under the category of mistake, but they did not except all from the category. If they did not use the word "mistake," they did use the words "error," "goof," "missing" something, or "overlooking" something. They had notions of what every competent physician should know or be able to do, and they were both ashamed of themselves when they deviated from those norms and grieved or angered at colleagues who deviated. What was the character of these norms, or rules?

At the very least, there were expectations of elementary knowledge of what are serious symptoms requiring attention. Deviation was blatant or gross.

> If somebody calls up and says, "I have severe chest pains, I can't breathe," or if the wife calls up and says the husband is turning blue, if the physician doesn't go out then, he is guilty of many things, among them malpractice. I don't know whether that sort of thing ever happens. Perhaps nothing that blatant. (#56—PRIMARY PRACTITIONER)

Such failure shows "that you're stupid, a fumbler or [commit] mistakes where you just didn't know some basic information" (#9—PRIMARY PRACTITIONER).

It is important to realize that this notion of deviation from normal procedure (and normal judgment of what to do when faced by a given problem) did *not* get invoked only when the outcome for the patient was poor. The judgment that it was a mistake was made no matter what the outcome. But apparently action against the performer was contemplated only if the mistake has an untoward outcome.

> Someone did something I wouldn't have done and which wasn't in line with good surgical practice. It was an error of judgment. Nothing happened. The patient did well, and the physician had his minor reasons for not doing what everyone else would have done, and he got away with it. But if he hadn't gotten away with it he would have been censured for what he did. (#47—CONSULTANT)

Another physician described the rule generally accepted in ophthalmology for testing ocular pressure. When that rule was violated consistently, the tendency was to impute a mistake due to deficiency in judgment or competence.

> I see mistakes in my own department. There is one physician whom I consider inadequate. . . . As far as I can tell from the record, [he] never uses the instrument to test for it. Like the doctor who is being sued, he used his fingers to measure pressure, which is a notoriously unreliable way. . . . You have to occasionally, but it is not the accepted routine way. If you do it routinely, it is not good practice. (#44—CONSULTANT)

Similarly, in other specialties, there were other comparatively clear procedures that, if ignored or left unused, reflected seriously on the knowledge, judgment, or conscientiousness of the doctor. A gynecologist described how he learned that failure to probe the cervix of a woman he examined led to missing evidence of cancer.

> I found out from a man not in the group that I did miss something. There was apparently more bleeding, and her family took her to this man he gave me a call. He had known me as a resident, and he said, "You know, this is one of those instances where you have to shove a probe into a closed cervix to get the tissue." This man got cancer cells out of the uterus. Now of course I was most chagrined. . . . He was very nice about it, but he made it very clear he felt I was in error. I didn't argue the point. (#43—CONSULTANT)

Apart from failure to use generally agreed upon, known procedures due to imputed ignorance or poor judgment, there was failure in the practice of the procedures. In the surgical specialties the contrast was sometimes made between an error in judgment and an error of technique. Here, the line between normal and deviant mistakes seemed to depend on the precise procedure involved. Some physicians spoke of an error of technique as a "natural hazard" or normal mistake that could happen to anyone.

> Then there are errors of procedure too. A man can put a needle in a little too far, which could lead to the death of a patient or perhaps to his blindness. These things happen to all of us. (#35—CONSULTANT)

> A technical error, an error of technique or something, a slip, an accident or something could happen, certainly. But that wouldn't be classified as a mistake. This is one of the natural hazards, and there would be no way of preventing that except to see that the man doing the surgery was a competent man. (#46—CONSULTANT)

But in at least some contexts, an error in performance was treated as a reflection of inadequacy rather than as a normal contingency of work. By and large, while they differed in detail, the physicians gave the impression that there is a certain body of knowledge and procedure which may be taken to be routine or standard, therefore constituting a set of rules for acceptable performance. Deviations from these rules were likely to be seen as mistakes or errors that are not a normal and therefore excusable part of the everyday contingencies of medical work.

What complicated such deviations far more than appears at first sight, however, was the question of judgment. One's judgment is involved in deciding to use one technique or another, and one's judgment is involved in determining, in the light of all the circumstances and risks involved in its use and the precision required in its user, whether or not the decision to use the technique was faulty. And it is precisely judgment which cannot be reduced to the unambiguous rules of technical procedure, which cannot be memorized, and which cannot, through drill, be trained to invariantly correct performance by supervised repetition of a set of physical actions. It is precisely because judgment is so intangible that ultimate recourse to it as an arbiter of mistakes in effect made otherwise deviant mistakes normal mistakes by contracting that portion of the universe of work which may be said to be subject to definite rules.

JUDGMENT AND THE NORMALIZATION OF MISTAKES

Because the pressure to take some action rather than to wait and do nothing is ubiquitous in medicine, it is essentially in the light of the available evidence *at the time of the action,* rather than after the fact, that a person's judgment is evaluated. Thus, while a surgeon conceded that he mistakenly removed an appendix, he argued that his judgment to do so was reasonable in the light of the available evidence and the alternatives and risks open to him:

> A recent mistake would be a case which I kept out of for two days and I finally went in because of the elevated count and the temperature and the persistent tenderness. I went in because I was afraid to stay out, really. It wasn't an acute AP. It was my fault. . . . Actually, it was an error postoperatively speaking, an error in retrospect. (#48—CONSULTANT)

Thus, some normal mistakes, involving errors of omission and commission, were those in which one of a number of alternatives was exercised in the light of available evidence only to be shown as the inappropriate alternative by later findings. A decision based on such judgment might have been in error, but the error was considered honest as well as adequately, even if not extraordinarily, competent. Better judgment would presumably have led to the correct decision at the outset, but since it was all a matter of such an intangible as judgment, the fact of an error became neutralized. It became a so-called error.

> Mistakes of judgment may occur. It might be an error in judgment, but that so-called error might be truly a question of a difference of opinion. (#46—CONSULTANT)

The word "judgment" therefore can be made synonymous with "a matter of opinion." so that no stable criterion for decision is assumed and, within general limits of known alternatives, every decision is equally correct at the time it is made. Only the outcome allows talk of "error": in the decision-making process itself at the time it occurs, there can be only different opinions, not mistaken choices.

Differences of opinion were clearly recognized and were discussed on the basis of an understanding that there is comparatively, but not wholly, ambiguous evidence and somewhat, but not wholly, incomplete knowledge that precludes knowing with certainty what exists inside the body or what result will follow what alternative. The absolute number of alternatives is limited by common knowledge, but the choice of alternatives depends on one's opinion. And so an "error" is normalized as an "opinion."

> I did have a case recently in which there was a consultation and in effect an error. A woman was pregnant, and the question came up of a fibroid tumor or an ovarian cyst. My impression was of a fibroid tumor. But in the course of my uncertainty I had #40 see it, and he thought it was an ovarian cyst and that it should come out. I was delighted to go ahead with another consultation with a man outside the group who saw her, and he wasn't sure either. Since there was so much question about it she consulted still another man on my advice, and he felt it was an ovarian cyst and should be operated on. So I did, and it turned out to be a fibroid. (#42—CONSULTANT)

The idea of judgment could, by pointing to the complexity of the problem and the ambiguity of the evidence, make an error honest, intelligent, and so excusable, and a mistaken decision made at a given point in time when action must be taken could thus be interpreted legitimately as something that could happen to anyone or as a matter of opinion. Indeed, except in the most blatant and gross cases, the idea of judgment could remove any real reproach from the recognition of a mistake, since a matter of opinion or a matter stemming from normal human frailty could hardly stigmatize one's competence.

> In general, when there are oversights, they are freely granted by the physician. It's not as much of a stigma as you might think. If you miss something, you miss it, and I think people will admit this freely. I can't think of any mistake that wouldn't be included under this cover of general openness. One time a guy called me and asked about thyroid, and since I had once examined this patient, I looked at my notes and there was nothing about thyroid enlargement. I could have missed it. It could have grown within the year. I just don't know. (#17—PRIMARY PRACTITIONER)

Also present, however, was an idea of the way one uses one's judgment in evaluating the evidence: one exercises sufficiently sophisticated suspicion to recognize the possibility of certain alternatives. Since judgment and not mere gross physical indications, measured laboratory tests, and machine tracings that a computer could use for diagnosis was involved, when one had good judgment one would operate in more than a mechanical way.

It seemed almost a ritual, perhaps a way of neutralizing censure by self or others, for the physicians to say that they learned something from their mistake and to imply that the same mistake would not happen again. But the ambiguity of the available evidence that created an honest error had not changed, which implies that if a physician learned something from his mistake, perhaps his error was not so honest as it appeared, and certainly it was not something that could have "happened to anyone."

The ambiguity introduced into the idea of error or mistake by the idea of judgment is such that the possibility of utilizing consistent technical rules for evaluating and controlling mistakes seems to be very much reduced, if not precluded for all practical purposes. As Feinstein (1967: 26–27) put it, "If the clinician seems knowledgeable and authoritative, and if his reputation and results seem good, he can be condoned the most flagrant imprecisions, vagueness, and inconsistency in his conduct of therapy. The clinician does not even use a scientific name for his method of designing, executing and appraising therapeutic experiments. He calls it *clinical judgment*."

With the rules removed, the criteria for evaluating one's own and one's colleagues' work become so permissive as to allow extremely wide variation in performance. Only gross or blatant acts of ignorance and inattention which all physicians would be united in recognizing and condemning remained securely in the category of deviant mistakes, but they were unlikely to be performed by any normal physician with an average medical education. Most of what remained beyond that seemed to be normalized. These events remained mistakes or errors, they were deviations from normal work expectations, but they did not call for reproach.

9:

The Bases for Colleague Evaluation

What I have shown in the last chapter should not be taken as an argument that the physicians did not evaluate one another's performance. It would be patently false to argue that. Rather, it was argued that the physicians' way of seeing themselves, their colleagues, and their work was such that only a comparatively small segment of the universe of work which failed to conform to expectations was likely to be considered appropriate for the exercise of negative sanctions—for direct criticism or worse. The remainder of that universe, along with the universe of routinely or unusually successful work, was evaluated also, and these evaluations were, as we shall see, of some importance to the relations among the physicians.

We are all familiar with the fact of reputation and prestige in the medical world. If judgment were suspended, all colleagues would be equal in one another's eyes. But as Rhea and I have shown elsewhere (Freidson and Rhea, 1965), some physicians are judged to be above average in competence, others only average, and a few below average. Given judgment or evaluation by shared criteria, social control becomes possible. Indeed, proponents of group practice claim that working together as an organized collegium facilitates mutual control of performance by colleagues, thereby improving the quality of medical care. However, as Greenlick put it in a recent review of evidence (Greenlick: 1972:104), "much has been asserted in the polemics surrounding prepaid group practice concerning colleague interaction as an important determinant of quality in such systems, even though there is little empirical evidence concerning this point."

That some process of social control exists is of interest, certainly, but far more important is the substance of that process. How strong is it? What are the bases on which evaluation of colleagues takes place? When is pressure to change exercised, and what sanctions are employed and what avoided? Here, I shall present data bearing on that issue of detail, in this chapter describing the kinds of information used for the evaluation of colleague performance and in the next exploring the extent to which the circulation of information about performance in the medical group was extensive enough to make available to all physicians sufficient data to incline them to take part in the systematic exercise of sanctions.

THE SOURCES OF EVALUATIVE INFORMATION

There seemed to be a fair amount of consensus among the physicians about the kinds of information they used to assess the quality of their colleagues' performance. The kinds of information were formal educational and training credentials, such as the medical school attended, the hospital at which the residency was served, and certification by a specialty board; patients' evaluation of and reports about physician performance; the evaluative gossip of other colleagues; and, most important of all, one's own personal experience working and talking with the individual himself. Physicians also used the medical record, which will be treated separately in another chapter, as a source of information about colleagues' performance.

Of course, all sources do not provide the same kind of information, and all physicians were not agreed on the importance and reliability of the various sources. Board certification, for example, may be taken to reflect a certain level of advanced training which bears on competence but little, at all, on a physician's conscientiousness and effectiveness in managing patients. And not all physicians were agreed that board certification is a reliable indicator of competence. Thus, to merely list the sources of information used to evaluate colleagues is but to begin analysis. Let us examine each source of information more carefully.

FORMAL CREDENTIALS

The most readily available source of information that was used to assess colleagues was their formal credentials—the medical degree itself and specialty board status being the most important credentials. The medical group would not consider hiring a licensed physician unless he also had the training and experience that would make him eligible to take specialty board examinations. It in fact preferred hiring those who had taken their "boards" and had been certified in their specialty. Such certification was seen as an assurance of a certain minimum competence that was superior to that of the person without it. Given its requirements, the very fact that the medical group had hired a physician was itself held to be testimony of the competence of all of its members.

> If he's been certified, that doesn't make him the best in the world, but within certain limits he has qualified and passed inspection and examination and is safe within limits. He wouldn't be here in the first place if he didn't have the qualifications. (#46—CONSULTANT)

Apart from the diploma, the formal license to practice, and the certificate, refinements were introduced by reference to the reputations of the institutions issuing them. An M.D. degree from a foreign versus an American school or from a modest medical school versus an Ivy League school implied less prestige and even a lower level of competence. The same was the case for doing internship and residency training at a community rather than a university hospital. And it was also assumed that a physician with attending privileges or on the staff of a university hospital was somehow better qualified than someone with less prestigious affiliations. Thus, all those with the same nominal degrees, licenses, and certificates could be differentiated nonetheless. And within these differentiations could be found still others based on class standing, seniority, and rank.

Formal credentials, appointments, and ranks are the stuff that is easily accessible to anyone who cares to look them up in the various directories and registers. They are very gross and crude, as is the assumption that they reflect some definite *minimal* standard. Most physicians qualified their citation of training and certification as grounds for evaluating the competence of colleagues by asserting it as the first step in a more extensive process of forming an opinion. Someone newly hired by the medical group was often known initially to his new colleagues only by his formal credentials. They were all that was available at that stage of opinion formation, not the best but the first information. Later, in the process of interaction with the colleague, one would find out more.

> Generally speaking, there are a couple of ways of forming opinions about doctors. One is I guess by his background, his training. This is probably the initial factor, which is very often wrong. But that's probably the first information you have. Secondly, you see patients that they handle and how they

handle them, and you are impressed with that or you are impressed by informal discussions around the hall or you are impressed by some more formal
discussions at conferences. (#1—PRIMARY PRACTITIONER)

Formal credentials, then, were background data. What were the fore-
ground data?

HEARSAY: PATIENTS

An early resource in the process of developing an opinion about a
colleague was the patient. It was only the patient who could tell what
went on behind the closed door of the consulting room, and while the
rules of etiquette required circumspection in *talking* to the patient about
a colleague, they did not preclude the cautious *use* of the patient as a
source of perspective on a colleague's performance. Indeed, even if one
deprecated the patient as a source of reliable information about technical
performance, or competence, the patient was perhaps the major source
of information about the skill, compassion, and conscientiousness
employed by colleagues in dealing with, or managing, patients.

Patients could, of course, complain to one physician about another's
manner, and on occasion they did precisely that. A number of physicians cited this source of information.

> In the process of seeing a good many of the other men's patients, getting the
> patients' feelings toward their own doctor, you form a pretty good idea of
> what kind of medicine he is practicing, more so than you would in private
> practice, where you rarely get to see anybody else's patients unless you are a
> consultant. (L12—PRIMARY PRACTITIONER)

In general, patient complaints about colleagues were discounted by
those who heard them, questions being raised about the patient's un-
realistic expectations or distorted judgment. Nonetheless, sometimes
such complaints were attended to in the light of what was already known
about the colleagues involved. Individual patient complaints about individual colleagues would, while being ignored for the moment, be stored
up in some way, and if the group physician heard a number of such
complaints about the same person, he would then be likely to believe
that something was really wrong.

One doctor of the group, I don't ever recall having a patient who has gone to see him ever coming back saying a nice word about him. Now the average patient won't say anything about a doctor. He'll say, "Well, he's seen me," and that's that. But three out of four people whom I refer to this fellow would come back and say, "Gee, there is something wrong with him. He is very nasty to patients, he is very short and abrupt, not courteous. He didn't even give me a chance to talk." There *is* something wrong with that doctor. (#26—CONSULTANT)

Finally, I may note that, while patients might have supplied information bearing primarily on colleagues' modes of relating to patients, they may also have carried information about technical performance. When a patient requested a housecall or was referred to a physician by another doctor for a consultation, the physician could learn much about his colleague's behavior that brought the patient to him and even, on occasion, taking the patient's opinion with a grain of salt, could learn something about the therapeutic judgment of the other physician.

You pick up errors of omission as follows. A kid will come in with a sore throat on a Saturday morning, and you look at him and he looks bad and you say, "Well, he's got a sore throat. Does this happen often?" They say, "Oh, yes." And you say, "How many times?" And they say, "Oh, six or eight." And you say, "What did #69 (their usual physician) say about it?" They say, "Oh, he said, 'Take this medicine,' and whenever he gets a cold he should take this and do this," but no reference to ENT. No question about whether hearing has been impaired. (#15—PRIMARY PRACTITIONER)

Such simple information, if the questioning physician was prepared to believe it, provided the basis for believing that the colleague committed errors of omission by not checking on the possibility that frequent infection might have damaged hearing. Such information, however, was unlikely to be considered an authoritative source for evaluation.

HEARSAY: COLLEAGUES

If patients did not yield authoritative information, what about colleagues? Individuals not familiar with a particular colleague were able to obtain information about him from other colleagues. They may have known of his reputation with other colleagues and thus knew how others evaluated him. Given the size and character of the medical group, reputation and colleague gossip may have been all the information available by which some individuals could have evaluated others. Physicians in more than one specialty had so little contact with those in others that they could not get enough first-hand information to allow them to develop an opinion without reliance on reputation (cf. Freidson and Rhea, 1965). As I have already pointed out, obstetrics-gynecology and pediatrics had very little contact with each other, nor did pediatrics and internal medicine. Indeed, there was also comparatively little contact between internal medicine and OB-GYN because the latter usually assumed medical responsibility for women while they were pregnant, not sharing it with the former; it may have taken a longer period of time for a family doctor to collect impressions of the performance of an obstetrician, who holds onto a case for many months before returning it, than impressions of, say, an orthopedist or ENT consultant. Indeed, sufficient time was a prerequisite for the accumulation of first-hand contacts, so when there was turnover of staff, there may have been a comparatively widespread sense of unfamiliarity with all but the long-tenured people.

Thus, in many cases, the only basis on which one could evaluate another in the medical group was by his reputation with mutual colleagues. Furthermore, the differences in specialized knowledge between specialties frequently led to the necessity of suspending personal evaluation of competence, even if not of conscientiousness and of skill in dealing with patients, and relying instead on reputation among better-qualified colleagues.

> Look, I'm a doctor, but I don't know how well I can evaluate a gynecologist. I'm not a gynecologist. It's very difficult for me to evaluate the competence of a gynecologist in a lot of things. I don't know how I could do it. [EF: So in this sense your evaluation really is of the way he handled patients and the problems created for you in handling the patient?] Absolutely right. (#20—PRIMARY PRACTITIONER)

Therefore, an indispensible source of opinion about both new colleagues and colleagues in specialties with which the physician felt unfamiliar lay in the reputation sustained by colleague gossip. It was by such talk that reputation got built up and circulated to those not yet in a position themselves to evaluate and judge a person. But what was the substance of the colleague talk from which reputation stemmed?

It is difficult to delineate colleague talk clearly and precisely, for the rules of etiquette played a sufficient part in it that it was not entirely open and graphic. In general talk among acquaintances, there seemed to be some limitation placed on negative remarks about a named individual's competence, though negative remarks about his manner of dealing with patients and colleagues were not uncommon.

> It's relatively rare I think that we talk about other people in the group from the point of view of competence. If there is talk, there may be talk about one of the specialties like GU handling so-and-so lousy, and if we bring it up someone may bring up other patients that they have had that they have given a rough time to. (#7—PRIMARY PRACTITIONER)

A rather important source of open, critical evaluation lay in the talk of the house staff of a nearby hospital in which many of the physicians had staff appointments. The house staff was, of course, somewhat removed from and less committed to the colleague network of the medical group, and also they were in a strategic position to observe critical elements of performance. Those physicians who had a reasonably good relationship with members of the house staff therefore had access to rather incisive sources of information about colleagues' reputations.

By and large, however, given the dominant restraint of etiquette on open and critical discussion of colleagues' failings, the most important source of physicians' access to others' evaluation of colleagues lay in close and respected friends. Their friends would be frank and open in their evaluation, trusting them to keep the information confidential. They, in turn, knowing their friends well, could have more faith in their evaluation than they might have had in the opinions of others whom they knew and respected less.

> I'm very friendly with #34, who gets referrals from all of the specialties. He is a clever man with excellent judgment, and he often tells me stories, you know, of what people have referred and whom he thinks is a very smart internist, let's say. . . . It sticks to you even if it is not always personal experience, because personal experience with internists, except for some discussions, I do not have. We have no common field. (#23—PRIMARY PRACTITIONER)

In cases in which a negative evaluation was voiced by someone whose criteria of evaluation were not clear—a person whom one did not know well—the tendency was to consider the evaluation somewhat skeptically, suspending acceptance and use of the evaluation until a number of others corroborated it.

FIRST-HAND EXPERIENCE

Since, as I have noted, not all physicians had the opportunity to work directly with all other physicians in the medical group, formal credentials, patients' reports, and colleague talk were often the only sources of information by which they could evaluate the likely quality of performance of many of their colleagues. Indeed, the same was true for their evaluations of the performance of some physicians with whom they did work in a referral relationship, for example, when the specialty involved was considered too esoteric for other specialists to be able to assess it securely. As I have already noted, however, credentials were deprecated as being no more than minimal indices of likely performance, and patient information was used only warily and selectively. The same may be said for reputation and colleague talk; over and over again the physicians deprecated the reliability of reputation and gossip, as ubiquitous as they were. Over and over again they asserted that the only really reliable source of evaluation lay in their own personal, first-hand experience of working and talking with colleagues. The individual's own first-hand experience was the ultimate arbiter.

> Other people's opinions about a man don't make any difference. Your opinions about another doctor are based upon your experience. It would be foolish of me to form an opinion because somebody said this or that. It's like everything else in daily life too. I think the important thing here is first-hand experience. (#36—CONSULTANT)

Many physicians were inclined to claim that they suspended judgment without such direct experience and that they tested others' opinions against their own first-hand experience with the person involved.

> You form an opinion about a man first of all from the general opinion that others have that the guy is good. But you know, some people say this one is very good, and you see what he has to say and if it sounds like he knows what he is talking about and you get advice you can use, then it sort of confirms this. (#9—PRIMARY PRACTITIONER)

I will discuss the structuring of first-hand experience in more detail in
the next chapter, but here it may be pointed out that it accumulated in
different ways, involving different bits of information and proceeding at
a different pace for different individuals. The referral, in which two
physicians saw the same patient, was clearly a major source of information about the way each approached the problem. For consultants, one
element of evaluation was their sense of how conscientious the referrers
were being in referring rather than themselves treating the patient. Lack
of conscientiousness was presumed in an instance in which it was discovered that a referral was made without benefit of examination of the
record.

> He once referred me a hydrocele as an emergency as a possible hernia on
> which there was a note immediately above his which said, "Hydrocele preva-
> lent five years," having not even read the chart. (L9—CONSULTANT)

Apart from evaluation of the conscientiousness of the referrer, there was
evaluation of the competence of the referrer. This was done by assessment of the way the physician had managed the case before he referred it
and by what he might have overlooked in his management. An intangible
but commonly cited criterion of competence was the general medical
intelligence and logic with which the referrer talked to the consultant
about the case. The ultimate test seemed to be the way the referrer
discussed and managed the occasional complicated case, a test that was
not easy to apply to all referrers because some specialties did not come
across enough complicated cases to refer.

> I can evaluate internal medicine better than pediatrics because the cases I get
> from them have a great many more complications. From pediatrics you get
> strabismus, conjunctivitis, and a few other things. Question of a brain tumor
> perhaps. But you get much more complication in internal medicine, so you
> can tell, I think, more that is involved in the doctor's judgment there. (#35—
> CONSULTANT)

By the same token, the *referrers* came into contact with information
that allowed them to evaluate the performance of their consultants.
Here, as in the opposite case, some referrers expressed reservations
about their capacity to evaluate the technical competence of consulting
specialists. A surgeon reiterated the point from his own perspective,
specifying the criteria a referring internist could legitimately use to
evaluate the quality of his work.

I get an impression of a man almost immediately if I get a direct referral, because I can tell by the way he gives me the history of the patient; by the way he talks I know that he knows him. . . . I imagine it's easier for me than for a medical man to get an impression of the surgeon because the medical man brings the patient to the surgeon, and in bringing him he gives information or doesn't. I guess they can form an opinion by what I have to say about the case. On the other hand, they can't very well form one on my capabilities in the operating room. They know the surgeon on the floor, at the bedside, and on the telephone, but very few follow their patients into the operating room. And if they did watch, very few would know what they are watching. So that the medical man's opinion is only determined by the number of survivals or deaths or lack of morbidity. (#48—CONSULTANT)

In the absence of ability to evaluate much of the technique of a colleague, it is not surprising that there was emphasis on good results, crude as this evaluation may have been in that it ignored the sometimes tenuous connection between outcome and good performance. In this, the referring physician was inclined to have much the same perspective on a colleague's performance as does a layman. Were it not for his commitment to the basic rule of trust, which inclines him to normalize mistakes, the referring physician would likely have been impossibly critical of his consultant's mistakes. And as we shall see, consultants hid their mistakes from their referrers. Etiquette or no etiquette, referrers used quasi-statistical methods of assessing results to evaluate their consultants, however they may have tempered the severity of their evaluations by admitting that they themselves were ultimately not in a position to judge and that results were very crude measures of adequate performance.

After all, when I send a case down to ENT, he treats them in a certain fashion and I can form an opinion as to whether he treated them properly and what the results were, and after a while you get some pretty good ideas. If I got a hundred tonsillectomies, I have a pretty good idea of whether the ENT man can do a tonsillectomy or not. I think that holds true of everything, surgeons, orthopedists, skin people. Patients actually come back to you and complain. Now I send a man, let's say, to the GU service, and I don't know how many prostates they have done for me, but I have pretty good ideas about how many patients come back to me and complain, "Gee, the operation, I'm still urinating with difficulty," or "I still have burning in urination." If this happens often enough, it raises doubts in my mind. The same thing goes for surgery. If a patient has what looks like an appendix to me, and the surgeon stalls and stalls and then operates, and this is repeated many times, then you get certain ideas about the surgeon. (#22—PRIMARY PRACTITIONER)

Referrers and consultants each represented both a different field of knowledge and a different perspective on the case. While each saw the same patient and interacted with the other around that patient, each represented a different component of the division of labor and probably was not capable of taking the same approach as the other. Being complementary rather than directly the same in knowledge and approach, it may have been that they evaluated each other and discussed the common case on the basis of only a very general shared medical knowledge, the social and psychological demands of patient management, and the administrative requirements of the group practice. Indeed, some of the physicians claimed that only colleagues in the *same* specialty could evaluate each other accurately.

In group rather than solo practice, it is believed possible for colleagues in the same specialty to observe one another's performance on a routine basis. Not all physicians agreed that they could really observe and evaluate one another, but even those who claimed that they did not really know very much about their colleagues noted that cross-talk and sharing of patients had on occasion provided reasonable grounds for evaluating colleagues. One, somewhat maliciously, discussed the information about the performance of one former colleague which was made available by rotated emergency and vacation coverage of patients.

> When #15 went on vacation one summer he asked if I would cover him. Of course I said I would. As a result, during the time when he went away, whenever I got a call from one of his patients or saw one of them I'd jot it down in a little book. When he got back from his vacation, I suggested we have lunch together and sit down and discuss his patients. But when I got through with the first three or four names I closed the book because it was obvious that he doesn't remember his patients. He works fantastically fast in the office. He can see double the number of patients of anyone else in the office because he didn't involve himself with anything. (L30—PRIMARY PRACTITIONER)

The most ubiquitous source of information that the physicians claimed formed the basic grounds for evaluating the competence of colleagues, however, lay in personally chatting with or consulting with a person about his cases. Of course, access to this kind of information is limited by social relationships as well as by accident. The substance of the interaction, often fleeting and casual and rarely sustained, nonetheless left its residue of impressions that constituted much of the source of the inquirer's evaluation of his colleague.

> You find out about a man by seeing him handle cases that were difficult, hearing him discuss patients in conferences at the hospital, following his reasoning, discussing patients with him privately, and so on. After talking to him for a while you realize how much he knows and how much he doesn't. If you speak to some of them and listen to them you realize there are some things where they are obviously deficient in knowledge. . . . There are people in the group from whom you get the feeling when they talk they are a little bit too vague to suit you, and when they discuss something they sound as if they might know it, but when you analyze it they haven't really said anything. (#4—PRIMARY PRACTITIONER)

Talk, of course, can be ubiquitous only when mutual schedules, time, and a modicum of sociability permit. Among the consultants, most of whom were part time and many of whom were on staggered hours so that all those in one specialty would rarely be at the medical group at the same time, there seemed to be little opportunity to gather evaluative information except at the hospital. It was only at the hospital, on the wards, in the operating room, and at conferences, where most physicians felt they could obtain the systematic first-hand information that provided the grounds for an adequate evaluation of colleague performance. The medical group was not considered a satisfactory source.

> It was easier for me to judge the ability of people when I was a resident in the hospital then it is here. When you are a resident, then you see everyone's patients. Here, you don't do that enough unless you happen to see them covering on a weekend or something or come across a patient, but then you don't have the chart, you don't have the history, and how can you make judgments on the management? (#14—PRIMARY PRACTITIONER)

Indeed, as we shall see, when pressed the group physicians tended to assert that in the last analysis, the hospital setting was the only situation that provided adequate information bearing on the quality of colleagues' performance. It was not interaction in the medical group itself which provided them with an adequate basis for evaluating their colleagues.

10:

Gaps in Information on Performance

Proponents of collective forms of medical practice tend to accept without serious question the assumption that merely by virtue of doctoring together under one roof, having the same patients, doctors will attain a higher quality of medical performance than would be the case if each practiced alone in his individual office. Group practice is thought to facilitate the social control of work by making performance more visible to others and therefore more responsive to critical evaluation. However, not all may be visible, and all that may be visible need not be attended to. As we saw in the last chapter, the practicing physicians themselves did not consider all the information available to be reliable enough to use as a basis for secure evaluation. Only first-hand experience with the work and talk of the individual would do. When such information was lacking, evaluation could be only tentative and informal, a question of mere opinion and so not a basis for controlling others. Of critical importance for the development of inclinations to exercise social control, therefore, was the extent to which mutual first-hand experience with the work and talk of colleagues was distributed throughout the group, for without it, social control could not take place on a truly collective, or group, basis. *Assumptions about effective social control taking place among colleagues are based solely on faith if they do not rest on detailed, empirical data on how various kinds of information about performance are selected and patterned by various kinds of work arrangements and by the workers' own willingness to display their performance and to communicate their knowledge of others' performance to their colleagues.*

Such issues are almost impossible to address except by reference to an abstract and hypothetical rather than an empirical criterion of completeness. That is, we must assume the possibility of a perfectly complete distribution of information about performance in order to assess what exists as a deviation from such perfection. It was, of course, in reality impossible for all physicians to observe all the performance of all others. But by considering complete information as a possibility, one can better identify the degree and substance of the selectivity of the process which did exist in reality. Thus, we can ask about deviation from universal distribution by asking after the pattern of selectivity to be found in the distribution of information about performance.

Since there were different situations in which information was displayed and perceived, I shall begin my analysis in this chapter by exploring the patterning of exchanges of first-hand information about performance in purposive, consultative interaction and then move on to less formal modes of interaction. I shall point to the selective patterning of particular kinds of interaction which thereby limited direct contact between some kinds of physicians and, where possible, I shall point to the selection of the information conveyed in such interaction, thereby restricting the material available for evaluation. Finally, focusing on performance itself, I shall show evidence that some kinds of information about performance were withheld from other physicians by the performer and by those who learned about it.

FORMAL CONSULTATION

A critical source of information about performance stems from the formal act of referring a patient to a colleague for consultation. As long as a physician himself treats a patient and keeps the patient from seeing other physicians, his colleagues may not observe, let alone evaluate, his performance. Referrals, of course, and the interaction between referrer and consultant around a case, do more than only organize the care of the patient. They also make some facet of the performance of each physician visible to the other and therefore make it possible for each to evaluate the other on the basis of first-hand experience. Formal consultation is thus a basic mode of distributing first-hand information in medical practice in general.[1] In the medical group, however, as I pointed out in an earlier chapter, routine referrals to consultants, particularly in periods of work pressure, tended to minimize interaction, limiting it to a written referral slip and a brief note on the patient's chart. Much of the communication tended to be very perfunctory. Thus, for our purposes it is necessary to distinguish among various kinds of consultation in the medical group. One informant contrasted several:

---

[1] For a recent study of referral patterns in a suburban area, see Shortell, n.d.; for a study in West Germany, see Hummel et al., 1970.

If one of the doctors wanted me to see a case other than routine he'd generally call me about it. Another kind of contact is quite by accident. I'll see a man in the hall, and I'll talk to him about a case or he'll talk to me. But we haven't actually gone looking for each other. The third way of informing each other is through the charts. In other words, the consultation is through the routine channels, and I haven't spoken to the doctor about it and I get what information I can from the chart. I get the most information from the man who calls me specifically about a case. I get a little bit less from chance meetings in the hall because we are usually going some place and we don't have that much time for talking. And then I get certainly least from the charts. (#39—CONSULTANT)

Let us begin with an examination of the formal referral and consultation, which is usually a two-person relationship joined together by the patient who is seen by both and about whom they confer. Such referrals not only facilitate the care of the patient and the exchange of technical information but also convey, each to each, information about the conscientiousness, judgment, knowledge, and skill of the physicians involved. Prepaid group practice is said to facilitate referral and so to facilitate the display of physician performance to colleagues. However, in the medical group, while referral was very common, the information conveyed about the referred case was often perfunctory, if not inadequate, so that insofar as most referrals were routine, they could *not* be seen to serve as important sources of first-hand information about performance. It was in the exceptional referral—in the more complex case—in which consultation was accompanied by discussion and sufficient interaction was likely to take place for referrer and consultant each to feel he had gained some reliable notion of the capabilities of the other. Nonroutine referrals and consultations between primary practitioners and consultants thus formed one important source of direct experience with colleagues in the medical group, but *they composed a distinct minority of all referrals*.

Furthermore, referral did not make information about the performance of each practitioner available to *all* others. The division of labor was such that pediatricians and internists worked as parallel services, rarely referring to each other and thus rarely having an opportunity to consult each other and so gain first-hand experience with one another's performance. Therefore, while most consultants were likely to have had some first-hand experience with the performance of all pediatricians and internists, and all pediatricians and internists were likely to have had some first-hand experience with most consultants, many if not most consultants were unlikely to have gained much first-hand experience with the performance of those in other specialties, and many if not most pediatricians were unlikely to have gained much first-hand experience with the performance of internists, and vice versa.

Apart from referral and consultation between specialties, there was consultation between colleagues *within* specialties. The possibility for extensive consultation within a single specialty is said to be another of the distinct advantages of prepaid group practice. However, even though no economic competition discouraged sharing cases—as is said to be the case in solo, entrepreneurial practice—among the physicians in the medical group, professional pride did seem to interfere with consultation. The person who had been given the special status of consultant for those in his own specialty described with accuracy the attitude toward him which his colleagues expressed to us in the course of our interviews with them.

> There probably isn't enough consultation in medicine. Originally the administration hoped that I could have some administrative position in relation to, let's say, hospitalized patients, where I would have to see each one that was hospitalized and oversee the patient. There were some that didn't necessarily have the type of work-up that in retrospect he should have got, but there was tremendous objection from most of the family doctors to that. They felt their toes were being stepped on. They're internists and they feel they know how to work up a patient, and they didn't want to have a boss in that sense. So it was left, when they feel they need a consultant, they would call me. (#20—PRIMARY PRACTITIONER)

In general, my impression was that *within* every specialty it was rare that a consultation took place in which a formal referral of a patient was made. Such a referral was problematic because of the tendency of each physician to feel that his colleagues in the same specialty were no more competent than he and therefore that referral was unnecessary. Only outsiders might serve such a function.

> In general I don't consider the other men in the service as being any more knowledgeable than I am. So when I run into a real problem I want an outside consultation. (#44—CONSULTANT)

The major exception to this rule occurred when there were legal or patient-management problems. In such cases, the senior person, or the chief of service, was consulted because of the greater weight his recorded opinion might have and because of some sense that, due to protocol, it was the senior person who "should" receive such referrals. Thus, the potential for formal consultation within specialties at the medical group did not seem to be fully or extensively utilized, each specialist working more or less by himself without much sharing of patients with other specialists except in the parallel, noninteractive sharing that occurred through rotated night and weekend emergency service. And, interestingly enough, the latter were precisely those duties that the physicians of the medical group sought to drop by hiring others from outside the medical group to replace themselves.

In general, it seems fair to say that circumstances in which two practitioners both directly examined the same patient and discussed the issues involved in the case with the deliberate end of arriving at some joint decision on its management formed a rather small proportion of the total universe of everyday work situations in the medical group. By far the bulk of such consultations occurred between specialties rather than within specialties, and they did not occur between every specialty and every other specialty. Thus, *formal consultation*, which had the greatest potential for making available extensive and direct information about the performance of colleagues, *was distributed very unevenly throughout the medical group, and in those segments where it did occur, routinization more often than not led to the minimization of such information.*

INFORMAL CONSULTATION

Apart from communication between colleagues about a patient each had seen, there was a less formal and less easily defined form of communication—consultation without referral.[2] In such a circumstance, the consultant did not usually see the patient. This kind of consultation differed from that in which referral took place in that the problem involved was not one defined as requiring examination or treatment of the patient by the consultant. The person seeking advice assumed that he

---

[2]For useful parallel observations on consultation in a nonmedical setting, see Blau, 1955; in a medical setting, see Goss, 1959:79–105.

was competent enough to keep the case but that he nonetheless needed supplementary judgment and information. He knew enough about the case and the issues involved to be able to describe it accurately and completely enough for another to understand the problem, and he wanted the other to give advice about the problem which could be used by the advice-seeker. The consultant might have had some specialized knowledge or experience that the advice-seeker lacked, but it was of such a nature that it could be transmitted verbally to the advice-seeker and then used without the consultant's help.

Such consultation without referral tended to be rather informal: one measure of this informality is the frequent absence of mention of the consultation on the official medical record. Sometimes such a consultation entailed deliberately seeking out a person to gain his advice on a particular problem that could not wait.

> I had a recent experience of a girl with what looked like a strep infection but with atypical symptoms and a disturbing throat culture, which indicated a possibility of infectious mononucleosis. About this time I called up #29 and described this to him because of the question involved. I had to make a decision that day, and he advised me that he has seen several cases like this that were infectious mononucleosis. As it turns out the tests came back a few days later and they all confirmed the diagnosis. Now in this case you didn't have to send the patient to him, he was just very helpful to talk to on the phone. (#21—PRIMARY PRACTITIONER)

And, for those questions that could wait, there was the possibility of storing them up so as to be able to ask a particular specialist when one happened to see him.

> If I have something that's bothering me and I never happen to be in when #27 is around, and I happen to spot him and I could remember what I want to ask him, I will. You know, nail him along the way. #51 the same way. This I could say I do more of. If I'm really up a tree, then, you know, I put in a call. But if it is something so-so, well, I would say about every three or four months, if it is quiet and #27 is in and not too busy, and if I'm just discussing something specific, I'll stand around and just talk to him for a while and usually while I'm talking to him, all the things I've been wanting to ask him for the past few months will come to mind and then I get them off my chest and that takes care of it for a while. The meeting just happens. You see him crossing the street or getting out of a car. You see him wandering around in the middle of the hall. And I'll chase after him. (#15—PRIMARY PRACTITIONER)

And there were spur-of-the-moment occasions when a colleague was present and available and when the discussion might be quite casual. Casual or not, all these types of advice-seeking were relatively purposive, dealing with particular problems and seeking advice about them from a given individual. On occasion, however, advice-seeking situations were purely sociable rather than consultative in that an interesting case was made available to another's inspection because of its sheer intellectual value. Interesting cases were treated virtually as gifts between equals, however, and so they depended upon reciprocity for their continued presentation.

> When it comes to a very complicated case, very often it is not so much calling somebody in for consultation as to say, "Look what I have, how interesting it is." I did call #20 in to look at my cases a few years ago until I decided it was one-sided and I dropped it more and more. I called him in not because I couldn't handle it but because this was a very interesting case, and he was very pleased. He said, "That's very interesting, thank you very much." But he didn't call me in, so after a while I dropped it. (#10—PRIMARY PRACTITIONER)

Functional considerations of who was useful to consult, formal considerations of who had to be consulted pro forma, intellectual considerations of who would enjoy seeing the case, and social considerations of who was owed a look at a case or was likely to reciprocate when he had the chance constituted some of the complex considerations involved in the process of displaying and receiving information bearing on medical performance in the informal consultations that did not form part of the formal medical record but composed a great part of the working physicians' experience with and consciousness of their colleagues in the medical group. In the case of formal consultation on general technical problems that anyone was competent to discuss, individuals' choices tended to be those whom they felt were approachable and easy to talk to. Their choices could have been but need not have been a matter of personal friendship and could have been but need not have been a matter of seniority and rank. On one service the senior person may have been avoided, while on another the senior person may have been used most often because face was lost less by asking a senior for advice than by asking a peer or a junior. But for minor problems one was more likely to use people with whom one was both friendly and equal. Quite naturally, specialized problems were taken up with those who had themselves devoted more attention than usual to these problems or who were interested in them.

Obviously, because of its very nature, informal consultation was not initiated by all possible parties with all possible others. Indeed, since it was not official or recorded, there was less need for it to follow formal specialty and rank criteria. And since it was, nonetheless, a concession of need for advice for information, a concession with which the physicians were not entirely comfortable in spite of their protestations (Blau, 1955:108–109; Goss, 1963:178–179), the tendency was to use more particularistic criteria for initiating it than might have been used for initiating formal referrals. Thus, *the patterning of this mode of exchanging information was less narrow, less determinate than that of the formal mode*. And it was considerably more subject to the accident of friendship, of meeting someone in the hall on a particular day, of having hours on the same day as someone else, and of having adjacent offices.

CASUAL SHOPTALK

In reviewing the material on consultation, I have devoted myself largely to advice-seeking, which tended to be initiated by one person for a limited, functional purpose. Advice-seeking, however, is a comparatively formal mode of interaction even when it takes place informally, without referral. Some of what might be called "consultation" was not so much advice-seeking as it was sociable discussion among fellow workers, or casual shoptalk. Such discussion might have contained within it the request for and granting of advice or information, but it would probably not have taken place between the two people involved if they had not happened to come together when they did. It was often embedded in social, nonfunctional talk. Much corridor or luncheon-table interaction was of this nature, almost always informal and involving more than two people. Unlike an ordinary consultation, which was more the intentional seeking of advice from one by another and which took place as a two-person exchange from which others were excluded, these informal conversations were unplanned and, even if they were two-person exchanges, occurred in the company of other colleagues who listened and sometimes commented on what they heard. In such conversations, the participants displayed their knowledge and acumen to more colleagues than just the one being consulted or consulting them.

The first thing to observe about such casual shoptalk was that a rather limited number of the physicians in the medical group participated in it extensively. It was rare to see one of the part-time consultants sitting at the luncheon table where one found, almost daily, a cadre of full-time primary practitioners. Furthermore, more internists than pediatricians stayed to eat at the luncheon table, as did more male practitioners than females. Apart from the composition of the luncheon groups, however, the mere fact of colleagues meeting and sitting together at a table in the cafeteria led to the exchange of talk beyond the social boundaries of friendship and the functional boundaries of the normal division of labor. Pediatricians chatted with internists, and members of the same specialty chatted with one another. Their exchanges were characterized as small talk or chitchat, but they both educated one another by their comments and tested one another by their questions in ways that spilled over the functional borders of formal consultation.

Such talk was not considered so important as to be defined as consultation, and it included as much, if not more, politics, family, vacations, and hobbies as medicine, but it did include medicine and the practical problems of medical work. The going fees for private patients were discussed on more than one occasion (and such discussion led some individuals to raise their fees). Many problems of practice in the group were discussed, frequently in a jocular, facetious tone but one that nonetheless was instructive.

> About the tricks of the trade, we talk about that. We talk about that more in a joking manner than anything else. We complain about the workload and some of the things we do to try to save time, like not allow a patient to even sit down. (#7—PRIMARY PRACTITIONER)

Such conversation allowed the individuals participating in it to gain some perspective on their difficulties with patients by normalizing them—at the very least gaining catharsis and, even better, comfort and support from complaining publicly (cf. Blau, 1955:89–91).

> I think we discussed questions of whether we did the right thing by a patient with our colleagues to protect ourselves, but we discuss always to justify ourselves. In other words, did I make that housecall, should I have made that housecall? And then you want support. . . . So the tendency is when you have gotten angry with a patient, when you've been a little terse, a little fast, if

you have been a little discourteous, the tendency is to discuss this with somebody else, more or less to get support. (#12—PRIMARY PRACTITIONER)

In addition to having interviews with the physicians in which we asked them to discuss and classify their varied contacts with colleagues, we took notes on much of the shoptalk that we observed at formal medical-group meetings (usually before the proceedings or just after they had ended), in hallways, and at the cafeteria luncheon tables. It is of course impossible to be precise about the relative distribution of topics in the universe of such exchanges, but my own impression was that talk about medical work composed a small amount of the total. More important was the impression that, in most of the medical shoptalk, the rule of etiquette dominated interaction and restrained what was said in the discussions. That is to say, disagreement with an individual might have been expressed to his face, but only neutrally, as another opinion rather than as a contradiction reflecting on his judgment.

Difficulties in managing patients were almost always responded to supportively in the presence of the person discussing them. And in the case of a mistake that an individual admitted to while seeking support, the tendency was to normalize it by declaring or implying that it was something that could and did happen to anyone, as the following field notes illustrate.

At the luncheon table, #7 and #3, joined by #6. Before #6 came, the talk was of gasoline and automobiles. #6 came up looking harassed, as usual, and said, "Jesus, what a day! I just finished up. Twelve people this morning and every one of them with pathology. In one case I was going to skip a pelvic and get her out, but I did it and there it was." There was some commiseration, and he continued, "You know, #17 just had a complaint, and is he mad. It was one of those patients he's sat and listened to for years about nothing, and just today he got a letter from her telling him he missed a sacroiliac. She was in [another] hospital and wanted him to pay the bill. And he looked in her chart, and he couldn't find a mention of any symptoms like that. I told him he ought to be grateful because [practicing] here [in the medical group] he could find out what happened to his patients. In private practice he would never find out." Expostulations—"Jesus," "goddamned patients"—were followed by #6 stating that "those damned things were real easy to miss because you send them off to the orthopedist. You should be able to pick it up." #3 said, "But you can do a myelogram," and #6 said, "A good examination or a neurological exam should do it. I missed a lot of those. [Turning to #7] How many of those have you missed, #7?" #7 was noncommittal but left the impression that he had missed some. "How about you, #3?" #3 said, "None, to my knowledge," then hesitated and said, "But I haven't been here long enough to tell. But I think I've diagnosed them more often than they've been really found."

An unusual case, such as that of a thirty-five-year-old woman, very active, with a complaint about her shoulder turning out to have a very serious heart condition, was displayed verbally with great pride by the responsible physician who had "caught it," while a physician who had lost a patient publicly rehearsed self-defenses while colleagues sympathized.

> At lunch #4 told a story of a patient who came in complaining of chest pains. He did several cardiograms on him with no results, but the patient finally came in again and had a real infarct. He was hospitalized for two weeks, during which time there were no more symptoms, no cardiogram variations. He was put on anticoagulants and sent home. Two weeks later, another physician on duty got a call that he has chest pains again. He lived two blocks away from the medical group, but by the time the physician got there he was dead. #4 said, "And what could I do? When I discharged him I told him not to worry, that since he'd been walking around so long with it it must be slight. I had to work to get him and his family to prevent putting him on mothballs. I told him not to really exert himself, but otherwise live normally." #10 said something not entirely audible about the inadequacy of anticoagulants, the others making no more than sympathetic noises, and the conversation briefly touched on experimental work in the hospital relevant to the issue of coagulation and an article someone read about research on heart disease in zoo animals before shifting entirely back to the original topic of work coverage problems.

CONSTRAINTS ON INFORMATION AND DISPLAY

In all of the contexts I have attempted to describe, information about cases and their management was exchanged between colleagues. The information certainly facilitated medical care and on occasion contributed to the education of at least one of the participants in the exchange. Participation in consultation and conversation, however, besides being an exchange of information also constituted a display to colleagues of one's knowledge, skill, and judgment, a display that constituted the first-hand or direct experience with colleague performance which the physician considered to be the authoritative ground for his evaluation of another. I have already suggested some of the obvious ways in which participation in such interaction was patterned—since not all physicians interacted with all others, not all could get the direct experience with others which would allow them to feel that they had grounds for consequential evaluation. Thus, many felt that they must either suspend judgment about a colleague or else use other grounds for evaluation. What I wish to suggest now, however, is that *in addition to there being constraints on who could be in interaction with others so as to exchange such first-hand information, there were constraints on the information that was exchanged, producing systematic omissions in what was displayed and evaluated.*

It should not be forgotten that the essential issue being explored here is that of the prerequisites for social control. I have been asking how the physicians in the medical group could discover poor performance on the basis of the information conveyed in their interactions. I have been focusing on the distribution and substance of first-hand experience with colleagues because it was a prerequisite for the development of a sufficiently secure foundation for evaluation to incline the physicians to undertake the deliberate exercise of social control over a colleague. What I have pointed out about the distribution of consultation and shoptalk should come as no surprise. It is obvious, as I found, that universal distribution was impossible and that distribution had to be limited and patterned by a variety of factors—by the division of labor, seniority, friendship, and the like.

It is just as obvious that the substance of the information being distributed would have been controlled so far as possible by the people involved and at risk. There is no reason to expect physicians to be much more open with colleagues about those of their inadequacies of which they are aware than we would expect any other human beings to be. Assuming that the physicians did attempt to control the information they conveyed in interaction, therefore, in some of our questioning we focused on the information they conveyed about the kind of performance that the lay person would call a "mistake." That is, the physicians were asked whether or not and in what context they talked to others about mistakes—whether, in other words, they displayed mistakes in the course of consultation and discussion with their colleagues or whether they attempted to conceal them.

The essence of their answers was related to their largely implicit criteria for distinguishing types of mistakes. One, for example, claimed that he did not feel he had to hide his mistakes but did not discuss them generally.

> I think I have enough security to feel not anxious to hide my mistakes. A doctor makes mistakes, and I feel I try as hard as humanly possible to avoid them and I feel when one comes up that never in my career I felt I must hide it. But of course I don't go around talking about it generally. (#1—PRIMARY PRACTITIONER)

Clearly, while there was some talk about mistakes, it was selective in character. We have already seen evidence that the physicians did tell colleagues who were by no means their close friends and confidants about things they had overlooked and about occasions on which they had made mistakes in their diagnosis and treatment. But did they talk to others about everything?

What seemed to be important in discriminating between mistakes that were displayed and those that were not was the extent to which the mistake could be normalized. When a mistake is normalized it does not function as a reflection on the essential competence of the person involved. The field note on "missing a sacroiliac," several pages back, illustrated rather well how normalization and face-saving occurred in public, and in Chapter 8 other examples were presented. *Mistakes that tended to be discussed with others were mistakes that were normalizable*. The physician reported in the field note to have missed a sacroiliac reported missing still another condition without claiming any reluctance to mention it. The same physician, however, protected another colleague from disclosure that he had missed a thyroid, as we shall see below.

Not all physicians seemed to feel that they would mention their mistakes to others, but the problem was what they meant by "mistake." One who claimed in an interview that "doctors generally aren't likely to discuss the fact that they might not have paid attention to some symptom" (#24—PRIMARY PRACTITIONER) and who claimed that he would not discuss it nonetheless himself spoke more than once in his interviews of having missed an acute glaucoma. What is more important, our field observations show that his miss was apparently well known to many of his colleagues, since it was mentioned in public and they identified him as the person. The context in which he discussed his mistake and in which it was mentioned by others suggested that it served as a symbolic example of a typical and acceptable contingency of medical work. More than one physician had his own personal miss or normal mistake to discuss in interviews and refer to in public. Such mistakes *were* talked about in general.

All mistakes were not normal, however, and the deviant mistake was the one that physicians seemed more inclined to hide.

> I'd discuss with others the kind of mistake that others would make. I wouldn't want to discuss one [I made] that was absolutely stupid. You know, something that shows that you're stupid, a fumbler, or a mistake where I just didn't know some basic information. I wouldn't want to discuss this—to broadcast it that I was stupid. I would discuss things with people who I felt would excuse me for making the mistake. (#9—PRIMARY PRACTITIONER)

Deviant mistakes would be discussed only with close friends who could be trusted to be sympathetic and supportive because of their special relationship to the deviant, not because of a mere colleague relationship. They would not be made known to mere colleagues. Indeed, it is likely that, insofar as possible, deviant mistakes would be systematically purged from the information conveyed in consultation and discussion between colleagues. Perhaps this was why, in the last chapter, one physician described how part of his method of evaluating his colleagues lay in being sensitive to gaps in their discussion, to strategic vaguenesses.

Finally, it seems useful to point out that the entire collegium of the medical group did not have the same concept of deviant mistakes. Each specialty seemed to have its own special normal mistakes, based on its conception of the ordinary contingencies of its specialized work. These conceptions were not necessarily shared by the members of other specialties, which meant that some of what, for members of one specialty, were normal mistakes, mistakes that members might freely concede and discuss among themselves, ran the risk of seeming to be deviant mistakes in the eyes of colleagues outside that specialty. There was a tendency, therefore, for consultants to conceal what they themselves regarded as normal mistakes from the physicians who referred to them.

I would talk about my mistakes to personal friends, but not necessarily with referring physicians. The referring physician is so narrow-minded that he would take this error of judgment—well, some of them unfortunately idealize the man they are referring to. They foolishly think he is perfect or near perfect and all that sort of nonsense. . . . You've got to keep them in the dark. But we did discuss these things freely among surgeons. (#41—CONSULTANT)

It seems accurate to say that, quite apart from being selective in their distribution across the entire collegium, informal discussion and consultation in the medical group were highly selective and defensive in their content. Some of what a layman would call mistakes or errors in performance were freely conveyed in such interaction, but they were accepted in a comparatively uncritical, supportive manner rather than being criticized as reflections on the competence of the physician committing them. In cases in which a physician felt that colleagues—in the same or in a different specialty—would not agree to normalize his mistake, however, he would try to prevent its becoming known to them. If it concerned him so much that he felt obliged to discuss it, he would restrict his confession and discussion to colleagues who were especially close friends—to confidants who could be trusted to keep their knowledge secret. Thus, *unusually critical information about performance was, insofar as possible, withheld from the conversations and informal consultations that constituted a good portion of the first-hand experience with each other which was the physicians' most authoritative source of information about the quality of care their colleagues gave.*

The only source of relatively complete first-hand experience with colleagues which could be affected only minimally by the way its participants chose to display themselves was formal consultation with referral. In that situation, referrer and consultant each could examine both the patient and the medical record independently of the other doctor and could evaluate the other independently of the way he displayed himself. The distribution of formal consultation, however, was as we have seen limited by the nature of the division of labor and by the comparatively large number of physicians in each of the major specialty services. And communication was detailed only in nonroutine cases. Thus, in the normal course of events it would take a rather long time for direct, nonroutine consultation to take place among a large proportion of the physicians of the medical group, a long time for each to feel that he had had direct, first-hand experience with many others in circumstances in which performance was directly assessible rather than merely inferable from the display of talk, talk that was potentially dangerous to reputation. The distribution of such experience would not be likely to sustain an effectively organized process of social control.

RESTRICTIONS ON SHARING FIRST-HAND INFORMATION

It would seem that the only way by which such first-hand information about performance as could be obtained from formal consultation could have been quickly and extensively conveyed through the collegium lay in its transmission by its receivers to those who had had no immediate occasion to obtain it themselves. Only by such communication could the patterned bias of consultation be rectified and the slow pace at which information was normally accumulated be speeded up. But by and large this did not occur in the medical group. The rules of etiquette effectively prevented the transmission of such information, though some did get through. Most reported discussion of the unethical or incompetent behavior of others was with colleagues who were close friends, and even there the particular physician involved was not always named. The norm of protecting one's colleagues was firmly adhered to.

Many secrets about physician performance were kept rather well in the medical group. During our study we learned of individuals who seemed to have acted outrageously to patients, falsified their administrative service records, accepted money from patients, and had been dangerously neglectful. We learned that they were, on occasion, encouraged to resign from the medical group, but not all did so. In our investigation of the circulation of information about performance, however, after as much careful probing as we could do without ourselves providing the information to the physicians, we found that far more than a simple majority of the group physicians seemed to know nothing about most of the behavior we learned about. What was perhaps even more revealing was that most physicians did not seem to know of even serious cases of repeated poor performance which occurred in their own specialties, let alone in others. Obviously there were serious barriers to the transmission of information about critical areas of physician performance. Those physicians who discovered poor performance were not inclined to mention it to others.

This disinclination to share with colleagues first-hand information bearing on poor performance was explained by reference to the self-conceptions underlying the rules of etiquette—the view the physicians had of themselves and their work.

> Well, you talk about mistakes. Maybe that's what interests you. I saw this young girl with a CA of the thyroid yesterday, probably a CA. I'm going to operate next week. I went over the chart very carefully to see that she's been treated, and I couldn't believe that this thing had blossomed, as the chart said, just in the past few weeks. She wasn't sent to me by her regular family doctor but by a subspecialist consultant. After I had seen her he came in and said, "Well, what are you going to do?" I said, "I'll take care of it. . . . " So I said, "Tell me, do you think this has all come up just these last few weeks? She has been under treatment for years. Don't you think that was there to begin with and it should have been noticed and observed?" He said, "Look, the less said about it the better. The man who sent her to me feels horrible about it. He realizes now he missed something and he said, 'Forget it. Don't say anything about it.' He really feels badly about it, you see. . . . " All right, he knows. What more can you do? After a man knows and he realizes, you are not going to go in and twist a knife in his back. He really in my opinion made a very serious error there. This is the first time I've had anything to do with this man. I mean, every once in a while in my opinion one of the medical men in the group makes a mistake, and, as you say, I don't know what's done about it. I don't know what you *can* do about it. I talk about it to him, but. . . . I don't go around telling other people. I don't think that's good. (#47—CONSULTANT)

The physicians collected their first-hand experience with others as their positions in the division of labor permitted, but they did not communicate much of its substance or their evaluation of it to others unless, as we shall see, special conditions held. Under normal circumstances, the tendency was for each physician to accumulate and store his own experience, without sharing anything critical with others. Thus, in the group practice, which provided extraordinary *potential* for collecting and sharing information bearing on performance and for controlling the quality of performance collectively, *much of the patterning of both information and control remained in fact dyadic, almost as it would be had there been no group practice at all.*

11:
The Threat of the Medical Record

Thus far in my discussion of the foundation of social control in the medical group, I have deliberately avoided any serious discussion of a special source of information the importance of which was emphasized by both physicians of the medical group and other proponents of group practice—namely, the chart, or the medical record. I have reserved discussion for this chapter because the chart, in being a record, had a potential for evaluation and control which was quite different from that of any other kind of information. The everyday activities of the physician left their only lasting trace in the medical record. Furthermore, the medical record was, at the time at least, a *natural* precipitate of everyday work, not a response to the administrative requirements of some announced review procedure. It was quite different also from the kind of data one could obtain from it by the device of collating selected items and presenting them statistically. But, as a record, it was subject to inspection by the physicians themselves and by any others who could gain access to it and was examined as a representation of work performed. It could be used by the group physicians for informing and guiding their own internal process of social control and also could be used by review committees set up by outside organizations to evaluate group performance and guide an external process of social control. Apart from the credentials of the physicians, which were a matter of record, and recorded complaints of patients, no other kind of information for assessing physician performance reviewed in the past two chapters had such permanence as did the medical record. Indeed, present-day health policy emphasizes the strategic character of the medical record for use in monitoring the quality of medical care.

In this chapter, then, I will focus on the medical record itself. I will first discuss what the physicians indicated to be the process by which the record was created—that is, what was put into it—and then turn to the way the physicians responded to the idea of using the record as a source of information for assessing colleague performance. Finally, I shall turn to analyzing the way the physicians responded to the idea of "medical audit"—of the systematic and self-conscious monitoring of records as a

167

means for controlling performance. In brief, I shall show that the physicians regarded the record as a natural accretion of everyday work activity, to be treated as such rather than to be used as a qualitative or quantitative measure of that work. While they would, and did, use it in the natural course of their work to assess the performance of colleagues, they denied both the value and the propriety of doing so systematically in the absence of some special question about a given individual or case. Used in any other than the natural way, the record was regarded as a profound threat to their autonomy.

THE MEDICAL RECORD

Of all the sources of information about performance which were to be found in the medical group, the unit medical record, or the chart, was the most systematic and objective.[1] It was systematic in that every patient who was treated had his own chart, on which every visit was noted along with the complaint, the diagnosis, elements of the physician's examination, and recommendations for treatment. If tests were ordered, the reports of their findings were appended to the chart. If a referral was made, the consultant entered his findings and recommendations into the same chart. However short the record may have fallen of being complete (Garfinkel, 1967), it did constitute the *only* thing in the medical group which was designed to collect and record all medically relevant information on the treatment of every patient. It was an accumulation of information from all doctors who saw an individual and so contained more information than any particular physician could be expected to have obtained from personal experience with the patient. While in theory the primary practitioners coordinated all services and so were supposed to be familiar with everything bearing on the treatment of their patients, even if we assume their memory to have been as precise and detailed as the chart, a primary practitioner may have left the group, died, or retired or patient might have changed his doctor. The record remained. In its *systematic* coverage of care, then, the chart recorded an amount of information that surpassed that which any individual physician could have been expected to know or remember.

---

[1]Records have not received much attention from sociologists. For a recent collection of studies, see Wheeler, 1970.

Furthermore, the chart was also *objective* in the sense that the information was recorded permanently at the time of its collection. However selective that record, once made it was not subject to the distortion and selective bias for which the memory of human beings, physicians or not, is notorious. And it was also objective in the sense that it was, while being confidential and privileged, nonetheless virtually automatically open to scrutiny by qualified persons: any colleague in the medical group could ask for and examine any medical record. Whenever some issue—legal, administrative, or medical—arose about a case, the medical record could be used as a primary source of evidence on when a patient had been seen, who had seen him, what his complaint had been, how he had been examined, and what had been done for him. In that it was both more systematic and more objective than any individual's experience and recollection, then, it constituted a unique source of information about the medical performance of all physicians in the group and thus a unique resource for determining whether poor performance existed.

Finally, I may point out that the notations on the chart provided physicians in the medical group with what they themselves considered to be direct evidence of the quality of the work of their colleagues. They could examine their colleagues' notes directly and concretely and evaluate the notes in the light of their own knowledge and judgment, independent of the opinions of others. In some cases a physician may have been able to examine the patient involved at the same time as he could examine and evaluate the note in the chart written about the patient by his colleague. Additional information available from the chart, such as the results of tests, and the larger picture obtained from the cumulative record, further increased the potential value of the chart for assessing colleague performance. As an informational resource, it would seem to have been superior to the formal consultation, since it was available without formal consultation. And it could make information about performance available to all physicians in the group who cared to look at it closely; in contrast, the distribution of formal consultation was limited by the division of labor.

Nonetheless, the medical record was not used deliberately and systematically by the group physicians as a source of information about performance. A committee of physicians was once constituted to review randomly selected charts, but after about a year of operation it was disbanded for "lack of time." Chart review by a committee of distinguished outside consultants was carried out under the auspices of the insurance plan and was accepted by the physicians in the medical group when the findings were positive, but it was rejected out of hand when the findings were critical of colleagues. Thus, the evidence of performance based on the medical record was not considered more authoritative than other kinds of evidence even though it was, taken alone, more systematic, objective, and accessible than any other kinds of evidence. Indeed, it is by examining the physicians' use of the medical record as a source of information about colleague performance, by examining their mode of evaluating and using it, and by examining their response to the systematic use of evidence from the chart to evaluate performance in the form of chart review that we shall find what seemed to be the essential rationale for guiding and sustaining the particular mode of social control of the collegium in the medical group.

THE SUBSTANCE OF THE RECORD

In the medical group, the chart was created for and served more than one purpose. As in any kind of medical practice in the United States, the chart was created as a record of the contact between doctor and patient. In that record were placed those events or items of information and judgment which the physician wanted to preserve so as to be able to refer to them on future occasions of contact with that patient. Also placed in it were those events or items of information and judgment which the physician wanted on record in the event of some future legal action against him. In ordinary solo medical practice, this is presumably as far as the chart must go to serve its medical and legal purposes. When a solo practitioner wishes to refer a patient to a consultant, a phone call or a letter, but not the chart itself, provides the necessary information to the consultant, as a letter or phone call transmits information from consultant to referrer. But, in the medical group, where the chart accompanied the patient as he went on referrals to consultants, the chart served as the medium of communication. As we have seen, the notations on the chart were often the sole source of information for the consultant and the referrer. Phone calls or personal conversations were used to supplement the chart only when the case was nonroutine in character.

As we have already seen, many of the physicians complained about the inadequacy of the written record. Consultants complained that information bearing on the reasons for referral was sometimes missing, and primary practitioners complained that consultants sometimes did not write into the record sufficiently complete and legible information on their findings and recommendations. Indeed, some primary practitioners complained that they did not understand the consultant's notes—as when, for example, a numerical value of a specialized test or finding was presented without explanation. Telephone conversations and other un-recorded information seemed critical for the nonroutine case, not only because of the complex problem involved but also because of the perfunctory character of the notes on the chart.

This is not to say that the chart was used for only the most perfunctory communication between physicians. When a physician unwillingly refer-red a demanding patient, he sometimes used the chart to communicate his problem in order to be excused by the consultant for referring an ostensibly unnecessary case and to solicit support from the consultant in soothing the patient and discouraging his demands. Sometimes rather tactless remarks about the propriety of the referrer were written into the record by angry consultants, and sometimes, in seasons of the year when time permitted, witty remarks were written into the record about what were thought to be neurotic patients for the appreciative and sympathetic eyes of colleagues, as the following excerpt from a chart shows:

APRIL 21. Hemorrhoid problems at twenty. Twelve to 15 years ago left ingui-nal hernia was diagnosed. Patient has slight pulling sensation in left groin. No hernia found. Ring slightly relaxed. No hernia on the right either. In addition, the patient presents, from a slip of paper, the following fantastic complaints: (1) When he sings he has a slight soreness and some other indescribable sensation in his throat. Advice: Don't sing. (2) When he dances, his feet hurt. Advice: Don't dance. (3) When he rides the bicycle, his nose runs. Advice: Don't ride the bicycle. Aside from the above advice, which I somehow refrain from giving him, I had no suggestion for the handling of these distressing complaints. /s/ #24

MAY 2. No hernia on either side. The above note of #24 is appreciated by the consultant surgeon, who likes to have a good laugh occasionally. /s/ #47

Nonetheless, by and large, the medical record was rather abbreviated in character, created more as an aid to work than as a faithful record of work. While it may have been, as some claimed, that in the medical group they wrote more extensive notes into the chart than they did in their private practices because in the medical group the chart was to be used by other physicians, the notes tended to be rather scantier than what the physicians themselves agreed would be complete or optimal. Most often the explanation for the charts' brevity lay in the workload— that there was simply not enough time to write a "good note."

EVALUATION OF COLLEAGUES BY THE RECORD

Whatever its limitations, the record was a frequently cited source of information by which colleagues could be evaluated. Most of the physicians referred to the unit medical record as a unique resource for mutual evaluation and review—as an important element of practice in the medical group which "kept them on their toes."

> What keeps you on your toes? An inner desire to do good practice, of course. And also the exposure of your charts to the other physicians. The other family doctors will be seeing these people from time to time, looking over your notes. Just as I gather an opinion of a man from his notes, they gather an opinion of me. (#43—CONSULTANT)

Evaluation of colleagues from their notations focused on a variety of elements, including the style of writing a note.

> One thing you use to build up a picture of a doctor is the chart itself, the care with which the note is written, and this is an index of the quality of the work of the other physician. . . . If I were really rushed I just wouldn't have the time to sit down and formulate and organize a good note. (L20—CONSULTANT)

Most physicians assumed that the record was a faithful enough and accurate enough representation of the doctor's work for their purposes and so considered it to be an important source of insight into his competence and conscientiousness which they could use independently of any other information.

> I learn a great deal about my colleagues from the charts. How they go about their work, what they've done, have they sloughed over certain things, just not done things. (#37—CONSULTANT)

The chart, then, was considered a valuable source of information about performance to be used in the course of work. But if it were to be used only in the normal course of providing care and to be read in a purely functional way as one was dealing with the problem at hand at the time, it would be, as a source of information about performance, merely a complement to formal consultation. Exposure to information about performance embedded in the chart would, under these circumstances, follow the channels of the division of labor, as did formal consultation. And, in fact, comments about the chart were distributed in the same pattern as comments about formal consultation were distributed. Consultants more often spoke of seeing the chart notes written by referrers than of seeing those of other consultants, and primary practitioners more often spoke of seeing the notes of consultants than the notes of their colleagues who were also primary practitioners. For the primary practitioners, most talk was of the *potentiality* of charts being seen by their colleagues in medicine or pediatrics.

> Actually, we are only exposed here in a relative sense. One's patients are at times covered by other doctors. Charts are always available to another doctor, and he can have the need for review over a patient's history and your management of it. (#21—PRIMARY PRACTITIONER)

The paucity of talk about actually reading other colleagues' notes suggested that this was not a common or routine occurrence.

Ostensibly, then, the chart notes distributed information about performance little better than did interaction in formal consultation. The record, however, differed from the interaction of formal consultation in being a *record*. That is, it could be examined by those who were not involved in the particular formal consultation. The consultant could, *if* he had the time and inclination, read the notes of other consultants to whom he did not refer. Just as a physician who had no occasion to cover a colleague in his own specialty or refer to others in another, parallel specialty, could gain first-hand information about such persons by listening to their shoptalk at the luncheon table, so inspection of some of the chart notes of otherwise unknown colleagues could conceivably have served as an additional—indeed, a considerably superior—source of information. After all, the chart was always available in the file, and, unlike such informal conversation at lunch, it was focused on medical matters.

The medical record thus had enormous potential for compensating for the serious limitations in distribution of other kinds of information about colleague performance through the medical group. But it was in fact used only passively, serving as a resource for the daily work of consultation. Its considerable potential was unutilized by the members of the medical group. The chart and colleague notes on it were examined in the course of caring for a patient but were not otherwise examined.

THE PROBLEM OF CHART REVIEW

The term "chart review" is usually used to describe a formal process by which specially selected and designated physicians assume the task of systematically examining medical records for the explicit purposes of assessing their completeness and, less commonly, assessing the quality of the performance of the physicians who created the records. An individual may perform a chart review, but it is more common for a committee to do so. Chart review is considered by academics and medical policy-makers to be an essential method of assessing and controlling the quality of medical care, and its presence in a medical institution is considered to mark a high quality of care. Nonetheless, the physicians of the medical group, taken collectively, were quite ambivalent about the evaluation of performance by review of the record, whether performed informally or formally, by peers or seniors, by insiders or outsiders. Indeed, the idea of chart review threatened their most basic conceptions of themselves as physicians.

Let us begin consideration of the collection of information about performance through chart review by returning to the most informal mode of review—namely, a review by a physician who, wishing to evaluate his colleagues, deliberately examines their chart notes for that purpose. An excellent young physician, frequently irreverent about other issues his colleagues took seriously, was shocked by the suggestion that this be done.

[BR: How do you form an opinion about a man you don't think so much of?] I see him in the hospital and in minor ways here. [BR: Do you make any point of checking your opinion?] Checking my opinion? No, how could I do that? [BR: You check records and medical jackets.] How would that help me? [BR: Well, you could work directly with him. Another way to find out would be to look in the jackets of some of the patients he works with.] I have a feeling that's not etiquette. In fact I think it's prying. I really do. I know a couple of physicians around here who do that, #4, for example. I think that's crazy. You've got to have a reason, a very good reason to want to check on somebody. . . . [BR: Then your opinions are formed passively? You don't seek information? It just comes to you?] It comes to you in a variety of ways. For instance, you see patients of other doctors, and you'll get their charts, and if you look through their charts, read a few notes, you get an impression of how he's handling the patients, know what he is doing and what you would do. You see, most of the doctors here are good. I guess if I were working with a bunch of bums it might be different. I might have to check. But they check them before they get in the group here. (#13—PRIMARY PRACTITIONER)

The record was thus a legitimate enough source of information about colleague performance, but it was legitimate to examine only a record that normally came into one's hands in the course of work. To make an effort to seek out any other record and examine it was prying.

This is not to say that any chart review by an individual was considered inappropriate. When an individual had "a very good reason to want to check on somebody," it was routine to review a particular chart or set of charts. That very good reason was provided by such special events as a death, a serious complaint, a threat to sue, and the like.

The ward patients complained that the man took too long to operate. The question came up should he be dropped [from the staff]. I had gotten him appointed to the staff here, so they came to me with the problem. I said, "Now, let me take all the patients he's had in the last two years and see if his work is inferior." It turns out his mortality was no greater, his morbidity no greater, and his results just as good. There was just one thing—he was slow in the operating room. . . . He didn't seem inferior to me. . . . But I had to have some concrete method of proof. . . . So things had to be brought out on a point-by-point chart review. (#47—CONSULTANT)

In such a circumstance, review of charts provided evidence more authoritative than personal opinion about the surgeon's capability. Chart review was in fact most appropriate under such circumstances, when it was used to resolve the issue *after* a question was raised. Chart review as such was not questionable; what was questionable was review instituted for the purpose of actively *looking* for problems, for surveillance, for checking up in the absence of any definite suspicion of poor performance.

Not all functions of chart review were equally disturbing. All the physicians recognized how important adequate records were for defending themselves against a malpractice suit, and some physicians therefore felt that chart review concerned with the completeness of the record would be beneficial to themselves. The physicians themselves complained of the incompleteness of the record hindering communication among those cooperating in the care of patients, and so some felt that chart review could be beneficial by stimulating the writing of better notes. Poor notes, however, were also used as an argument *against* chart review. The notes were conceded to be poor, and it was argued that, given the pressure of time and workload, they were in fact impossible to maintain at the expected level of completeness.

> You can't keep good records. It is physically impossible. These people haven't the slightest idea how one practices medicine. You can't give a patient an hour and then go and write a nice, long, three- or four-page note. So their objection is always, "Why wasn't this done?" Lots of times it *was* done, but it wasn't written down. You can't do it. You can't ask doctors to see 20 people in three or four hours and expect them to have perfect medical records. I write "Px negative" or "Px as noted a year ago at this date." But I can't write it all out. It's ridiculous. (L16—Consultant)

The argument that it was impossible to write complete notes in fact got converted into an argument that the chart review itself was invalid *because* it relied on the evidence of the record alone. Indeed, it was considered almost unfair that the record be used to evaluate performance. The same consultant who claimed to learn an enormous amount from the chart about the acumen of his colleagues expressed skepticism about the chart's value in surveillance.

In our interviews, we asked the physicians not only what they thought of the chart review carried out by visiting committees on behalf of MSP, but also what they thought of the idea of the group itself developing its own internal chart review. In general, the opinion seemed to be that chart review could be palatable only if it were carried out by respected senior men, or "superiors." "Audit of record by colleagues rather than by superiors would be degrading" (L6—Primary Practitioner). But perhaps more important than who should perform the review was the way it would be performed and the way the results were to be used. Any overtone of using fixed, formal criteria for evaluating the record was resented, as was the idea of using the results of review as a basis for disciplining or in some way pressuring the physician.

The criteria used in chart review should not be trivial or rigid and should leave much leeway to individual discretion. The use of trivial and rigid criteria was called "pure bureaucracy."

This MSP chart review of my service was ridiculous. . . . They said we took out a lot of specimens and didn't send them over to the path lab. This is ridiculous because I send over any black thing that might be involved, but we take out dozens and dozens of sebaceous cysts. To send them over adds to our work, their work, and our expense. . . . So of course they said I was doing things wrong, and after that I sent over everything I took out, but it's not necessary. This came just from a chart, and this is the awful thing I remember from the review. It disturbed me greatly. I mean, this is pure bureaucracy. (#47—CONSULTANT)

Furthermore, unless done in the spirit of education, chart review could seem too much like a police action to be palatable.

I don't believe in chart reviews. It gets the machine too much involved. It's hard to stomach. . . . But it could be done gracefully if it were put in a constructive way in discussing the problem cases with someone who is universally respected. Rather than being a policeman, it should be the role of an educator. (L6—PRIMARY PRACTITIONER)

Indeed, done in such a properly professional spirit, the results of the review could be treated as advice, to be freely rejected by the person reviewed if he so chose. The autonomy of the individual's judgment must remain untouched.

I suppose the MSP audit is all right. If they want to do the study and make recommendations, let 'em. We don't have to follow them. That's the point. . . . I don't mind if anyone makes suggestions or looks at my records or patients. That's fine. (#39—CONSULTANT)

Finally, it is worth noting that it was very common for the argument to be made that chart review might be appropriate where physicians were not so carefully chosen, did not have such superior credentials, and did not work in teaching hospitals, but that it was unnecessary in the medical group we studied. Indeed, it was argued in addition that chart review within the medical group was unnecessary because close review of the really important, serious cases took place routinely in the hospital. And there, chart review was less important than the examination of the patient by the whole staff. The house staff of the hospital assured the quality of care more by relying on direct apprehension of the case than by relying on the chart.

THE THREAT IN CHART REVIEW

It seems to me indicative of deeper objections to chart review than merely differences of opinion about the proper way of setting it up that the physicians' comments were typically constructed on two levels. They tended to begin with a very personal, almost emotional, reaction around some point and then, as if they were pulling themselves together, to move on to a practical objection or an implicit objection made by specifying how chart review might be undertaken so as to be made acceptable. The structure of these comments suggested that chart review posed a real threat to the physicians' conceptions of themselves and their work. To them, it violated both the rule of trust in their competence and conscientiousness and the rule for conceiving of their work as so complex as to depend on judgment rather than standardized rules for procedure.

Chart review made them uncomfortable also because it took them back to the time when they were still students who, *because* they were students, were supervised and reviewed. As certified, licensed physicians with good credentials, they felt entitled to be treated like grown-ups, adults who might be trusted. To be reviewed was to be treated as if one were still in training, still a child.

> It makes me uncomfortable to think of chart review going on. I can't say why. I did that when I was chief resident physician in a hospital for my assistant residents and the interns, and that was done for me by the chief resident when I was in training. But once a man is in practice we have to draw the line somewhere. Once a man has reached his point of qualification, we presume that outside agencies have done the job for us in that sense, and I don't know how review could work anyway. (#43—Consultant)

As a reflection of lack of trust, chart review took on the character of oppressive surveillance. In this context, words like "Gestapo" and "police action" appeared. Finally, insofar as chart review is systematic in character and is predicated on some comparatively standardized conception of both records and procedures, its outcome was seen to be pure bureaucracy. Such an emphasis on standard routine was at once "ridiculous and childish" and a threat to the physician's prerogative of making his own choices in instances in which there could have been a legitimate difference of opinion.

Formal chart review designed to evaluate the quality of physician performance thus seemed to strike at the very core of the way physicians conceived of themselves and their work. It implied that they were not to be trusted; that, as when they were students, they had not yet grown up and were not yet capable of responsible, unsupervised performance; and that their work was rather more standardizable than was compatible with their emphasis on first-hand experience and the normality of mistakes.

In responding to the idea of chart review, the physicians were put into a kind of dilemma, for, as practitioners who were responsive to the standards of academic medicine, they had to pay at least lip service to the value of the idea. But some of their most treasured conceptions were threatened by it. The ambivalent resolution of the dilemma seemed to lie in subscribing to it in principle but rejecting it in the particular instance of themselves and their medical group, on the basis of ostensibly practical arguments. They argued that they were better-than-ordinary physicians whose superior credentials precluded the need for review, that, in any event, review of the serious and important cases went on in the hospitals where they worked, that anyway performance was largely a function of the physician's inner motivation and could not be changed by review, and that reliance for review on the medical record was inappropriate because the record did not reflect enough of all that went on in their work to be used to evaluate them. Thus was the legitimacy of the use of the medical record for supervisory review denied.

THE RESPONSE TO A CHART REVIEW

If the legitimacy of the use of the medical record to review the quality of performance was denied, then we should expect that the outcome of such review would be defied. And this in fact was the case in an instance we observed. While we were studying the medical group, an external audit was carried out for one of the consultant services, and the confidential report that was transmitted to the director was rather critical of the quality of the records as well as of the quality of performance. The Executive Committee met to decide what to do about the report and its critical recommendations. The mood throughout the meeting was one of solidarity with the criticized colleagues and hostility to the audit. Throughout the discussion that took place before replies to the report were formulated was the constant theme of the inadequacy of records as a source of knowledge about how cases were *really* handled. As one of the criticized consultants put it, "It's one thing to go by a certain set of rules; it's another thing to have the patient sitting there." And as a supportive primary practitioner put it, "The record just doesn't have in it my phone calls, the 10 minutes I spend talking to a consultant about a case."

Once the Executive Committee got down to business, it proceeded to "refute" the report's criticism and recommendations. The report first criticized the heavy workload carried by the physicians involved, one so heavy that, it asserted, patients got a less-than-thorough examination and chart notes themselves were too brief. It suggested that the part-time specialists increase their working time at the medical group (which they did not want to do). One of the consultants defended his practice by saying that patient care was not generally "shaved," though it might occasionally be, and suggested that the issue really lay in the brevity of the chart notes that the reviewer read and from which he inferred excessive time pressure. However, the consultant went on, brief notes were all he needed for his work: "Long notes are time-consuming, but notes aren't made for the evaluator, they are made for communication with other doctors in the medical group. Are notes made to help patient care, or are they made so that an evaluator can look at them once every few years?" Several other group physicians testified to the excellence of the notes of the criticized service, and the report's criticism and recommendation were rejected.

The second recommendation, apparently based on lack of documentation of consultation in the record, was that consultation and review of the cases requiring surgery be carried out with the referring primary practitioner before the patient was hospitalized. It was rejected with the statement, "This is always done and very thoroughly." The third recommendation was for a more aggressive use of an observational procedure on patients suffering certain symptoms, and it was rejected with the comment that the consultants involved did not believe that the procedure should be used routinely. The fourth recommendation was based on the observation (from the charts) that the primary practitioners were treating conditions that might better be managed by the consultants themselves and that, at the very least, the consultants should give the practitioners a series of lectures on the proper methods of managing such conditions. That recommendation was also rejected on the basis of an assertion that there was a very close liaison between the primary and consulting services and that the primary practitioners were of superior competence. Only the final, fifth recommendation, that a follow-up system be improved so as to assure that patients returned for recommended care, was accepted.

CONFLICTING ASSUMPTIONS ABOUT REVIEW

In considering the Executive Committee's response to the report of the chart review of one specialty service, we should not make the mistake of assuming that the response was entirely negative. The report did succeed in stimulating the institution of a follow-up system that on previous occasions had been rejected by the physicians when suggested by one of their own. However, the other recommendations of the report were rejected. The reason for this seemed to be too complex to allow one to impute crude self-interest, simple self-protectiveness, ignorance, or indifference to the physicians of the medical group. At bottom lay a sharp conflict between the assumptions of an outside consultant making a formal chart review and those of the working collegium of the medical group. Formal review assumed that the essentials of performance could be found in the medical record and that systematic samples of medical records, properly reviewed, would produce an accurate and reliable picture of the important elements of an individual's performance. Obviously, the record must be complete for such a review to work; and so, if for no other reason than that they could do their work, the reviewers pressed for more complete records.

The working physicians, however, made different assumptions. To them, the work of doctoring in all its ramifications was what was at issue, and both filling out the chart and using it were only two small segments of that work of doctoring. It was no accident that, in commenting on chart review, many physicians referred to what they knew about a patient that was *not* in the chart to be reviewed. As complete as we can imagine a chart to be, there will always be things the physician knows about a patient and his dealings with him and things he knows about a colleague and his dealings with him which will not be on the chart. In the experience of doctoring, the chart represents but a slice of medical work, only a segment of the accumulated mass of information from diverse sources met with in the normal course of work. It was work *experience*, not the chart, that was the reality for the physicians. They perceived correctly that the reviewers relied on what happened to be in the chart and so could only guess about the events and processes that lay outside it. And they were also well aware of the reality of doctoring, which was of such a character that reliance on the chart alone for guiding work decisions would be highly dangerous. On that basis, they insisted on allowing *their* reality, not the reviewers', to be the arbiter.

These very profound differences in assumptions and perspectives were clearly expressed in an interview in which a physician was put on the defensive by the interviewer's questioning of the objectivity and reliability of everyday knowledge about colleagues. And, in the course of the discussion, the issue of responding to criticism by an outside chart-reviewer was also described very clearly as being based on practical epistemology: "Either everybody in the group is wrong, or the survey is wrong."

#1: You know, [MSP did review one service] and they recommended that we get rid of one man, although they didn't come out that bluntly. . . .

EF: Have you gotten good marks in the past, or have you ever had any problems like that [before]?

#1: We've had excellent marks. We have had superior ratings on everything.

EF: Do you feel the investigating function is appropriate?

#1: It seems reasonable enough. I don't suppose it is thorough, but it seemed reasonable enough until we got the bad mark, and then it made us mad. [EF smiles.] Really, I'm serious about that, because if we come out with good marks it is all right. What I said at the meeting, and I'll still say it, is that if you work with a specialist for 10 years and you can't find anything wrong with him, then either everybody in the group is wrong or the survey is wrong. You know we have 30 [full-time] doctors here.

EF: It is a very difficult problem. You make your own systematic efforts in [an internal chart review] committee to investigate care, and you just sort of let it slide. The only evidence, and those you think highly of, are what you might call clinical knowledge, when you work with somebody and you see his chart, you know him as an individual, you get sort of a vague feeling which is difficult to document. Now this is a different kind of knowledge than the sort which a consultant who looks at charts would get. But, you see, the only systematic source, in a sense an objective and detached source, would be the consultant [reviewer].

#1: No, you are wrong.

EF: These are different methods. One is systematic and the other isn't.

#1: From that point of view, none of us is the least bit interested in whether a guy writes good notes or not. We are much more interested in whether a patient was properly diagnosed and treated, and released.

EF: When you take dictation, don't you need notes?

#1: Sure you do, but it is a matter of putting what is more important first. Naturally you do. When you say a vague feeling from yourself, it is not quite correct, what you are saying, because whenever a problem comes up, there is much more than that. There is direct contact with him, talking with him, and his visiting your patient and your knowing what he did and how he did it and what complications the patient developed, and so on.

At bottom, two different kinds of experience conflict when a chart-review report criticizes working physicians. Reviewers and physicians have different bases of evaluation, and when a colleague is criticized who the physicians all think excellent, their own mode of collecting and evaluating their experiences is threatened. To accept the result would require a profound reorganization of the way they worked and the way they judged work.

THE CHART AS TOOL, WEAPON, AND COVER

As we saw in an earlier chapter, the physicians denied the legitimacy of *formal authority* over most spheres of their work. In this chapter we saw more: we saw that they also denied the legitimacy of the use of systematic and *formal methods* of evaluating them, even when eminent colleagues were the ones to use these methods. Essentially, what they insisted on was the complete avoidance of formal method. They insisted instead on the reliance on informal methods of accumulating information about colleagues, of exchanging their information selectively, and of developing subjective opinions about their own and others' qualities as physicians. They insisted on avoiding the active collection of information, the systematic distribution of such information, and the deliberate collation of that information to produce an authoritative evaluation. Such processes violated the basic rule of trust. The chart, like all other sources of information, had to remain a tool of work; it could not be detached from that activity to be turned against them as a weapon.

This study was carried out at a time when there was no strong national pressure for greater accountability on the part of community physicians. In that the medical group I studied was accountable to an outside review group, it was the exception. If anything, the physicians of the medical group were more likely to be amenable to review procedures than was the ordinary solo practitioner of the time. While it is possible that physicians have changed since then, because of some new social consciousness or changes in training and the professional climate of practice, there is no systematic, empirical evidence to indicate it. The few studies of physicians which are available tend to support my findings. Mumford (1970), for example, presented a persuasive contrast between a university and a community hospital, showing that, in comparison to the elite, research-oriented staff of the university hospital, the attending physicians of the community hospital, oriented to community practice, deprecated the importance of medical records and put their completion lowest on their list of priorities. In a more recent study of the staff of five comprehensive clinics, Nathanson and Becker (1973) showed that those who were most strongly oriented to patient care rather than research kept the most incomplete medical records.

Thus, while significant changes are now taking place in the administrative review of community-physician performance, there is no reliable evidence that corresponding changes are taking place in the basic conceptions that everyday community practitioners hold of themselves and their work. If they, like the doctors of our medical group, insist on the primacy of their first-hand experience at work, the ultimate validity of their personal judgment, and their right to trust, it is difficult to see how they will respond to the imposition of formal review procedures by any other mode than the age-old practice of all workers, medical or otherwise—anticipating and conforming to the letter of requirements where absolutely necessary, but carrying on their own work life the way they see fit underneath that opaque and protective formalism.

Just as there has been defensive record-keeping to cover oneself against possible malpractice suits, so there will be concern to cover oneself in the record against periodic review. But, as one of the physicians asked, "Are notes made to help patient care, or are they made so that an evaluator can look at them?" I have no doubt that, where it is required, records will be kept in such a way that an evaluator can find little to fault: what was a tool in the medical group at the time we studied it will become more of a cover. What will go on behind that cover is likely to be a somewhat different reality.

12:
The Functional and Symbolic Properties of Sanctions

The detailed analysis of the foundations for social control in the medical group has lead the exposition through the examination of a series of topics that may be regarded as essential elements of any process of social control. First, there were what might be called the written and unwritten laws of the organization: the rules that attempted to specify proper performance. As we saw, there were written rules indicating working hours and similar contractual issues; and there were a variety of informal, unwritten understandings indicating how physicians were expected to relate to one another and to patients, when mistakes at work were deviant and thus to be controlled, and when they were not.

Social control cannot operate on the basis of prescriptive rules alone, however. Rules cannot be enforced if there is no way of learning about the way people perform. Agents of social control must be able to observe or otherwise learn about performance in order to determine whether rule violation has occurred. The concrete way in which information about performance was collected and distributed in the medical group thus constituted a critical element shaping the precise way the process of social control could function. In addition, the way available information was evaluated in the medical group as acceptable evidence of performance—the rules of evidence, as it were—was another factor of obvious importance for determining the substance of the process of social control.

Given rules that specify the norms for performance, given information about performance becoming available to the members of the medical group, given evaluation of the evidence leading to the conclusion that rule violation has occurred, social control can be seen to follow as a response to that rule violation. But any number of responses are possible. On occasion in history, physicians who have failed to cure patients have been fined, beaten, flayed alive, forced to refund their fees, publicly ridiculed, thrown out of windows, required to pay heavy sums for damages, and so on. Why was one sanction employed and not another? The responses to ascribed rule violation chosen by agents of social control in a particular setting must themselves also be explained: no single response is automatic and inevitable.

It may seem that one can deal with the issue simply by describing the penalties specified for various rule violations. As it happened in the medical group, there was no set of statutes that described rule violations and the penalties attached to them, but even if there had been one, it would not have encompassed the entire universe of responses to rule violations, many of which always occur informally and without conscious codification. Furthermore, the response chosen is inevitably discretionary rather than automatic because the meaning of the violation must be evaluated. Formal penalties are unlikely to be invoked and, if invoked, are unlikely to be used if the participants of a collectivity believe that the penalties are inappropriate or unjust. As the history of criminal law shows, when specific mandatory penalties for specific crimes are believed to be too severe, then few persons are convicted— even arrested and charged—for the commission of such crimes. And while the specific rule violation as an act does not change, rather than a charge being entered which would, if sustained, entail a severe penalty, the charge may be reduced—that is, the specific rule violation imputed to the individual may be changed so that penalties acceptable to the participants can be employed—and the record of offense may be made to show a lesser violation.

Whatever may exist as formal rules and regulations, therefore, one may not understand the real process of social control by reference to those rules alone, and one may not take at face value the records purporting to reflect the process of social control. One must first know whether the participants are in general agreement with the propriety of the rules, including those specifying penalties, and even if so, whether the rule infractions were such that consensus about their commission is readily established. In a previous chapter, I described the physicians' conception of the propriety of the formal contractual rules and of the use of formal methods of collecting, reviewing, and judging information about performance. Here, I wish to focus on the physicians' conceptions of the proper modes of responding to ascribed rule violations.

As I have already indicated, one can respond to a particular ascribed rule violation in many ways. How might we make sense of these alternatives, however? No doubt there are a number of ways of doing this, but here I wish to employ the criteria of the physicians themselves. Essentially, I wish to show that they used both *functional* and *symbolic* criteria for deciding how to respond to rule violations. The functional criteria concerned whether or not sanctions would "do any good"—that is, lead to the rectification or control of undesirable performance or not. To the physicians, sanctions could not be functionally effective if they were not fitted to the physicians' own source of motivation or incentive to perform their work suitably. They rejected the use of sanctions for purely punitive purposes. The symbolic criteria concerned the morality of the application of particular sanctions to physicians: the physicians rejected the use of some kinds of sanctions on the ground that they would not be right for the kind of person the physician was. As I shall try to show, the conjunction of symbolic with functional criteria created distinct limitations on the kind of social control that was acceptable to the physicians.

SOURCES OF DOING GOOD WORK

Insofar as it was the physicians themselves who were responsible for identifying some kinds of rule violations and assessing their seriousness, and insofar as they collectively could exercise their own modes of social control, publicly protest formal administrative attempts at control, and publicly and privately resist formal control, their own conceptions were of critical importance to our understanding of the special character of social control in the medical group. Assuming for the moment that the physicians were all agreed that certain kinds of behavior were clearly violations of desirable rules, the question is, what would they agree is appropriate to do in order to prevent such behavior or, if it did occur, to prevent its recurrence? Most of the physicians were prone to answer that question by reference to the way they believed physicians as persons were motivated to perform acceptably. To them the issue was which sanctions would be functional or effective, and effectiveness was determined by what was important to the physician as they conceived of him, what motivated him to perform well.

In the course of our interviews, we asked most of the physicians what it was that motivated them and their colleagues to "keep on their toes," or to perform their work well. As may be expected from the general character of the question, a wide variety of concrete answers were given, some being quite abstract and others dwelling on a few very concrete aspects of medical work. Taking all the responses together, however, it seemed that three sources of motivation, alone or in various combinations, exhausted the entire range. First, there was *biography*: physicians were seen to be impelled to work as they do by their personalities and their training. Understanding that it was the basic medical training of the individual physicians that gave them the resources of knowledge, skill, and judgment they used in the course of their work, the interviewees explained performance by reference to that past training in interaction with individual character or personality, a factor that determined how a physician would be able to *use* his basic resources of knowledge, skill, intelligence, and the like. Commitment to doing work according to particular standards was often characterized as "compulsiveness" and "conscience."

Second, physicians emphasized as a source of good performance the element of pride in one's reputation, sensitivity to the opinions others had of one's work. Rather than being formed and set by one's biography, one instead remains sensitive to one's immediate *social environment*, showing concern that one's colleagues think well of one's work.

Third, the source of at least some elements of good performance was seen to be *material self-interest*: this primitive conception of performance needs no introductory explanation. This influence on good performance was least important in the view of most of the physicians. Let us turn now to each of these sources of motivation.

BIOGRAPHY

Most of the physicians emphasized above all other sources of motivation to perform well the physician himself as an individual, believing that he performs more or less independently of the situation he is in and, particularly, independently of the social pressures connected with that situation. Like his basic medical training, his basic character was seen as a more or less permanent and only minimally changeable part of him. A biography, after all, is not usually considered to be something that can be changed. Those who emphasized biography thus minimized situational sources of influence on performance, as did the physician who protested our question, "What keeps doctors in the group on their toes?"

It's a very false outlook on life to ask how people keep on their toes. The impression I get is that you've got somebody over there with a lightning-rod keeping them on their toes. If you have good doctors, conscientious and well-qualified and working with the group, they are going to give a good job. It doesn't make any difference whether they're working in the group or alone. If you have a good, conscientious man, he's got to do the same job. He won't give the schmaltz when he is working with the group, but he is going to practice good medicine. It's the only way he knows how to practice. (L16—CONSULTANT)

Quite consistent with this view was the fact that those who emphasized conscientiousness were inclined to deny that working in the medical group had any significant impact on performance.

In the course of elaborating on the significance of his basic character to the way a physician performs, there frequently was denial of the significance of other motives commonly advanced by proponents of group practice, including the desire to maintain a good reputation among colleagues. The physician was visualized as someone who is guided only by his unchangeable inner needs. He works the way he does because he has no other choice. Given his basic medical education, he is literally compelled to use it in only one way, inflexibly.

The thing that keeps me on my toes is first of all personality—the compulsion, you know. If one is compulsive about certain things, he wants his chart on his patient just right. . . . A well-trained doctor wouldn't be lazy. Usually to be a good doctor, you have to be compulsive. (#3—PRIMARY PRACTITIONER)

So strong is that compulsive conscientiousness that, no matter what the circumstances, the physician feels that he must perform in the same way: he is unable to divide himself and have two standards of performance without, as one physician put it, destroying himself.

You can divide doctors into two groups. The conscientious slob is always the butt of humor, and that goes back to as far as when people laughed. On the other hand, the conscienceless sharpy has always been a source of a certain amount of envy. I have friends—I have a couple figuring how the hell they can face themselves across the sink in the mirror in the morning . . . but whom I envy a little bit for what they've been able to do materially with their most fantastically poor equipment and the most fantastically poor use of conscience. I can't—it boils down to simply that. MSP can't control how many of their people are going to be [conscientious] slobs and drudges and how many of them sharpies and stockholders . . . how many are going to set up a basic idea of trying to do as good medicine as they are able and how many not. The first thing I realized was that if I started to split myself and say that I have a five-dollar approach and a two-dollar approach, sooner or later I'm going to do the two-dollar approach all the way through and then the two-dollar approach is going to be worth 50 cents. You can destroy yourself that way. (#27—CONSULTANT)

For our present purpose, the most important characteristic of this view of physicians' motivation was its immutability. The view of biography was that it could not be changed. Physicians were fully formed adults, no longer able to change. To those subscribing to the biographical view, physicians either were or were not compulsive, well-trained, conscientious, or mature. A physician who orders "too many" tests, for example, could be seen as someone who is basically insecure or immature. So can one who refers "too much" and one who refers "too little." As we shall see, those holding the biographical view argued that no sanctions of any kind could change a physician's performance.

SOCIAL ENVIRONMENT

Almost as frequently mentioned as the physician's biography was the motivation provided by concern with the approval or disrespect of others. In the case of the personal compulsions of character, the controlling sanction is conscience, guilt or appeal to conscience. In the case of concern with the opinions and esteem of others, the controlling sanction instead is shame, though words such as "pride" and "self-respect" were more likely than "shame" to be used by the physicians. But, of course, in being concerned for his reputation, the physician is being responsive to the evaluative actions of others. He is oriented to the social setting or environment of his work and may be presumed to change his performance as the pressures of that social environment change. In the case of biography, on the other hand, the social setting of work was a comparatively unimportant influence on performance. But the interrelation of the two sources of motivation was complex and their relative influence sometimes difficult to discern.

As we have already seen, some physicians denied that they were motivated by the esteem of any other physician, let alone those in the medical group. There was, however, an ambiguous kind of negotiation that even those who denied responsiveness to the opinions of others discussed—a negotiation of latent standards. The physician's basic training and conscientiousness remained unchanged, but a colleague's appeal to standards might activate what was latent in biography and lead to efforts at change. This was seen not as a responsiveness to external influence, however, so much as a desire to improve oneself by one's own internalized standards.

> It's hard to answer what makes doctors behave themselves. I don't recall ever thinking I'd want to get away with anything. Of course, in a group you are under close surveillance. Other physicians will see your patients. But I don't know how consciously this idea operates, perhaps unconsciously, I don't know. I have always taken pride in maintaining a fairly good record. . . . But that's the way I am. . . . Something that griped me in other people's charts was that they'd just jot down something like "a virus infection." You don't know why the patient came in or what it was or what was done. I brought this up at one of the meetings . . . and they started . . . writing down more material. So in a way maybe they were looking good for me? Oh, I think they were just interested in improvement. (L15— PRIMARY PRACTITIONER)

In other words, he did not shame the others into keeping better records: rather, their training made them sensitive to the functional need for technical improvement. Similarly, the assertedly self-guided physician refers not to his sensitivity to others' opinions but to the standards he himself accepts.

> You are trying to do what in your opinion is right and good in complete medical care. I personally don't give a damn about impressing anybody. If you feel that you are doing right and up to what you can do, then that's it. The thing is that I would want to be sure that what I was doing is the best I could do. I'm not interested in impressing anybody. Of course, your own standards should be high enough so that they are equal to those at the mean or those at the top of your field. (#31—CONSULTANT)

Patently, those who emphasized biography and the biographically formed self also engaged in some kind of negotiation with the colleagues around them, no matter how they chose to interpret the negotiation.

Once it is conceded that the individual engages in interaction with others which influences his performance or his view of performance, it becomes quite important to define who those others are. Most proponents of group practice assume that the physicians of the medical group constitute the most important source of stimulation for and pressure on medical performance. This was not always the case in the medical group we studied. In fact, there was no real consensus among the physicians about the significance of the medical group as the major source of respect and standards responsible for keeping them on their toes. For many, particularly but by no means exclusively the part-time physicians, the medical group was not so much a true reference group as it was a physical, administrative, and economic convenience.

A minority of the physicians reported that the esteem of *group* colleagues was of major importance to them. The most prominent characteristic of those emphasizing the importance of the esteem of group colleagues was seniority. The older, long-tenured, full-time physicians were more prone than others to refer to the medical group as their reference group and to emphasize the sense of watching and being watched within the group. Even among these physicians, however, there was recognition of the importance of the opinions and responses of physicians at the hospital.

The middle-aged, medium-length-tenure physicians and the young, more academically oriented physicians—of whom the youngest, at least, were least committed to the medical group—tended instead to locate the colleague esteem and pressure of greatest importance to them in the hospital where they worked rather than in the medical group. The respect of the physicians on the hospital staff who see their "important," which is to say, hospitalized, cases was primary to them. And among those physicians were not only their peers, but also a critical house staff. The hospital was referred to by the consultants as the only place responsible for keeping them on their toes, perhaps because they did not feel that those who referred to them could judge them. Specifically mentioned as the most ubiquitous agents of shame and even humiliation were the house staff members, who, as students, have the license to ask questions that colleagues may feel more constrained to avoid. As students, they can ask an attending physician questions in areas in which he may be weak and can ask also for public justification of some of his medical decisions.

MATERIAL SELF-INTEREST

Finally, we may turn to the material aspects of practice as an imputed source of motivation to perform well. The most obvious of such aspects appealing to extrinsic self-interest is money, and we have already seen in earlier chapters how some physicians felt that, in private practice, the reward of a fee could at the very least compensate for delivering a housecall when it was not considered medically necessary. Some felt, furthermore, that insofar as income was assured at the medical group, the physician lacked any additional incentive to work well beyond their inherent dedication to perform at their best level.

Typically, however, almost all the physicians were loath to consider material self-interest to be directly connected with performance. That is, no one went so far as to assert that the basic quality of performance varied directly with the amount of monetary compensation. While money was seen as an incentive, it was considered supplementary to a more basic motive of dedication, conscientiousness, or the like. Satisfactory monetary reward, in conjunction with adequate work time, was seen to contribute perhaps to the motivation to perform at one's very best, but the lack of financial reward was not seen to undermine the motivation to perform *acceptably*. No one claimed that physicians were motivated to work well solely by the money they made or by fear of generating an official patient complaint, administrative reprimand, or malpractice suit. Anger or frustration at what were perceived to be inadequate rewards or unjust handicaps or penalties might operate to the detriment of performance, but their effects were secondary rather than primary, physicians' basic motivation stemming more from inner need or pride.

THE EVALUATION OF SANCTIONS

From the discussion thus far, it is possible to highlight the issues by posing a stark and oversimple set of equivalencies between one's conception of sources of motivation and one's choice of functionally effective sanctions. If one believes that biography is the essential source of motivation to perform well, then one should feel fatalistic about the use of any sanctions at all, short of expulsion from the group, resisting the use of any sanctions because they are ineffective. If, conversely, one believes that social pressure is the essential source of motivation to perform well, then one should feel that activities designed to bring the sanctions of collegial pressure to bear on an offender would be useful. One could conceive of such activities as being graded in intensity, from the least to the most collegial pressure. Similarly, if one believes that material self-interest is the essential source of motivation to perform well, one should feel that monetary sanctions, graded in intensity, would be functionally appropriate for the control and remedy of poor performance.

I have already indicated that no such simple set of equivalencies existed among the physicians; but, by keeping it in front of our eyes as we examine physicians' own responses to sanctions, we can more easily sort out the strands of their thinking. Most important, this formulation allows us to distinguish an entirely different criterion for evaluating sanctions which was employed by the physicians at the same time that they used functional criteria. The physicians evaluated sanctions or the possibility of sanctions not only by asking, What good would it do? If they had used criteria of effectiveness alone, they would not have rejected many possible sanctions. In fact, they also used the criterion of "rightness"—whether or not the sanctions were appropriate for physicians, given the kind of person they felt the physician was. That is, while the physicians were concerned that the punishment fit the crime, they were concerned also that the punishment fit the criminal. To them, the physician fell into what Dibble (1973: 519–520) called a special "classificatory category" of offender, which was explicitly distinguished from the categories into which children, clerks, and factory workers fall. That classificatory category had a distinct influence on the selection of sanctions: it established the ground for rejecting the use of some sanctions as symbolically inappropriate for the kind of person the physician is.

I am suggesting, in short, that in considering the possibility of employing sanctions to control undesirable performance, the physicians used two separate criteria. One, based on their conception of what motivates good performance, evaluated possible sanctions by their effective connection with such motivation. The other evaluated possible sanctions by their appropriateness for the kind of person the doctor was felt to be— their propriety for use on doctors rather than on children or clerks. Those two criteria were so closely intertwined in the physicians' comments as to make it almost impossible to discuss them separately, but the analytical difference is essential for our understanding of the source of the inconsistency, ambivalence, and contradiction embedded in the physicians' responses toward social control in the medical group.

If one believes that people are motivated to perform well by only one of a number of possible stimuli, then it follows that one will not consider

all kinds of rewards, threats, or punishments to be effective means for
stimulating good performance. Indeed, incompatible sanctions most
likely would be considered useless and self-defeating: only compatible
sanctions would be considered to be reasonable. Thus, those physicians
who believed in the biographical source of physician performance
thought that, if a physician was not basically conscientious, there was no
sanction that would lead him to become conscientious. By the same
token, if he ordered too many expensive laboratory tests or overrefers,
his behavior was a function of either his basic insecurity or the habitual
way he has come to practice medicine; in neither case could anything be
done to change him. "You can't change people's ways of practicing
medicine." (#18—PRIMARY PRACTITIONER). Sanctions, social or financial, were considered useless. Those physicians who held this view
argued quite consistently that the only solution to undesirable performance was to expel the offender from the group if they could, or
otherwise to live with him. Neither positive nor negative sanctions of
any kind were likely to have much effect, and they would be resisted.

Not all those who emphasized the motivation and habits of the physician felt helpless, however. Many felt that motivation and habits were
amenable to tempering. To such physicians, effective modes of improving individuals' performance had to be addressed to their personality and
their conscience. One possibility for change was colleague exhortation
designed to awaken individuals' sleeping consciences and thus get them
to improve their performance. And among those few who felt that some
improvement of performance was possible even when it stemmed from
individual character or personality, the proper method was thought to be
not sanctioning but psychotherapy. Being aware of one's personal problems, confessing them, and asserting that they were being worked on in
psychotherapy was an explanation of and excuse for criticized performance which was readily accepted by offended colleagues, at least for a
time. In areas of performance in which technical knowledge and skill
rather than conscientiousness were presumed to be involved, those
physicians who thought that improvement was possible urged colleague
pressure posed in the spirit of education.

But not all physicians felt that either nothing could be done about poor
performance or that all that could be done was to send an offender off for
postgraduate medical education or psychotherapy. Many physicians felt
that individuals could be moved by colleague and economic pressure.
However, there were distinct limits on the kind of pressure they would

condone, limits best understood by focusing on the physicians' responses to two rather crude suggestions that carry to their logical conclusion the ideas of sanctions based on colleague pressure and economic pressure.

EVALUATING AN EXTREME SOCIAL SANCTION

The first suggestion (occasionally practiced by the administration) was based on the notion that, if physicians knew that their undesirable performance were to be made known to all their colleagues, they would be motivated by shame or pride to avoid it. One concrete manifestation of such an attempt to generate shame lay in the posting, on the physicians' bulletin board, of lists of practitioners ranked by the ratio of services provided to their panel size, the number of laboratory tests ordered, and the like. When this was actually done, code letters were used instead of the physicians' own names, making it impossible for colleagues to recognize who stood high or low on the list. We asked some of those we interviewed, "Why not post the actual physicians' names so all could know how all performed?" The physicians' answers were generally of the same rhetorical structure as the one I pointed out in my discussion of responses to formal chart review—part technical questioning whether the number of services, tests ordered, and the like had a uniform meaning, part doubt that publicity would really change anyone's performance, and part an appeal to the propriety of doing such a thing to physicians.

No matter what the issue, one emphasis was shared by almost all of the physicians—namely, that no effort to change performance be made which was systematically designed to establish *formal* pressures that would embarrass physicians by making their deficiencies known to their colleagues. In the matter of tests and X rays, argued a number of physicians, no shame would be felt, in any case, because a person's standing on a posted list need not necessarily reflect negatively on him. They felt that statistical measures, like much in medicine, were too amgibuous and their meaning too variable to reflect on performance in such a way as to elicit shame in the offender.

In one physician tests might be a real compulsive thoroughness and in another just an effort to handle the patients as quickly as possible, to satisfy him and get rid of him or send him to another doctor. It's pretty hard to know from statistics alone. (#21—PRIMARY PRACTITIONER)

Some physicians expressed uncertainty about the possibility of laying down precise rules about the ordering of test and X rays, while others assessed the ordering of tests and X rays as an intimate part of the individual's work style which is essentially unchangeable.

Above all, the proper way of coping with ordering an excessive number of tests was to adopt an informal, confidential approach that did not shame the offender in public.

It wouldn't be proper to post a record of the number of tests made or special services by the name of each physician. There is no need to embarrass anybody. I think they did it once when they published a PBI list and the number they ordered. But it was a ludicrous thing to do, it could be embarrassing. . . . There should be some sort of control over tests and X rays, done in committee. If one doctor spoke to another, he might come around saying, "You ordered so many GI series, do you think that it should be the first part of the work-up, or do you think it could wait awhile? Or do you think you ought to see the patient two or three times before ordering it? . . ." I think if a committee existed and individuals on the committee could go around and mention this, very informally. (#11—PRIMARY PRACTITIONER)

Informality and confidentiality were the keys to "proper" methods of exerting colleague pressure. A formal, written, and public report, as resulted from the chart reviews of the MSP visitors, was undesirable.

Several issues seemed to be involved in these responses to formal modes of publicizing comparisons of performance throughout the collegium of the medical group. First, formality, by the nature of the case, implied fixed criteria with fixed or at least limited meaning. As we have already seen in the cases of the medical record and the ordering of tests and X rays, the physicians were convinced that such fixed criteria as the number of tests one orders or whether or not one sends all excised tissue to the pathology laboratory did not have invariant meanings or make sense in the context of everyday practice and so could be deprecated as a legitimate measure by which to evaluate performance. A practitioner high on a list of number of tests ordered which was circulated to colleagues need not feel ashamed of himself, nor need his colleagues take his listed standing as a reflection of poor performance. Thus, the list could fail to have the intended effect of mobilizing colleague pressure on standards of performance by expanding the circulation of reliable information about performance.

Second, the procedure of formal written collation and reporting of performance was itself considered to be a violation of the rules of etiquette that specify how one interacts with physicians. It embarrassed the individuals, it was insulting, and it was, above all, childish, violating the rule of trust.

> One thing you have to assume is that the man is doing conscientious work. You have to not make him feel he is going to get a lollypop or 16 cigar coupons if he gets a big enough number of housecalls, or he is giong to get his head patted. It's junk. It isn't mature. (#27—CONSULTANT)

Of course, from the point of view of social control, it was precisely embarrassment that the administration intended by the posting of names. The assumption was that, if practitioners cared about their colleagues' opinions and if information about performance was widely circulated, then they would try harder to improve their performance. The assumption that physicians are responsive to their colleagues' opinions was, as we have been, one that many physicians also held, and the posting of names a logical outcome of it. But it was carried too far past the limits imposed by etiquette. At the very least, then, the idea of deliberate publicity about performance occasioned uneasiness, and it more often occasioned outrage.

Finally, it must be noted that, in light of the physicians' belief that the use of fixed criteria for evaluating performance was of questionable value, the likelihood of evoking widespread peer pressure by publicized formal listings was also questionable. In light of both the possible ineffectiveness of the method and the distinct barrier posed by the rules of etiquette, it follows that physicians who approved of the effort to control performance were most likely to recommend an individual, confidential approach in which an individual is talked to *in camera*. Such a procedure was seen to allow flexible exploration of the meaning of recorded performance so as to avoid bureaucracy. Furthermore, it precluded general embarrassment, and it allowed attempts at educating the physician. Thus, while physicians were thought to be responsive to the opinions of colleagues and could be motivated to change their performance by colleague pressure, both their dignity as physicians and the ambiguous character of the criteria by which one person's performance could be compared to another's precluded acceptance of formal sanctions designed to mobilize the opinion of the entire collegium.

EVALUATING AN EXTREME ECONOMIC SANCTION

The other suggestion for sanctions focused explicitly on decisions the physician made which led to economic penalties for the medical group—instances in which the physician refused to render a service such as a housecall, which a patient was later able to show was necessary. The suggestion was made during an Executive Committee meeting that, if a patient successfully claimed compensation from the medical group for what he had to pay to obtain from an outside doctor a service refused by his group physician, the refusing physician rather than the group as a whole should pay the claim. It was, as one physician argued, only fair: why should all pay for one person's reluctance to provide service?

No action was taken on the suggestion, but we posed it to some of the physicians to see how they would respond. The response was all but unanimous. Sanctions using economic penalties were rejected. Even though many of them felt that the lack of positive economic incentives influenced performance negatively, all but one of the primary practitioners were opposed to the suggestion that they be held responsible for paying their patients' claims for compensation. Even the physician who pointed out in the Executive Committee meeting how unfair the situation was did not suggest that individual physicians be held responsible for claims. Again, the issues lay in the perceived injustice of using mechanical, formal criteria to assign responsibility, in the difficulty of deciding even on a case-by-case basis, and in the impropriety of using such a sanction on a physician.

> I'd simply react against the proposal to make physicians pay patients' claims. It's the attitude toward the physician involved in it. It reduces his stature. It demeans him. It subjects him to a type of humiliation. It's inevitable that a physician at some time or another is inclined to resist making a housecall. There would be no way to judge it. There is no one who couldn't say, "There but for the grace of God go I." I've done the same thing. (#21—PRIMARY PRACTITIONER)

Great emphasis was placed on the inappropriate character of the sanction of economic penalty. Most common was reference to its offensiveness, which demeaned the doctor by treating him like a child.

To have the doctor pay the family for its use of another doctor is petty. This is the type of thing, "Well, you don't give the child chewing gum for a day." It's infantile. You don't resolve the problem by having somebody pay 10 dollars. . . . It's more the conscience of the individual. . . . The doctor should be called in, and it should be brought to his attention that this is happening, then it depends on his conscience. It's too easy if it's just 10 dollars and you're let off. It's the conscience of the doctor being brought to the administration and your other colleagues. This is what's the important point. (#12—PRIMARY PRACTITIONER)

It follows, of course, that since physicians are not children, their performance cannot be improved by treating them like children, by material punishment. Even if the economic sanction were not insulting, degrading, childish, and the like—even, that is, if it had no negative affect attached ot it—it would not work because physicians' performance was not seen to be motivated by fear of economic loss. Colleague approval and, at bottom, one's own conscience were the ultimate sources of motivation to perform well.

Thus, attempts to publicize poor performance among the collegium so as to generate extensive criticism were rejected as inappropriate, as going too far. Attempts to correct it by financial penalty were also rejected as both ineffective and inappropriate. If the ordinary processes of circulating information about performance (consultants, shoptalk, medical records) and the informal, confidential processes of talking to an offender—all guided by the rules of etiquette—brought no satisfaction, then the offender was to be considered defective, to be considered beyond the pale, and to be ejected. No attempt to increase the scope of the circulation of information about performance to systematize and formalize the selection and application of sanctions designed to correct undesirable performance was acceptable.

Given conceptions of what keeps doctors on their toes, specific sanctions follow as putatively effective modes of dealing with poor performance. But the "categorical classification" of the physician as a special kind of person—a classification implicit in the rules of etiquette—prevent the systematic articulation of sanctions into a rationalized set of procedures for guiding a predictable system of social control. Understanding this, we can turn in Part IV to examination of the sanctioning processes that actually went on in the medical group. This examination will enable me to conclude with an evaluation of the process of social control among the professionals of the medical group.

IV:

Sanctions and Control by Professionals

13:
The Variety of Professional Sanctions

In Part III I attempted to describe and analyze both the structure of relationships among the physicians of the medical group which could permit the transmission of information about performance and the modes by which the physicians evaluated and selected their experience with one another insofar as the experience bore on medical performance. I attempted to describe, in essence, those beliefs and practices that placed limits on the kind of social control that was *possible* in the medical group—the analogues to law and surveillance, which direct and place limits on the possibilities of enforcement. The analysis, taking all the chapters together, suggested that a series of interpretive screens were interposed between the practicing physicians and their awareness and perception of the performance of their colleagues. The interpretive rules led to normalization of actions that by lay standards could be called "mistakes" and so functioned to reduce the universe of what could be perceived as poor performance requiring control. In turn, the rules of etiquette limited the way the universe of performance could be observed by others. And as we saw in the last chapters, should poor or otherwise objectionable performance pass through all these screens and be perceived, public, formal, and deliberately systematic methods of control were rejected on the basis both of propriety and of imputed effectiveness.

None of this is to say that there was no process of social control in the medical group. It is unimaginable that human groups could function without some kind of controlling mechanism. Rather, the analysis has sought to describe the factors that shaped the characteristics of the particular kind of social control that did exist, that selected that particular method out of the entire range of possibilities. The analysis has also put us in a position to finally turn to examining the outcome—the system of enforcement that did exist in the medical group. In this chapter I shall describe the major sanctions the physicians used in efforts to influence colleagues whose performance had offended them and then describe the natural history of efforts at influence. Then, in the next chapter, I shall try to show how various problems of physician performance were managed.

MODES OF PEER CONTROL

Analysis of the physicians' discussion of their working relationships with colleagues and of their modes of responding to behavior that offended or upset them requires us to distinguish two essentially different classes of response. One was indirect and only covertly sanctioning, in that, while it did involve the withdrawal of rewards from the offender, withdrawal of rewards was done in such a way that the offender may not even have been aware that rewards were being deliberately withdrawn or, if aware of that, not aware that an offense of his was the reason for withdrawal. It involved *the withdrawal of reciprocity in areas of work in which cooperation was optional*. The other class of sanction was direct and open, in that *the offended physician openly complained about or criticized* the behavior that had offended him, thereby directly threatening the offender's self-esteem, his reputation with his colleagues, and even his status in the medical group. The former class of responses was composed of essentially individual, private acts influencing only the relationship between the offended and the offender. The latter class of responses included a range of acts that could draw in the participation of a variety of other colleagues, functionaries, and committees.

The Favor System

Many of the unannounced sanctions were those that have already been discussed in earlier chapters as elements of cooperation in work. Some forms of cooperation were virtually obligatory for those under contract in the medical group: physician A could hardly refuse to see a properly referred and scheduled patient from physician B just because the latter had once offended him. Other forms of cooperation, however, were almost completely voluntary and could be withheld at will. Many of these voluntary modes of cooperation were part of what might be called the economy of personal favors in the medical group.

The personal favor consisted in doing something for someone else which was not an ordinarily required part of one's obligations. Typically, it was initiated by a request from a colleague, accompanied by such phrases as "do me a favor" or "as a personal favor to me." Much of the flexibility of work in the group hinged on such a system of favors, since the physicians were often allowed the privilege of not fulfilling their contractual obligations so long as they were able to persuade colleagues to do the work in their place or cover for them.

> I know that any of the men would always come to my help if I'm really in a jam. . . . Even if I'm very tired one night. . . . Anyone of them would be glad to take over for me, if, let's say, I have a cold or I've been up all night, and I just can't work. (#43—CONSULTANT)

And the favor system was invoked to bypass normal appointment delays when one wished to have a patient seen quickly by a consultant or, in fee-for-service practice, seen without charge.

> When I had a patient who I thought was in trouble, and I knew the specialists were harassed, overworked, and overburdened, and the patient couldn't get an appointment for weeks, and I felt the patient really needed a doctor, I would call the specialist and ask him to look him over. This would be on a personal basis. It depended on whether the specialist and I got along well. . . . You couldn't quite do it without bringing in favors. When I could get this done, then I would owe that specialist a favor, and then it would wind up I had X number of favors that I owed him. (L11—PRIMARY PRACTITIONER)

By and large, it seemed to be difficult to refuse a colleague's direct request for a favor.

> Just yesterday #10 called me up and asked me to take two weeks of service time for him, as a bolt out of the blue, which I didn't have the nerve to refuse. This was doing it as a personal favor, to give him a chance to get away for a vacation, which he can't do unless he finds coverage. (#7—PRIMARY PRACTITIONER)

Nonetheless, requests for favors did not seem to have been made indiscriminately. There was reluctance to ask favors from (and become obligated to) those with whom one did not have a good relationship. Contributing to the ambiguity of the favor system was the fact that, on occasion, extra work could be done without explicit reference to its being a favor, and, when it was not reciprocated by some extra consideration on a subsequent occasion, the donor of what was regarded as an implicit favor could feel a great deal of resentment. Given the ambiguity of the currency of the system, however, it seemed to be that only in a clear instance of being refused an explicitly requested (and labeled) favor was license given to refuse a favor asked by the initial refuser.

> If you are working with a man and he doesn't want to do something, you say, "I'm busy too." If he asks you to go on a call, he says, "I have a patient and I don't want to go over," you say, "I'm busy too." You don't do him a favor. (#3—PRIMARY PRACTITIONER)

Coverage and helping out were not all that was involved in favors. Making and granting referrals were also, on occasion, seen as favors. As we saw in Chapter Five, the referral was, in a medical group in which fees were not involved, often routine to the point of being mechanical. Nonetheless, there were occasions in which physicians asked another physician to accept a referral as a favor to them. Accepting such a referral constituted a favor because the individual granting it did not have to accept it at the time it was requested.

By the same token, however, asking someone to examine an especially interesting case constituted *offering* a favor in that it expressed esteem for the taste and competence of the individual referred to. As we have already seen, the very fact that in the medical group it was difficult for the primary practitioners to refer to a particular physician made them sensitive about their status because they lacked an important sanction over consultants and because they could not exercise choice on the basis of their own preferences. Similarly, the consultants were not generally chosen as individuals, and thus they also were sensitive to the esteem of others. The special case, whether it was one that was intellectually interesting or a problem that was not regarded as properly treated through normal emergency coverage arrangements, became a token in the favor system which allowed the reciprocal expression of esteem between individuals under circumstances in which normal referrals could not allow this expression. In private practice, of course, the referral is, by the nature of the case, made to an individual, and issues of both personal friendship and esteem, in addition to financial reward, are also critical. Where the consultant lacked esteem for the referrer and could afford to lose his referrals he communicated this in one way or another short of telling the referrer outright that he did not want his cases.

Those [colleagues] who don't do a good job . . . for the most part have disappeared from my referrals. I didn't drive them away, but they become too embarrassed when they'd call me up and say, "I want to send you a patient with such and such," and I'd say, "Well, what did you do?" And they'd tell me a few things and I'd suggest other questions—"Did you check this, and did you check that?" Those who were not especially good doctors, I think, either were embarrassed [and stopped referring] or . . . are . . . practicing better medicine today because they have come to accept my questions. (L4—CONSULTANT)

The favor system was characteristically one that employed only positive sanctions, and it could be considered part of a process of social control only insofar as it was by its nature discriminatory in distributing rewards. The rewards of being a participant in a favor system were not distributed evenly throughout the collegium. Some individuals could feel excluded and resentful or contrite because of their limited participation in the favor system, but others could be entirely unaware of their position. All were faced with a rather ambiguous situation that was difficult to interpret and respond to directly because, except for refusal to do a favor or to reciprocate a favor, there was no definite criterion by which to assess one's position. As a technique, this form of exclusion was essentially passive and vague, communicating no reason for action—if it was action. It did not indicate what, if anything, had given offense, and so did not encourage the rectification of performance. Essentially, it avoided confrontation and segregated people from one another.

The Complaint System

Unlike the favor system, the complaint system did involve confrontation: direct criticism of the offender by the offended. It was most often referred to as "talking to" colleagues, and it was explicitly used as a method of attempting to influence the performance of an offender.

Basically, it's very simple the way you twist somebody's arm. Criticism by colleagues is an extremely effective way of doing it. (#1—PRIMARY PRACTITIONER)

The magnitude of this risk of embarrassment or shame seemed to be a function of the manner and context in which the criticism was made—

tactfully or not; in private or in public; as a helpful, educational act or as a demeaning or hostile act. Criticizing without tact or charity violated the norms of etiquette and was considered very offensive. The idea of talking to a person in an educational fashion, however, was more acceptable, for even if implicitly critical, the educational approach avoided the appearance of attack on the basic competence or conscientiousness of the offender.

> There shouldn't be any recriminations. . . . It does harm. Whenever a discussion leads—and now I'm taking a psychological slant—to attitudes of guilt, then it is no good. I think the discussion of a mistake has to be on the basis of what one has learned [from it]. (#36—CONSULTANT)

A joking manner of talking to an offender, which is more likely to occur among friends than among physicians who did not know one another well, was also reported as an acceptable manner of criticizing.

> Just the other day, my best friend in the group . . . dropped into my office and jokingly shook his finger at me because of some mishandling of a patient medically. (#13—PRIMARY PRACTITIONER)

Essentially, it was complaining or talking to a colleague who was believed to have erred which constituted the primary means of social control used by the physicians of the medical group. Furthermore, to both the offended and the offender, it was a conscious and deliberate attempt to correct performance. Thus, the use of the complaint system was much easier for us to observe in the field and to explore in our interviews than was the use of the favor system. It seemed that it was exercised on a very broad range, from informal, very private interaction between two people to much more formal interaction between people discussing their differences before the assembled Executive Committee, which itself also on occasion talked to accused offenders. Important as the favor system may have been, the complaint system seemed to have been considerably more central to the operation of social control among the physicians in the medical group. Let us examine the range of exercise of the complaint system in more detail.

LATENT OFFENSES

While an effort at social control virtually requires the perception of some offense for its justification, the perception of some offense does not require or automatically elicit an effort at social control. In the medical group a very large number of offenses did not seem to be followed by a complaint. Insofar as it was possible to tell, many were completely forgotten shortly after they occurred. Many, however, while not followed by a complaint at the time they occurred, were in fact stored away in memory for the guidance of response to future offenses. In storage, they constituted evidence for the *possible* institution of social controls. They may be called "latent offenses"—that is, offenses that are not responded to but nonetheless are preserved in memory for use as one of several justifications for later efforts at control.

> The first time this happens, you sort of remember. The second time you begin to look around. The third time you do something about it. (#6—PRIMARY PRACTITIONER)

It is difficult to be very precise in estimating how frequently something occurs to which no overt identifying response is made. It is impossible to estimate from our data the degree to which an overt complaint is *not* made about particular colleague actions—that is, we cannot easily estimate the *absence* of something. It would seem, however, that unexpressed recognition of offending performance is far more frequent than overt response to it as offense. Many physicians reported occasions in which they felt that it was quite possible that a colleague had sloughed off a housecall or emergency patient on them, but that they had said nothing about it to anyone, including the presumed offender.

> Sometimes you feel that your patient has asked for a housecall and hasn't received that housecall from the man on call, and you felt that maybe the housecall should have been made. Now, I never talk to anyone about that and never even talked to the man involved. (#22—PRIMARY PRACTITIONER)

There seemed to be no substantive pattern that would allow us to conclude that for some type of offense, sloughing off, for example, no complaint would be made the first time it was perceived, while for another kind of offense, upsetting a patient, for example, a complaint would follow immediately. Perhaps this fact—that the delineation of what constituted an indictable or complainable offense appeared to be fairly idosyncratic—was testimony to the informal character of this early stage in the process of social control. Among the consultants, for example, some bore unnecessary or inadequately worked-up referrals without complaint to the offenders, others telephoned the offenders almost as soon as the patient left the consulting room, and still others bore the offenses for a time and then gave vent to their accumulated complaints all at once. The same may be said for offenses involving sloughing off. It is my impression that one critical element predicting whether or not an offended colleague would directly talk to the perceived offender was the relationship between the offender and the person perceiving offense. The junior physicians seemed understandably reluctant to complain to or criticize seniors within their own specialty and even more reluctant to do so to senior colleagues outside their own specialty. Indeed, all but the most influential and senior physicians in the group seemed reluctant to take their complaints directly to offenders whom they did not know personally.

Apart from the constraint of status differences, a complex set of factors seemed to be responsible for both the large number of offenses overlooked and the reluctance to complain. A comparatively minor, unpremeditated offense, for example, was unlikely to be commented on.

> If it's a matter of principle I'll raise it with the other man or in public rather than sit on it. Or if it's an instance where somebody is involved in surgery or something of that business, I'll certainly raise it, and if I feel it is liable to be something that will be repeated, I'll raise it. If I feel it was just something, you know, happening without any forethought, unpremeditated, I'd probably not raise it at all. (#8—PRIMARY PRACTITIONER)

Understandable responses to a difficult situation could also be ignored, even if not forgotten. They were normal offenses, like normal mistakes, and were not to be commented on. As we have already seen in other contexts, a certain amount of overreferral may be considered to be normal, at least in certain circumstances.

As we might expect from our discussion of the physicians' conception of what it is that is responsible for keeping physicians on their toes, the inclination to complain about a perceived offense was also discouraged by the pervasive tendency to feel that complaining about the offense to the offender would not accomplish anything positive and so would not be worth the embarrassment of potential challenge or rejection. The ground for such reluctance to indict offenses was constituted by reference to human nature or to the offender's personality, neither of which could be changed. Indeed, if such behavior was a function of unchangeable biography, complaining about it to the offender would only lead to bad feelings without changing the behavior. The ground of biography was pervasive in explanations of why, after perceiving offense, the perceiver did not attempt to change the behavior of the offender. Changing ingrained habits being impossible, once a person is out in practice and is set in his ways, rather little can be done to either persuade him of his error or otherwise redirect his habits. Confronting an individual offender is, furthermore, embarrassing to both parties and unpleasant. If the offender is really beyond redemption, and confrontation would do no real good, why risk embarrassment from such a confrontation?

> I came to the conclusion that I'm not going to educate them. This is such a deep-seated personality problem and I would hurt them more than gain by their becoming self-conscious and the anxiety becoming more aggravated. Since there is no evil intent involved, there is nothing I can do to change their basic personality but to accept the situation as it is. ⟨ (#23—PRIMARY PRACTITIONER)

Such an attitude of resignation to the behavior of offenders was especially strengthened by anecdotal reference to propr failure at accomplishing much by complaining about offenses.

Finally, I might mention that the notion that complaining about an offense would not do anything to control offenses was reinforced by the notion that it was inappropriate for the physician to be involved in criticizing colleagues. A number of the physicians argued that it was not their function to attempt to change or punish the behavior of their colleagues. While in one case reluctance to say anything to another doctor was connected with genuine fear of the possibility of so angering some individuals that an unpleasant scene would result, more important than fear of an unpleasant situation was the conception of propriety or etiquette, which made even chiefs of service reluctant to attempt to exercise social control by talking to a colleague who was a persistent offender. In the medical group, where the practitioners had no choice but to deal with one another, the tendency seemed to be to avoid complaining directly *to* offenders but after a time to complain instead *about* the offender to others and most particularly to the administration.

I prefer that the administration take disciplinary action for the doctor because we are all very friendly with each other and it's very tough to work with people and discipline them at the same time. (#23—PRIMARY PRACTITIONER)

If it is a friend or a colleague toward whom one feels warm who has offended, then one's relationship may give one some license to talk to him in the interest of helping him, but the relationship has to be close enough to justify such potential embarrassment. Otherwise it would be better to swallow as many offenses as possible and avoid confrontation and its risks. Since work with the offender himself cannot be avoided in the medical group, confrontation may worsen work relationships and so must be avoided.

THE AVOIDANCE OF CONFRONTATION

The physicians' avoidance of confrontation by avoidance of direct efforts at responding to offense seems to stem in part from habits of action developed in solo, entrepreneurial practice. There, just as the fee barrier was an impersonal mechanism that discouraged patients from demanding services the physician did not want to give while relieving him of the necessity of confronting the patient and refusing the service, so was the solo referral mechanism a device by which the physician could sever relationships with a colleague who had given offense without having to confront him directly and complain about his offenses.

I never went directly to him and said, "Now look, cut this out." I never thought it was my place. You see how it would happen in private practice. In private practice I would send the patient to a consultant, and if the patient came back to me and said, "What kind of a guy is this?" or something specific to indicate he didn't care for him, if it happened a few times, every patient that I sent to this consultant wasn't pleased by him, why I'd stop sending patients to him at all. Period. I wouldn't feel it was my place to say anything to him. It would automatically work out that way. Here I didn't feel it was my place to go and yell at #49, and there was no way of steering patients away. . . . After a while, I got so annoyed I told the [appointment] secretary downstairs not to send my patients to #49, but what could I do? Write on the [referral slip], "Not #49?" That looks very bad. (L21—CONSULTANT)

While the medical group clearly lacked such "automatic" methods of denying service and suspending cooperative work relations, the etiquette of nonconfrontation appropriate to circumstances in which these automatic methods existed nonetheless persisted. The outcome in many instances was a veneer of cooperation underneath which were stored memories of offenses never directly expressed or resolved. In entrepreneurial practice, an effort at controlling offense could be made by avoidance or boycott (cf Freidson, 1970b). In the medical group, however, confrontation was avoided even though the possibility of using the method of the boycott did not exist.

Some effort to sanction the other by avoiding work relations was made, but ultimately it was impossible in the medical group. Closed-panel practice cannot survive if only popular or nonoffensive physicians are referred to: the workload of consultants in the same specialty would become impossibly unequal. Many physicians in the medical group were tempted to avoid those they felt to be offenders and so were prone to avoid referring to them and to refer to popular colleagues instead. When popular physicians began complaining about their heavy workloads, the administration occasionally had to send memoranda like the one below to referring physicians.

MEMO TO ALL FAMILY DOCTORS
SUBJECT: REFERRAL
Please do not refer to specialists, especially *Orthopedists* and *Obstetricians*, by name either on the referral forms you write or in your discussions with the patients. This practice clogs the schedules of favorites and makes it impossible to maintain appointment schedules.

Avoidance of cooperation also was impossible for physicians in the same specialty, who had to cover each other on emergency duty. As we have already seen, all was not mutual liking and respect within at least some of the specialty services. And offenses did arise which seemed too important to simply ignore. Rather than confront an individual whom one could not merely avoid, however, one instead made efforts to "work around" the offender. On some occasions we uncovered, colleagues avoided the embarrassment of direct criticism, but the immediate danger of the individual physician's poor performance was such that they made efforts to control or limit his future offenses by attempting, where possible, to supervise his work personally.

We had in our service a man who came out of his residency and worked in the group and he wasn't conscientious. He wasn't following up on his patients and

> he was doing poorly technically. . . . It got to the point where we had to go in and chaperone him with the patients in the operating room, and it was twice as much work for us. (L5—CONSULTANT)

In another case, an effort was made to prevent serious cases from falling into the hands of a physician colleagues thought poor, though, in the interest of avoiding the embarrassment and confrontation that would certainly have resulted had he been removed from emergency duty, he was kept on such duty and the risk was run that he might deal poorly with a serious case.

> I thought it would be better not to give him any big cases to do, and I cut down as much as I could. He is on emergencies, so I can't control that. If he's gotten an emergency he takes care of it. But we haven't referred him any major surgery since that time. (#47—CONSULTANT)

It is noteworthy that we could obtain from the physicians outside that specialty service no hint that they were aware of his colleagues' doubts about that individual's competence or that they had any similar reservations about him.

In all, it should be clear that a variety of elements were responsible for establishing a fairly high threshold to responding to offenses. In some instances, the offense was normalized as something that the offended person himself might do "unconsciously" or "in a weak moment" or "on a bad day," and thereby justification for complaining to the offender or about him to others was denied. In other instances, the offense was perceived as the outcome of the biography of the offender—his habits, training, or personality—which, since it could not be changed, provided justification on functional grounds for failing to respond to it by complaint. Finally, the very act of confronting the offender was distasteful, not only in normal personal terms but also by virtue of the basic professional norms of etiquette which make criticism of a colleague somehow inappropriate and not one's place to make. The result of all these factors was to allow a large number of offending actions to remain unexamined and unacknowledged and often to allow the covertly defined offenders to rest unaware of the fact that their actions were offensive to others. The offenses were prone to be only latent in character. But the covert mental dossier of unacknowledged offense did not disappear. It could grow, and, once past a certain threshold of accumulation, it could be used as the foundation for motivating, justifying, and sustaining overt responses of social control. Let us turn now to the development of these responses.

PERSONAL CONFRONTATIONS

While the bulk of offenses remained latent, composing the substructure of such things as the popularity and respect practitioners receive from their colleagues, some offenses did elicit an immediate critical response from the offended physician. Most of the practitioners claimed that they did sometimes talk to colleagues when they appeared to have sloughed off, overreferred, or managed a patient in such a way as to cause extra trouble for the others. Rather few claimed that they criticized colleagues for technical inadequacies, but most were sufficiently self-conscious about their special mode of practice in a prepaid medical group that they went on to say that they were more able to talk to colleagues in prepaid than in entrepreneurial practice because in the former they did not operate under the constraining fear of losing fees or referrals in retaliation for criticism.

> [EF: Do you and your colleagues ever discuss among yourselves the mistakes of the family doctors?] Oh, yes, we have several silly things. For example, a man who was a borderline prostate may have been given drugs that would further his condition and throw him into retention. That sort of thing. [EF: Do you ever go back to the family doctor and say, "Look, you made a mistake?"] Oh, yes, I'll talk to them about it. That's the nice thing about it. Most of them take it well. . . . But I would be rather reluctant [in fee-for-service practice] to go to someone who refers me a great deal of work and say, "For crying out loud, what did you do this for? Look what you did to him." They don't have to take that from me. (#37—CONSULTANT)

Most of the examples we collected of such talk in the medical group were described in terms that conveyed a neutral and educational rather than an angry and critical tone. Some, however, were higly emotional and critical and could be considered to be genuine confrontations that could ruffle feelings and relations for some time afterwards. Sometimes, as we have already seen elsewhere, the patient got caught in the middle and was used as the medium of confrontation. Great success in altering the referral habits of primary practitioners who sent the patients to them was reported by those few consultants who reported refusing to see patients who, in their eyes, were improperly referred.

> We stopped it by sending them back upstairs. We ranted a couple of times. I ranted. [My colleague] doesn't rant. He just sits, and blop, out the patient goes. After we sent them back upstairs three or four times, the only ones we get now is when they're unsuccessful. (#51—CONSULTANT)

Much of the talking to offenders described by the physicians was seen as a part of the ordinary interaction of everyday work relations. Emotion may have been connected with some of the offenses, but the talk nonetheless tended to be described in neutral terms as serving the periodic but normal need for inducing acceptable or cooperative behavior in colleagues. On occasion, however, talking to the individual proved ineffective—sometimes because he would not agree that he had truly committed an offense or performed improperly and sometimes because he continued to commit the same offense. The offended (and determined) physician then had to use other social resources in his attempt to alter the other's behavior.

> Educational programs of the family doctors don't really do too much good. I'll talk to the doctor himself. If there is a certain doctor, I'll call up and say, "Look, I've got three or four cases, and none of them is [what you referred for]. Don't you think it would be a good idea if you work on this yourself?" I think this carries more weight, and I much prefer to do it. However, I was getting a lot of work from [one service] the past three or four years, so I contacted [the chief]. . . . I'd say, "Look, this is a funny referral I got," and go into it. . . . But ordinarily I'd go directly to the physician himself. Of course, occasionally—it's happened occasionally—I get a patient referred to me without a thing written on the chart, so I went tearing down to the administrator. I said, "Here, take it. What kind of business is this?" I sort of raised hell. It got results because now we don't have that any more. I complain and I make it inconvenient for the doctor. (#33—CONSULTANT)

He may carry his complaint to the head of the offender's service, to the administration, or even to the Executive Committee.

Nonetheless, the physicians varied greatly in their tendency to seek out or call up an offender in order to talk to him about the charged offense. Some described themselves as cowards or as being passive and avoided, if they could, talking directly to a colleague who had offended them. Most likely, an offense had to have been extremely annoying or serious to have provoked them to complain. Other physicians were considerably more volatile and aggressive as individuals and called up or confronted a colleague upon the first offense, even when it was minor. Cutting across these individual differences, apparently, was the matter of seniority and status in the medical group. Both the "cowards" and the junior members of the staff—particularly those among the primary practitioners of the group—were less likely to complain directly to the individual offender than to complain *about* the offense of their own peers or sometimes to the senior members of their own specialties and the accessible and sympathetic administrators. Under such circumstances, control over the offense or the offender was not exercised, at least initially. Rather, what seemed to develop was the initial stage of a process of generating evidence of additional offenses on the part of an individual which, if successful, could develop into a collective process of social control.

THE DEVELOPMENT OF COLLECTIVE CONTROL

Confronted by what they believed to be an offense, some individuals who did not wish to undertake talking to the offender or some senior mediator also did not wish to merely overlook it or tuck it away in their memories as a latent offense. Rather, they talked about it to their peers—sometimes directly, naming the person, and sometimes indirectly, sometimes calculatingly and sometimes on the spur of the moment of their anger or disturbance. In one instance, where indictment would have entailed a fairly serious charge, a young practitioner deliberately canvassed some of his peers in order to see if they had had similarly suspicious experiences. Without their corroborative support, he noted, he would undertake no response to what he believed might have been a serious offense.

In case of a colleague who was really doing bad medicine, I'd talk to my colleagues. I'd say, "Did you notice so and so?" And I'd speak to another one and another one and see how they feel about it, you know. If there is not an agreement or opinion on it, I'd just keep quiet and watch until there is an agreement of opinion, and I'll try, you know, to talk things up, start some sort of dissent and have people start muttering about this guy, and eventually word would get to the administration and something would be done about it. In one case I had a consultant. One of my patients died in a funny way, and another died. There were some peculiar things that happened. I talked to some other people, and they said, "No, he is great." So nothing happened. They thought he was very good, and I guess he did do some good things. So I make it my business, you know, to watch and wait. I wouldn't take up a complaint about this man. I'd talk with other people and see if they had the same experiences, and if they do, start talking it up, you know. I certainly wouldn't bring a complaint if I didn't have any support. (#9—PRIMARY PRACTITIONER)

In another case involving a rather more pedestrian offense of slough-ing off housecalls onto colleagues on night duty, a physician described how the initial perception of offense remained latent until a sufficient number of similar instances had accumulated to form a consistent pat-tern of "being unreasonable." At that point, rather than choosing to complain oneself about the offender, the choice might instead be to canvass one's peers to see if they have had similar complaints. When one talked about the offender with others—peers or seniors—the sys-tematic accumulation of complaints could occur, with the latent offenses previously stored in memory being brought out into the open to be added to the indicting weight of those that led one to initiate the process. Even though any single charged offense may be impossible to prove, the reasoning went, it became "obvious from the volume [of similar com-plaints] that not all of them could be wrong" (#20—PRIMARY PRAC-TITIONER), and so it became possible to justify the initiation of a formal process of collective social control.

THE EXERCISE OF COLLECTIVE SOCIAL CONTROL

Once the physician felt that he had a reasonable basis for complaint and that he could not or did not gain satisfaction by himself confronting the offender, he could make his indictment formal by complaining to the Executive Committee. Usually the route led initially to the administra-tion, which, if the case could not be managed by private and informal meetings among the parties, would refer it to the Executive Committee.

If an internist is unloading patients or sloughing off, perhaps on the specialists, it usually goes to the administration, which brings it up at the Executive Committee and then, when it involves family doctors, at the monthly meeting of the Executive Committee when the family doctors are invited. The specialist who has the complaint about too many referrals is then invited to be at that meeting so that he can have an overall discussion about what the problem is. (#20—PRIMARY PRACTITIONER)

At most of the meetings of the Executive Committee which we observed, the procedure was to try to avoid confrontation based on a single individual's complaint. Rather, members of the Executive Committee would canvass their colleagues for complaints about the charged offender so as to represent the experience of as many physicians as possible. That canvass was an action through which still more latent offenses could become manifest.

> I thought it was improperly handled by the specialist. Obviously [the patient] was left with the impression from the way he spoke that I was silly sending her over [to him]. I didn't know the consultant so I didn't discuss it directly with him. But I did mention it to one of the Executive Committee members when I was asked a year or two later if I had any complaints about this doctor. At the time I didn't mention it to anybody. . . . There was a number of doctors that complained about this. . . . I didn't complain at all, although I did add my opinion on the subject when somebody was going around asking how I felt. (#11—PRIMARY PRACTITIONER)

In brief, "there is a snowballing of evidence; each man will bring up an incident and they accumulate at the meeting" (#41—CONSULTANT).

The charged offender was of course given an opportunity to present to the Executive Committee his side of the events for which he had been indicted, and, as I shall show in an analysis of exemplary cases in the next chapter, many accusations rested on evidence of such a nature that outrated denial was plausible.

> Once evidence piles up against a man, it always depends on the circumstances you are talking to him about. When it comes to an individual case, what are you going to say when a man says, "I didn't say that to the patient. That's a gross exaggeration. I didn't say that." (#21—PRIMARY PRACTITIONER)

Nonetheless, the process of generating both personal and official confrontation was so conservative that, by the time most cases had come before the Executive Committee, the climate of opinion and accumulation of evidence was such that while denial could save face and perhaps could deflect some of the subjective impact of the confrontation on the indicted offender, the mere occasion of being talked to could be a serious form of sanctioning.

The fact of being presented with a collectively sustained set of complaints was considered to be highly effective. Rarely was there an official invitation to resign from the medical group. Even more rarely was it considered necessary to actually "fire" an offender. Most offenders either changed sufficiently to reduce the level of complaint or left the medical group once they found a satisfactory alternative practice.

> He would have to be a rather peculiar type of individual if he is told we feel his practice of medicine wasn't right and he was persistent in his methods of practice. The administration has told him . . . since you haven't changed, we prefer that you resign rather than bring you up on charges. It would take an awfully peculiar individual to be so persistent as to want to go through the charges and not resign or change. (#20—PRIMARY PRACTITIONER)

The resignation of offenders *cannot* be expected to occur easily, of course, should the medical labor market be so restricted that few attractive outside practice opportunities exist to serve as safety valves for closed-panel institutions like the medical group.

14:

The Failure of Professional Sanctions

In the last chapter I distinguished among several techniques of social control without refering to the particular kinds of offense involved. I dealt with the way in which these techniques were used rather than with what they were used for. Now it seems useful to conclude the analysis by focusing attention on the substantive problems of the medical group described in Part II and asking how efforts at their control were organized and what techniques were used. Remembering that economic sanctions could not be used, since salary was an automatic function of seniority and specialty, I shall discuss the characteristic ways in which sanctions were used to control the problems of maintaining office hours and coverage, of ordering diagnostic tests and X rays, of making housecalls, and of referring to consultants. Then I will turn to the sanctions used to control the deviant performance of individual physicians[1], concentrating on several case histories that illustrated the range of sanctions actually available for use in the medical group and the manner in which they were used. That final step of the exposition will put me in the position of being able to make an evaluation and assessment of the peculiarities of the processes of professional social control we found in the medical group.

CONTROLLING HOURS

As we have seen, a constant problem for the administration was the tendency for physicians to seek to control their office hours in their own way, according to their own individual conceptions of patient need and demand. This attempt often meant that they would try to reduce the number of hours in which patients would be able to be scheduled by appointment or else would come in late for their scheduled hours and leave early. They justified their practice by indicating that unscheduled

---

[1]To avoid the possibility of identifying those individuals and thus honor my promise of confidentiality and anonymity, I shall omit some identifying details and alter others.

patients in fact arrived in sufficient numbers to require them to work in
their office for a longer time and see more patients than the appointment
schedule indicated. They felt that, if they had to work overtime on some
occasions, they were entitled to make up for it by coming in late for their
official hours. And they argued that they were able to see all their
patients, even if they gave each one less time.

To the administration, of course, the problem was to so plan
scheduled time as to make sure that a predictable number of patients
would be seen. If individual discretion in setting office hours was the
norm, then the number of patients for whom contractual responsibility
was assumed could not be predicted. And so the rule was established
that whenever physicians wished to change the day or time at which
they held their officially scheduled hours, their receptionist must report
the change to the administration. The administration then made sure that
the total number of new hours conformed to the physicians' obligations,
that the proposed hours themselves were not such as to leave certain
periods uncovered, that office space would be available, and the like.
Formally scheduled office hours were thus fairly closely controlled and
planned by administrative mechanisms, not by peer controls.

This was in itself an extremely delicate issue, for the physicians resented such control even when they recognized the legitimacy of the
administration's rationale. In turn, the administration was very sensitive
about its position. Early in the field study, for example, I received a call
from one of the administrators informing me that he had discovered that
two physicians I had approached for interviews had scheduled my interview in lieu of seeing patients, during their office hours. As we discussed
ways of avoiding this situation in the future, I asked him whether any
others I approached had scheduled me on patient time, and he said,
somewhat stiffly, "I don't know. I don't go around checking." Later,
however, I asked him how he learned of the two instances he mentioned,
and he said that the receptionist had notified him in one case, while in
the other he "might have noticed it while looking through appointment
books for something else."

Formally scheduled office hours, of course, were comparatively easy
to control administratively. Considerably less easy to control were tardiness and leaving the office early, if only because it was not easy to
obtain information about them. In the case of office hours rather than
emergency coverage hours, only the receptionist and the patient with an
appointment were likely to be aware of the physician's absence. But,

since the receptionist was not instructed to report the physician's absence, it was only the patient annoyed enough to complain who could be the ordinary source of such information to the administration. In an attempt to improve the administration's access to information, an official reported that at one time an attempt was made to have receptionists "clock" particular physicians who seemed to be more tardy than average, but "there was a tremendous fuss—it's a very threatening thing." One administrator commented on the practice by saying that "I prefer that receptionists don't [report on physicians' comings and goings] because this would create more friction than is necessary . . . . I'm not denying the fact that she is working for the group . . . . but this is not a relationship where she is a tattler." Receptionists in fact functioned to drain off patients' annoyance at being kept waiting, an action that in turn reduced patient complaints to the administration. They had no choice but to try to cool patients off by excusing the physician, for otherwise *they* were the targets of anger. As one administrative supervisor put it, "Where possible, we suggest the receptionist say that the doctor is delayed because of an emergency, and the patients can always understand that."

When a number of complaints about an individual's tardiness or leaving early managed to get through the net into the purview of the administration, an attempt was made to determine whether he continued to come in late, or leave early, by telephoning him during his scheduled hours. If there seemed to be a pattern of offenses, an administrator would wait until he happened to see the physician and ask him whether he might not like to change his hours, since he had been late or had been leaving early. Some bargain was usually struck, but if it could not be or if the new agreement also failed, then greater administrative pressure would be applied by having a more formal talk. In one case an attempt was made to trick a persistently tardy physician into being on time by having his hours scheduled for a later hour than he thought, so that, in being late for what he *believed* to be his hours, he was actually on time for his official hours!

By and large, the administration could do no more than deal with offenders individually, by talking to them. It did not have sufficient support from the collegium to ask it to talk to offenders and exercise peer sanctions. It would periodically point out to the assembled collegium that the problem was becoming critical, without singling out individual offenders, but it gained little sympathy. In late April of the first year of our study, the Executive Committee was told by an administrator that a "serious problem in the group has been getting worse: coming in late for hours." The physicians smiled and joked, and he went on to say, somewhat apologetically and defensively, "I know that at first it's a joke, that professionals can't keep exact hours, but it's getting very serious." He then asked a physician to work with an administrator to collect data on the problem for review by the Executive Committee.

The following week, there was discussion of a patient's letter that presented a mild and reasonable complaint about being kept waiting and a more extensive report on increasingly routine practices of arriving late at hours and scheduling appointments to end some time before hours were officially over. In comment on the report, the physicians of the Executive Committee complained, in turn, of overload and of an increase in unscheduled walk-ins, clearly being unwilling to sustain the administration by condemning the practice. The meeting was concluded by an administrator's suggestion that, at subsequent meetings before the summer vacation period, individual offenders be brought before the Executive Committee and asked to explain their time practice. Two weeks later, at a general meeting of family doctors, an administrator again referred to the growing problem of lateness and to the possibility of offenders being "invited" to attend an Executive Committee meeting to account for their practices (even though the Executive Committee had not actually agreed to the administrator's suggestion). Thus, the threat of collective pressure was made, but we had no record of the issue being raised again for the remainder of the year or of an offender being called up before the Executive Committee.

In sum, in the case of office hours there appeared to be no sustained method of systematically collecting information or of systematically exerting sanctions to correct deviance. In theory, the administration could have employed bureaucratic measures such as clocking arrivals and departures so as to account precisely for time and could have sanctioned the physicians by paying them solely for the time they were present during regular hours. But clocking, like "docking," was not feasible for profoundly felt ideological reasons. Nor could the potentially powerful sanctions of colleagues be mobilized, since cutting hours or arriving late and leaving early was practiced by most physicians on one occasion or another and represented, like medical mistakes, the right to discretionary flexibility. Furthermore, one practitioner's lateness rarely had much bearing on anyone other than patients. Only leaving early and being unavailable for an emergency walk-in posed inconvenience to colleagues.

Keeping strictly to hours, in short, was not a problem of colleague relations, and freedom about hours was seen too much as a professional prerogative. Strong colleague sanctions could not be mobilized to deal with this issue. All the administration could do to contain it was to periodically publicize the problem as serious and hint at apparently unenforceable peer sanctions. And all it could do with individual offenders was to talk with them in private, at once pleading and threatening. I attended one such private meeting devoted to turning on the heat to persuade a consultant to manage himself and one of his colleagues (and friends) in the same specialty.

ADMINISTRATOR: Look—

#87: Our service stinks.

ADMINISTRATOR: No, it's good, but you've been here a long time and you know what to get away with and how . . . . You're squeezing patients. [Your colleague] takes only three hours, not the five required, and he explodes when we scheduled those he left out one day for the next day because it ruins his schedule.

#87: We both admit we've cut hours. But up to now no patients have been harmed by this fact. There have been minimal complaints in the past year and a half.

ADMINISTRATOR: The two most serious cases of misdiagnosis in the group were made in your specialty.

#87: They weren't my cases.

ADMINISTRATOR: They were [your colleague's].

#87: [He] is the best man in the city.

ADMINISTRATOR: It's most likely to happen when you're squeezing patients . . . .

#87: But you shouldn't pile them on. If he sees a good list, he'll take more time.

ADMINISTRATOR: Are you kidding?

#87: I can't change his nature. He can cut through a lot of patients.

ADMINISTRATOR: You can't solve it by making his schedule shorter. . . . [He's] got to come in on time.

#87: He can't, he just can't. Our services have fallen down because there isn't room to say to a patient, "You come in again at such and such a time," He's a more popular guy than I am. . . .

ADMINISTRATOR: Not true. He can do it, but he doesn't want to.

#87: Then let him do it his own way. Now, the two serious cases, one was cancer of the _____?

ADMINISTRATOR: Yes. He just does the routine, he doesn't take the time. He can make the same mistake again.

Such exchanges, perhaps not always in as jocular and affectionate a tone of voice as I heard, were apparently effective enough to prevent repeated crises in the availability of appointment hours for contract patients, but they took a great deal of effort and seemed to succeed merely in containing the limits of offense rather than transforming the sources of offense.

CONTROLLING X RAYS AND LABORATORY TESTS

By the evaluative criteria used by administrative agencies, the medical group was likely to be considered to have failed to institute adequate controls over the ordering of X rays and laboratory tests. It was way above the norm in such orders. At the very beginning of the field study, a meeting was held at which it was announced that the medical group ordered *three* times as many laboratory tests and X rays as any other group providing services under an MSP contract and *ten* times as many as some groups. In the files we searched, we found a memorandum from as long as 12 years before our study which deplored the situation, asking that no more "than are necessary" be ordered but typically drawing back from giving the impression of laying down hard-and-fast rules. It stated that "no one is to be deprived of any procedure, including those mentioned above, when there is a valid reason." Perhaps that form of general exhortation worked to reduce orders, but certainly not for long. Typically, there was a cycle of pressure by exhortation, after which the number of orders apparently dropped somewhat. But over time the number of orders rose again, hortatory pressure followed, the number of orders dropped off for a time, then they rose again, and so on, with no permanent change in physician habits.

Throughout our study we observed meetings at which the topic of the extraordinarily large number of X rays and tests was brought up and its cost to the medical group noted. And the response was always one that neutralized the pressure—that the patients' well-being depended on the tests and X rays or that they were recommended by some medical authorities. The dialogue at one meeting was as follows:

ADMINISTRATOR: We've had the highest X-ray costs these past three months than ever.
#76: They're all sick people.
ADMINISTRATOR: Sure, I'm just bringing this to your attention.

#70: I order X-rays to cover myself legally. [Everyone else agrees.]
ADMINISTRATOR: How about GI series and the rest? You tend to re-ray people
   a lot. The frequency of re-raying is the source of the large number of orders.
#81: The X-ray man tells you to re-ray every six weeks.
ADMINISTRATOR: You must take the responsibility yourself. . . .
#90: Besides that, 75 PBIs were ordered and only one positive.
#86: But a lot of patients are being followed for hyperthyroid.

The meeting never returned to the subject.

Eight months later an administrator noted again that the group was faced with a critical financial drain caused by the large number of expensive tests ordered. But the discussion collapsed as the physicians turned to one another in little groups, exchanging anecdotes, telling jokes, seeking therapeutic advice, whereupon the meeting ended. A few months after that, at another family doctors' meeting, the administration announced that "42 PBIs were ordered during the previous month, and of those, three . . ." but before he could finish he was drowned out with laughter, and the meeting ended.

In all, any effort at arbitrary quota-setting was resisted almost automatically by virtually everyone because it constituted an attack on freedom of judgment and practice. And any effort to appeal to economic self-interest—a type of appeal that was never straightforward and positive but always ambivalent and defensive—met with a somewhat sanctimonious response by many doctors, particularly the full-time physicians. The one method of attempting to control the practice of ordering too many tests which did receive close attention was an effort at persuasion and education in which a particularly respected subspecialist or consultant was used as an ally. However, the discussion tended to be inconclusive, fragmenting into clusters of individuals exchanging opinions, and no meeting we observed ever concluded with a collective decision to adopt a particular policy designed to guide a more restrictive, discriminating use of orders for X rays and lab tests. Perhaps this was because, as I suggested in Chapter Five, orders for tests and X rays constituted as much a method of managing patients as a method for diagnosis. But, as a method of diagnosis, the right of each physician to hold an opinion and to make his own decisions about it led to rejection of any collective norm.

Overriding all three efforts at control—setting bureaucratic quotas or norms, appealing to economic self-interest, and educating—was the constraint of the service ethic and the aleatory excuse that "something might be found." The aleatory argument is a common one in all professional rhetoric: it is that if there is even a *slight* chance of discovering a dangerous condition early by a test, it should be done and expense be damned. In the medical group that argument, buttressed by case examples, was constantly invoked in defense of the free use of X rays and laboratory tests. Even one of the most vociferous critics of the practice, a physician who was intensely aware of and preoccupied with the high operating costs that reduced his income, found himself at an impasse:

> I just don't know what can be done about lab tests. I had an embarrassing experience. There was a friend of mine . . . and he is somebody who doesn't complain very much. You know, he underplays his symptoms. One day he came in and said, "You know, I have a funny pain in my stomach. I don't get it all the time, but it is a strange one I really haven't had before." His [group] doctor didn't feel anything in particular, and he said, "Why don't we do a complete GI series and a barium enema on you?" That came back and they found something really suspicious and a surgeon went in and came out with a colon the size of both my hands in the middle of which was a real cancer. He had this about five years ago, and there has been no recurrence since. I'm over a barrel. What can I do? This thing was picked up and could only have been picked up by having tests done at the time. And I know when I bring up this matter of lab tests in the Executive Committee, they keep saying, "Look, we have the highest rates of discovery of cancer of all the medical groups in the city. Now, even if we got just one in 100,000, isn't it worth it to spend all this money?" And what can I say?

These powerful reasons, combined with the disinclination (and probable inability) of the administration to impose bureaucratic quotas, reduced the exercise of social control largely to periodic reminders of the cost of tests and X rays to the group, citation of statistics, and the like, with the collegium playing little part in the effort. Such temporary pressure apparently had no long-lasting result, since it had to be repeated over and over again.

CONTROLLING HOUSECALLS

When we turn to housecalls, we turn to a problem of control which was rather different from that of controlling office hours and the ordering of tests and X rays, and while the balance against the imposition of precise rules was again, as in the case of ordering tests and X rays, weighted by an aleatory argument, it operated in precisely the reverse direction. The same excuse used for *providing* one service (ordering tests) was used for *withholding* another service (making housecalls). This was not irrational from the point of view of the physicians' economy of effort, since ordering tests saved the physicians time while making housecalls cost them time. Nonetheless, the acceptability of the aleatory argument hinges on benefit to the *individual* patient, to the one person in 100,000 whose life may be saved by a service. That was why the aleatory argument was used by an administrator to support the position that, in the case of housecalls, the benefit of the doubt ought to be given to the patient:

> There is this range down here where [the patient] says, "I'm getting something and I just don't know what's wrong with me. I just don't feel well and have a slight tickling cough, but I have no fever." And then the doctor says, "Well, even if I looked at you, I wouldn't be able to find anything," which is probably true. But if he is getting Waterhouse Frederickson Syndrome, which is almost inevitably fatal unless it is treated within the first two or three hours [the doctor *would* be able to find something]. And of course, there is only one case in 100 or 150,000 like that, when he should be seen at that particular time. A faint rash which he hasn't seen himself would be visible to the doctor, and the possibility enters the doctor's head that he might be treated and recover, whereas if he isn't seen, he dies. And that one case of measles that really isn't measles but is typhus fever or something like that, or Rocky Mountain Spotted Fever—he's got to see them.

Attempts to control housecalls in the medical group were primarily individual and went on in private. The physician who refused to go out would be approached by an administrator or a senior physician in his own specialty, and he would be talked to. Most commonly, the issue arose in the first place because of a patient's complaint, and, if it occurred during the course of an illness rather than after, an attempt was made to persuade the physician to go out, even if only for public relations purposes. On occasion, the physician was manipulated into dealing with the complaining patient by members of the administration who had received a call from the patient but lacked authority to settle the matter themselves. If the physician could not be persuaded to go on the merits of the case, he might be asked to go out as a favor to the official requesting it.

If complaints about one individual physician were especially common, or some instances of refusal proved to be such as to border on neglect or to lead to strong claims for payment of bills incurred by the use of an outside physician who made the call, the administrator might have a private meeting with the offender, during which he would ask for an explanation of the decision to refuse a call and seek a promise about decisions in the future. But, interestingly enough, it was not possible to find in our notes and records one reference to a physician being "brought up" before his assembled colleagues at a formal meeting because of the refusal of housecalls. If this occurred at all, it was patently rare. Refusal to make a housecall by itself seemed to be insufficient ground for the development of organized *colleague* pressure. To have been given colleague attention, the refusal to make a housecall had to have been accompanied by more heinous crimes, such as asking for a case of Scotch, collecting a fee for the call, or filling out record forms claiming that housecalls were made when they were in fact not made. Most important of all to the collegium was the involvement of another colleague whose patient was refused a call that the colleague then had to make himself. The vast majority of cases in which physicians were subjected to the ultimate stage of social pressure in the medical group— being brought up before the Executive Committee—were those in which one *physician* had complaints about another. Offending patients was not sufficient: physicians as well had to be offended. *Collective forms of professional control were brought into play primarily when the issue was that of intercollegial relations*, not that of patient relations or relations with the administration. Being tardy in hours, ordering a large number of tests and X rays, and refusing to make housecalls were by themselves insufficient grounds for the organized exercise of professional sanctions. Only the administration took active interest in them.

CONTROLLING COLLEAGUE RELATIONS

I have already indicated in earlier chapters how a variety of problems arose in the cooperation among colleagues—problems of coverage among colleagues in the same specialty and of consultation between specialties. Some of these problems could be controlled fairly well by rather mechanical administrative solutions, such as designing and requiring the use of a special referral slip for scheduling referrals to consultant services, developing a system for "flagging" medical charts so that the referrers could see the consultants' entries before the patient returned to them, and supervising coverage and "on call" schedules to make sure that there was no uncovered time period.

Within that framework, however, there were problems of sloughing off within particular specialties and between different specialties. Complaints about sloughing off generally involved colleagues in one's own specialty service and were generally handled informally. The offended complained to the offender, sometimes with the mediation and aid of the senior person of the service, sometimes with the mediation and aid of a member of the administration. In the case of overreferral, however, involving *inter*specialty relations, it was far more common for the issue to move past the stage of complaining in private to the offender into the official and collective, public stage of sanctioning. We observed a number of Executive Committee and general family doctor meetings at which representatives of a specialty described their problems with referrals, answered complaints by individual referrers in the audience, and attempted to persuade the primary practitioners to reduce their rate of referrals, particularly referrals without a prior work-up or examination. From the recurrence of such meetings, it would appear that their effect was short-term.

Beyond general problems of coverage within specialties and referral between specialties as units, which could be dealt with collectively, there were, of course, problems between individuals. I have already cited instances in which patients were sent back to the referring physician and in which the consultant made angry telephone calls to referring physicians. Few disputes went much beyond that stage, but some had to be taken to the Executive Committee for its review and recommendation. Characteristically, the initiation of a charge to be taken up by the Executive Committee reposed almost entirely in the hands of full-time, senior physicians. Our records indicated no case in which a junior physician was the initiating agent. Juniors were canvassed for complaints after the fact, when an attempt was made to collect a full bill of particulars on an individual offender, but otherwise they seemed to keep their mouths shut in public.

Formal meetings of the Executive Committee around such charges of offense by an individual physician took two forms. In one, the problem was to resolve a complaint and hopefully prevent the future occurrence of the offense charged. While in some cases, the offense charged might have been sanctioned so effectively that it did not recur, in all cases the outcome was to at the very least cool off the complaintant. In such meetings, the tone was more a blend of catharsis and conciliation than of organized sanctions focused on an offender. In one such meeting we observed, for example, the invited offender was told of the charge and the instance that precipitated it, and he, in turn, presented his side of the events at issue. Then he himself took the offensive and presented his own complaints about the referral habits of other physicians to him. At that point, the Executive Committee split into two groups—consultants, who supported the offender by telling of their own problems with referrers, and primary practitioners, who largely kept silent and did not support the senior primary practitioner who had made the precipitating charge. The meeting ended on a note that did not exonerate the offender's charged rudeness to a hastily referred patient or to the referrer, but that did draw attention and pressure off his offense by becoming generalized into a discussion of the general problem of the quality of referrals and of consultants' responses to unnecessary referrals. The particular complaint was not resolved directly, and business turned to the next item on the agenda. Thus, the heat was put on an individual, but with neither the intent nor the consequence of burning anyone. Since most of such heat was, over the years, addressed to the same mercurial or tactless individuals over and over again, one might guess that as a form of social control it was better designed to contain than to seriously reduce the likelihood of continued offense.

PRESSURES FOR RESIGNATION

In another form of Executive Committee meeting, the problem was less to modify the performance of an offender than to press him to leave the medical group. For those who had not yet gained tenure, a meeting of the Executive Committee was not usually necessary for getting them to resign. It was possible to have a private conversation with an undesirable physician during which his poor chances for gaining tenure would be revealed so that he would not be inclined to ask for a formal meeting with the Committee to discuss the charges against him. An administrator's notes described his private meeting with one offender:

> He asked me whether I would recommend his tenure to the Executive Committee. I said, "No, You've got to convince the Executive Committee yourself." I told him frankly that he could get another job, and it would be better for all concerned that he did.

Most persons in such a position proceeded to resign, letting it appear that they had done so willingly in order to graze in the greener pastures of fee-for-service practice outside the medical group.

Physicians who *had* tenure, however, were rather more difficult to eject from the medical group. Most resigned at their convenience, but it was possible to hang on, as one composite case[2] illustrates. A number of years before the beginning of the field study, a tenured member of the medical group was discovered to have neglected a seriously ill patient and to have fraudulently filled out certain MSP forms. Brought up before the Executive Committee, he did not deny his actions, but he asked for another chance and promised to resign if he misbehaved again. Six months later it was discovered that he had committed another comparatively serious offense, and, on being asked to resign, he began crying. He said he was going through a divorce, had children to take care of, and could not look for another position. He again promised to do better and indicated that he had just entered psychotherapy in the hope that it might improve his professional performance. Embarrassed by his tears and by the story of his personal troubles, the committee members agreed that he could stay. However, an undated letter of resignation was demanded from him, to be used on the next occasion on which he committed a similar offense.

The letter of resignation still reposed in a confidential file at the time of our study. It remained unused even though the physician continued to draw patient and colleague complaints. He did "behave" in that he was not discovered to have neglected a serious case or to have committed fraud, but he posed a continuous problem of management and coverage to both the administration and his colleagues in the same specialty. On yet another occasion of fresh offense, a senior person said to me that he didn't know what to do about it. "It's impossible when you get someone who is determined to hang on and is smart enough not to get caught in anything flagrant."

In that case and in others we observed or heard about, it appeared that effective collegial action was not possible because of the normative and structural characteristics of the medical group. Once the initial, "flagrant" offenses were not responded to by forced resignation, little else could be done. The bylaws of the medical group allowed a tenured physician to be ejected on the basis of a vote by the assembled col-

---

[2]Several cases about which we learned are mixed together into a single composite case so that the identification of individuals is prevented.

legium. The offenses the previously described individual committed six months after the original flagrant offenses were not sufficient to assure even a majority vote, let alone the three-quarters vote required by the bylaws. Indeed, upon a move to initiate a collective vote to revoke tenure, a group of colleagues signed a statement of support for the individual, citing his competence and their good relations with him. This step effectively discouraged attempts to use the formal mechanism for collective revokation of tenure.

Most offenses were of such a character as to involve personally a very small number of physicians in the medical group. The restriction of communication about grievances was such that rather few of the physicians were even aware that there was a history of persistent offense by this individual. Indeed, the offender had a good reputation among the majority of the physicians: some had only episodic, largely routine dealings with him, while others had only fleeting social contact without any consultation in which his work and mode of managing it could become directly known to them. Under such circumstances, it was little wonder that the decision was made to avoid bringing his ejection to a vote. Only flagrant or gross offenses were sufficient to mobilize collective modes of formal colleague sanctions. But gross offenses were by their nature so obvious and damning that if an individual were "caught red-handed" at them, he would be only too happy to resign and avoid their being publicized. It was the vast bulk of professional deviance that was difficult to sanction; the exception did not really require professional action.

THE COLLEGIUM AND THE ADMINISTRATION

Rather early in my analysis I argued that the exercise of formal administrative authority and of formal administrative sanctions was fairly insignificant in the medical group and that in order to understand the behavior of the physicians one had instead to understand the nature of the collegial system of social control. On that basis, I focused most of my attention on the collegial rules and norms, modes of surveillance, and modes of sanctioning. However, it should be apparent from the data I presented that the administration did serve critical functions in exercising what social control there was. The peculiar character of the colleague control system created a vacuum that only administrative initiative could fill. *Something* had to be done about at least some of the operating problems of the group. Though it was largely unable to employ *formal* sanctions, the administration did employ informal sanctions of some importance.

In essence, as I have shown here, the collegium consistently abdicated the role of exercising organized sanctions. The process of social control it sustained was designed to permit wide individual differences in performance. Its rules tolerated all but gross and obvious deviance in performance, so long as intercollegial relations remained manageable. Its system of surveillance was deliberately loose and unsystematic. And it denied the propriety of participating in the exercise of systematic sanctions intended to control variability in stances toward providing service. It did leave individuals free to exercise their own sanctions over colleagues who gave them offense. And, when conflict between colleagues became severe, the organized collegium, in the form of the Executive Committee, did participate in smoothing over the dispute if not actually adjudicating it. But basically the collegial system of social control was such as to leave individuals free to work in their own ways within the very broad limits set by obvious unethicality or incompetence. Thus, we can understand how, within the broad, external framework of constraint posed by the contractual scheme and the group-practice organization, the variety of stances toward service could exist. *The collegium was a largely neutral force in the social control of its members' performance.*

Given the general abdication of the collegium, the administration actually constituted the most important center of influence in the medical group. In the face of persistent problems with maintaining regular office hours, incurring heavy expenses for diagnostic tests, and generating heavy (and expensive) loads for consultants in the medical group, the administration was forced to attempt to at least contain the magnitude of those problems. It could not, as we saw in this chapter, mobilize organized collegial control processes, but had to make do with informal devices of its own. While its formal, bureaucratic authority was severely limited, its informal influence was pervasive. In the face of the permissive rules of the collegial system, it had to draw the line on a case-by-case basis. In the face of the deliberately fragmented character of the collegial surveillance system, the administration had to become the real collection point for information from patient and colleague complaints about individual performance.

In some of the interview material presented in earlier chapters, we saw that, while some offended physicians did not wish to confront the offenders, they did not wish to ignore the incident either. Some complained to friends or a senior colleague with whom they were close, but some also went to complain to one of the administrators. The administrators could serve this role in part because they were *not* colleagues, though also not outsiders. In addition to being the repository of some of the physicians' personal complaints and grievances, the administration was also the central repository of formal information bearing on the performance of all members of the collegium. It possessed information on the way physicians kept their hours, the number of housecalls they made, the number of diagnostic tests and X rays they ordered, and the like. And it was the central repository of complaints from patients about individual physicians—both those complaints transmitted by the insurance company's complaint office and those brought directly to it by an aggrieved patient.

Going to the administrators, then, constituted for the physicians the most natural and effective way of getting information and of getting informed advice about how to deal with colleagues who had offended them. Indeed, the tendency was for the physicians to register their complaints against colleagues with the administration instead of with their representatives on the Executive Committee. Characteristically, the administrators urged the offended physician himself to confront the offender, after assuring him that he had good grounds for his complaint; but the norms of etiquette, which made it embarrassing to confront a colleague, usually won out.

> I mentioned it to the administrator and he said, "We all know about it. You really ought to take it up with him." Well, I just never got to it. I cooled down, and as the days passed I saw less point in doing anything about it. (#21— PRIMARY PRACTITIONER)

Lacking real formal authority to intervene, the administration often attempted to get individual physicians and the Executive Committee to use professional sanctions, urging them to take the responsibility themselves, but more often than not it found the responsibility on its own shoulders.

In light of its strategic position in the communication network of the medical group, it was no wonder that it was largely the administration that was able to judge and even determine what formal modes of social control would be exercised in the group. The Executive Committee relied largely on the administration's advice before deciding to talk to an indicted offender. In fact, it often urged an administrator to have a private talk with a charged offender in the hope that it would not itself have to confront him. In the face of professional reluctance to confront (and sanction) offending colleagues, the administration found itself forced into the role of sanctioning offenders where it had to and where it could.

The ultimate outcome of stubborn cases of deviance in the group was the final testimony to the influence of the administration. Even after offenders had successfully defied threats to "put it to a vote," all but one offender did resign eventually rather than hang on. These resignations were largely a consequence of essentially administrative, not professional, measures and, what is more, of discretionary rather than rule-guided sanctions. These administrative measures consisted of denying requests for administrative favors in scheduling hours, vacation times, and the like and of interpreting the rules minimally and restrictively so as to deny the offender the privileges he believed to be his right and proper due. The method was employed, and could only be employed, by those with some connection with the bureaucratic apparatus. It manipulated those discretionary elements of the organization of work which made the difference between convenience and inconvenience and between the sense of being valued and respected and the sense of being unwanted and scorned. Ultimately, such informal and covert discretionary actions were responsible for the resignation of intransigent cases.

The collegium as such was largely a spectator, and it had rather little to do with what was, in practice rather than in theory, the ultimate sanction used in the medical group. Social control was thus left to often unwilling officials, and its exercise was pushed into the underground of administrative discretion by the reluctance of the collegium to participate in the process. The administration's role in the process of social control in the medical group was thus far greater than the limitations on its formal authority would have led us to expect. And the importance of its role was the direct outcome of the abdication of the collegium from exercising the effective self-government that it insisted was solely its own legitimate function.

15:
Human Service and the Fate of the Collegium

The basic issue underlying this book is the role of formal, administrative schemes in the control of work involving service to human beings and the role of the workers themselves in such a scheme of control. The formal fiscal and administrative characteristics of the organization we studied were and are considered to be a model for public policy, and by ordinary criteria prepaid group practice seems to have provided service of a higher than average quality (Roemer and Shonick, 1973). I do not contest that statement, even in the case of the particular prepaid medical group described here. I believe that on a number of grounds prepaid group practice constitutes a far more desirable administrative framework for medical care than does traditional individual practice. Even if the processes of collegial control in prepaid group practice leave something to be desired, as I suggest they do, it is likely that in individual, entrepreneurial practice they are considerably less adequate.

I do not mean to suggest, then, that such a formal framework is undesirable. Rather, I am arguing only that there are distinct and important limits to what such a framework can control. The physicians who work within it have sufficient latitude that important variations can exist in the way they cope with their problems of work, variations not desired or intended by those who formulate and administer the formal structure. While the administrative structure placed limits on what *could* take place, it could not determine the nature of the variation within those limits. Part of that incomplete bureaucratic control was unintentional, but the most important part was deliberately instituted on the basis of the assumption that the workers themselves—the physicians—were themselves best qualified to control their performance. And it was assumed that they were especially likely to control their own performance in a setting in which they all worked together in close proximity. In this book I have attempted to assess the nature of the self-regulatory process in that setting.

240

THE PROFESSIONAL SYSTEM OF CONTROL

At the core of the professional control system of the medical group was a set of rules for defining the limits of acceptable performance by reference to conceptions of self, one's colleagues, and the nature of medical work and work performance. These norms blurred and weakened the notion of collegial accountability upon which the effective operation of a control system must rely. The rules governing colleague relations—the rules of etiquette—limited the critical evaluation of colleagues' work and discouraged the expression of criticism. They seemed to take priority even over standards of technical performance, for when we followed out the limits of acceptable technical standards by exploring the meaning of mistakes, we found them normalized and relativized on such a broad front as to make them far less likely to be subject to reproach than were breaches of etiquette. The professional was treated as an individual free to follow his own judgment without constraint, so long as his behavior was short of blatant or gross deficiencies in performance and inconvenience to colleagues.

In evaluating colleague performance, the physicians employed their own concrete, personal, and therefore individual experience as the ultimate authority on which they would rely. The evaluative information about the performance of colleagues which was made available by the reports of colleagues and patients was discounted as inconclusive and unreliable. But, given the organization of the division of labor in the medical group, the distribution of what was considered to be conclusive and reliable evaluative information—direct, personal experience with colleagues' work—was seriously limited. The scope of each person's direct experience with the work of others rarely corresponded with that of others; it only sometimes overlapped with the personal experience of others; it sometimes did not overlap at all with that of any other individual. Thus, insofar as direct, personal experience with others' performance served as the primary criterion for secure evaluation of colleague performance, the convergence of judgment necessary for collective efforts at social control was not common. Obedience to the rules of etiquette discouraged critical attitudes toward colleagues, the communication of critical information to others about the performance of colleagues, the discussion of critical evaluations with colleagues, and the undertaking of collective social control. Etiquette was a more important norm than accountability, and it undermined attempts at critical evaluation and control by its characteristic rule of overlooking fault in order to maintain harmony within the collegium.

Ultimate reliance on the authority of personal experience without efforts to distribute the information to others and make it a topic of common discussion and evaluation thus seriously reduced the scope of who and what the physicians were willing to evaluate, while the norms of etiquette seriously limited the exercise of controls. Confrontation was distasteful even in private and almost unthinkable in public. The most acceptable and comfortable mechanism of control was that which could be practiced very easily in solo, fee-for-service practice—namely avoiding, or boycotting, an individual who has offended. But, in the closed-panel group practice, avoidance was difficult in many cases and impossible in others. In spite of the fact that the group practitioners had no choice but to deal with one another, they were nonetheless committed to rules of etiquette that made them unable to participate in more direct forms of social control.

THE COLLEGIUM AS A DELINQUENT COMMUNITY

The system of social control among the physicians in the medical group was founded on a consensus around the rules of etiquette governing colleague relations which permitted differences of opinion about the proper way of dealing with patients and also about technical standards of work performance. While there were disagreements about technical standards of work performance between specialties with overlapping jurisdictions and even in single specialties within which various schools or segments were contending for hegemony, there was fairly general agreement about the social norms that sustained the internal permissiveness of the social-control system. That general normative agreement constitutes part of the "community" that is often ascribed to professional identity and organization (e.g., Goode, 1957): it is an expression of the social solidarity of an organized occupation.

Given the general idea of collegial consensus, it may be noted that such a consensus operated in a way that has sometimes been described as conspiratorial. Professions have often been characterized as conspiracies against the laity, and the reluctance of physicians to cooperate with the courts by testifying against colleagues has been described as a conspiracy of silence. But this is not a characteristic of professions alone. Adam Smith rightly noted it as a potential characteristic of all groups with a common economic interest when he observed that "people of the same trade seldom meet together, even for merriment and diversion, but the conversation ends in a conspiracy against the public" (Smith, 1970: 232). Conspiracies, however, can be organized in different ways. All of them require some kind of effective internal solidarity in order to maintain a common front against those outside, but that internal solidarity can be created in a variety of ways. It can be created on the basis of force and maintained by the exercise of rigid hierarchical discipline over the members of the group. It can also be created on the basis of common recognition of interest and maintained by voluntary self-discipline on the part of group members. There are, no doubt, a number of bases for establishing solidarity in the face of perceived threat from the world outside the group and for ordering internal relations. What was peculiar about the organization among the physicians I described was not so much the existence of a common front of silence to the lay world as the fact that the rules of the collegium were designed also to leave each individual member a maximum amount of independence and autonomy.

This is a very special kind of community that, structurally and normatively, parallels that described by Jesse R. Pitts as the "delinquent community" of French schoolchildren in particular and French collectivities in general during the first half of the twentieth century. Parts of his description parallel our observations in a striking way:

> The school peer group is the prototype of the solidarity groups which exist in France beyond the [family]. They are characterized by jealous equalitarianism among the members . . . [a] conspiracy of silence against superior authority . . . in an effort to create for each member a zone of autonomy, of caprice, of creativity. . . . Any change that is apt to create new ambiguities of status, or restrict the individual zones of autonomy in favor of a systematized and rational approach to the problem, will be resisted with all the strength the group can muster. (Pitts, 1963: 259)

Crozier, commenting and elaborating on the usefulness of Pitts's characterization for understanding the cultural sources of the bureaucratic behavior of the personnel of the French organizations he studied, says that such a community possesses

a kind of implicit solidarity among all members of the same rank . . . a negative kind of solidarity, directed against superiors and against other groups,
[which] is extremely successful in preventing any attempt at leadership within
the group. (CROZIER, 1964: 219)

He goes on to note that this defensive solidarity involves the collective
obligation to protect each colleague's independence.[1] Different as may
be the circumstances and persons involved in our case from those
studied by Pitts and Crozier, it seems taxonomically accurate nonetheless to characterize the professional community of the medical group as
a delinquent community. Its norms and practices were such as to both
draw all members together defensively in a common front against the
outside world of the laity and, internally, to allow each his freedom to
act as he willed.

THE BACKGROUND OF THE PROFESSIONAL
DELINQUENT COMMUNITY

While Pitts and Crozier couched their explanatory analyses of French
delinquent communities in terms of their members' attempts to cope
with rigid and demanding administrative structures embodied in state-
controlled educational institutions and productive enterprises in the
France of the 1940s and 1950s, understanding the genesis of the delinquent
community of the physicians requires reference to quite different elements of economic organization. The origin of the delinquent community of the physicians lies in a position of vulnerable privilege rather than
in one of vulnerable subordination. Over the past hundred years
medicine has gained an effective occupational monopoly over practice,
protected by law but always subject to change by political power should
competing occupational lobbyists and organized consumers find their
causes strengthened by publicity given to inadequacies in the profession's performance.

As a political and economic community of interest, the profession has
been concerned with defending its privileged position by presenting a
united front to the outside so as to prevent the public from learning of its
occasional excesses and thus avoid damaging scandal. (See Carlin, 1966,

---

[1]See also the characterization of the trade associations of small shopkeepers as "individualistic collectivism" in Bechhofer and Elliott, 1968:196.

for evidence on the correlation between public scandal and professional sanctions.) Given the profession's monopoly provided by the state, protected from the competition of all other kinds of claimed healers, the historic arrangement *within* the organized occupation was designed to sustain some modicum of collegial equality by which each colleague would be sufficiently satisfied so as to be inclined to close ranks without defection to the outside. Much of what has been called "ethics," and certainly the commonly understood rules of etiquette, is designed to prevent "unfair" internal competition and preserve comparative equality of opportunity in the medical marketplace at the same time as it preserves an impeccable front of silence to the outside world. Licensing laws themselves preserve such internal equality by granting to all M.D.s the unrestricted right to cut or to dose in any way, irrespective of specialized training (cf. Derbyshire, 1969: x–xi).

The process of social control in the medical group, I suggest, was rooted directly in the norms and customs of that historical tradition. In traditional solo, fee-for-service practice, there was no reason to discuss differences of opinion, knowledge, and practice with patients or colleagues. The market could solve interpersonal relations automatically, without the necessity of physicians undertaking deliberate effort at solution of conflict by reaching a consensus that could lead to changes in behavior and new forms of cooperation. Given a fee barrier, one is relieved of the need to persuade patients that their desires for service are unnecessary: willingness to pay out of one's pocket and to fill one's pocket can be arbiters of necessity. Given independent, individual practice that leaves one nominally free to work or not work with a colleague, one need not take overt issue with a colleague's performance and have to hammer out some working consensus with him: "water seeks its own level," as one of the group physicians put it, and each goes his own way, minding and running his own business. Even though they were in a different kind of practice organization, most of the group physicians responded to their problems with patients and colleagues by invoking the norms and customs of entrepreneurial practice to define what professional work should be. To claim that the problem was created by the absence of the fee barrier and of "free" individual practice is to miss the point that those traditional elements of organization work only because of particular norms sustaining them. New norms about the nature of medical work, patient relations, and colleague relations would make traditional forms of organization just as problematic. The prepaid group practice required, but did not have, norms supporting the organization; without them, it could not reach its full potential.

THE DEVELOPMENT OF EXTERNAL CONTROLS

While the delinquent community of physicians that I described was similar in its structure to that of French schoolchildren, it differed in one very important way. The French schoolchildren were responding to a rigid, authoritarian educational system, but no analogous system imposed by outsiders has ever existed for medicine. At best, its delinquent community may be explained by reference to a sense of vulnerability to the possible imposition of such controls, an *anticipatory* response. The irony is that rather than defending the profession against the imposition of a rigid authoritarian framework, the anticipatory responses of the medical community have created part of the pressure for the institution of such a framework. The failure of the profession to control the availability, cost, and quality of the services of its members in the public interest—a failure tied directly to the internal laissez faire etiquette of its delinquent community—has contributed to the development in the United States of externally imposed requirements that may very well come to be, in the future, what the profession has always feared. It may thus have created what it has anticipated by the very defenses it erected!

In 1965, shortly after our study of the medical group was completed, national Medicare and Medicaid legislation made it possible for physicians and hospitals to be paid by federal funds for the care of the elderly and the indigent. What followed the legislation is well known: there was a sharp increase in costs. The enormous increase was not anticipated by those writing the legislation and quickly created both a fiscal crisis and a political scandal in which some persons charged physicians and hospitals with venality and irresponsibility.[2] Such charges were simplistic, as should be clear from the exposition of earlier chapters in this book. The imputation of purely selfish economic motives does not explain enough

---

[2] I do not mean to imply that the medical profession can be held responsible for all of the problems of cost, availability, and quality of health care in the United States. Hospital charges account for a far greater proportion of the health dollar than do physician charges. However, it should never be forgotten that physicians play a key role in hospitalizing patients, prescribing drugs, ordering diagnostic tests, and the like. While they may not profit from such charges, they are responsible for incurring them.

to be, by itself, a reliable guide to policy, for providing and ordering services is as much a way of coping with problems of work as it is a way of making money. A sudden increase in eligible patients less constrained than in the past by a personal fee barrier can create a problem of management which, as we saw, can be solved with the least effort by multiplying service units while reducing their duration, by ordering diagnostic tests, by making referrals, and by hospitalizing patients. (It should be remembered also that, in the United States, where the community physician is usually an attending staff member of a hospital, hospitalization stacks patients up where they can be visited all at once at the physician's convenience.)

By the same token, it should not have been surprising that no organized system of collegial influence was exercised to control claims. In the salaried, prepaid service-contract medical group, the fact of working cooperatively in the same building and with the same population of subscriber-patients made close control possible. Nonetheless, social control was loose, unorganized, and extremely permissive. In the far more common mode of solo, entrepreneurial practice, the possibility of control is much smaller, and one has little reason to assume that there would be more inclination there than in the medical group to exercise any significant professional self-regulation. There has in fact been little precedent for systematic professional self-regulation in medicine in the past (cf. Daniels, 1973; Lewis and Lewis, 1970).

Given the fact of precipitous increases in charges and services, which implied the lack of any internal professional self-regulation, federal legislation required the institution of formal, professional "utilization review" committees to review admissions to hospitals and other residential-care facilities. They had the task of reviewing physicians' decisions to hospitalize patients and, after admission, to review the length of time patients were kept in hospital. Review was to be based on professional criteria of medical necessity. By this means, it was believed, unnecessary hospital utilization, and so unnecessary costs, would be reduced.

The outcome was not as hoped. In the words of the Senate Committee on Finance, "utilization review activities have, generally speaking, been of a token nature and ineffective as a curb to unnecessary use of institutional care and services. Utilization review in medicare can be characterized as more form than substance" (Committee on Finance, U.S. Senate, 1972). Other institutional review committees—such as those

concerned with reviewing research proposals for their conformity with
regulations requiring the "protection of human subjects"—have also
appeared to suffer from the same inadequacies (cf. Barber et al., 1973;
Gray, 1975). Such an outcome is quite understandable if, first, we remember that the members of the utilization review committees were all
staff members of the same institution, with collegial ties; and if, second,
we assume that they shared the same sort of self-conceptions, work
norms, and conceptions of social control as described in this book. And,
as we saw, medical necessity is not a fixed, but a highly elastic, criterion.

The consequence of failure to establish effective professional control
through institutional review bodies led to new legislation in 1972 which
required the constitution of professional standard review organizations
(PSROs). (For a lucid summary, see Goran et al., 1975). These would
ordinarily be independent of particular hospitals, practice organizations,
or local medical societies. Once constituted, such PSROs were to collect data on the practice of all the physicians in their area who receive
reimbursement from Medicare and Medicaid programs. They were to
establish review standards pragmatically, on the basis of statistical
"profiles"—the "norms of care, diagnosis and treatment" employed by
those physicians—and then use these standards as a basis for reviewing
the medical necessity of decisions to hospitalize patients and to keep
them in hospital. Initially, standards were to be developed and employed
only for diagnoses involving admission to and stay in hospitals and other
expensive extended-care facilities, but it was intended that the PSROs
would eventually develop standards for ambulatory-care practices as
well. As for sanctions, the PSRO was empowered to recommend the
denial of payment for claims for services that do not conform to its
standards and even to exclude from eligibility to provide services on a
reimbursable basis practitioners or institutions that do not meet its standards.

One cannot envisage many details of the coming system very well at
present, for the legislation is ambiguous about many critical issues, and
the program will take time to become truly established. Nonetheless,
several elements of great importance are contained in it which merit
close attention. The legislation requires physicians to institute (1)
rationalized standards for performance, (2) a systematic method for carrying out indirect surveillance of performance, (3) procedures for formal
adjudication of evaluations of performance, and (4) the employment of

discrete economic sanctions. What is required is *the antithesis of the system of social control I described in the medical group, precisely the elements of control that the physicians heatedly rejected.* Essentially, it requires the bureaucratization of social control. And, compatible with bureaucratization, the entire process will be based on a system of written records—presumably the medical record and standardized forms by which the providers specify diagnosis and treatment and also claim service and seek reimbursement. It will be entirely separate from the interaction that goes on between doctors and patients in the course of work, being constructed as an administrative framework above and around it but presuming to measure and control it. It is an indirect, external control system.

THE INADEQUACY OF EXTERNAL CONTROLS

While the scheme may seem to be the answer to the problem of control raised by my description of the inadequate system of the medical group, it is nonetheless likely to accomplish less than is intended. Surely, given our data and their compatibility with the evidence of how physicians responded to Medicare and Medicaid, one may guess that, unless massive changes have taken place over the past few years in the basic attitudes of physicians toward their work, there are likely to be persistent difficulties of some importance in the operation of such a system. This is so because, while it is set up as a framework around day-to-day work, as was the contractual framework of the medical group, it is an indirect form of social control and thus cannot penetrate day-to-day work.

The scheme depends for its viability on the review of records. In order for it to do so, record-production is regarded as an unproblematically faithful reflection of practice rather than a selective construct *from* practice. As we have seen in Chapter 10, a record is a *construction*, not a reflection, of work, and its substance will vary as the purpose of its producer varies (cf. Garfinkel, 1967; Wheeler, 1970). Thompson (1967:124) noted that "distortion of organizational records is a widespread phenomenon. . . . We should expect 'favorable biases' to appear wherever rewards are influenced by records, and alternative ways of reporting are available." While I have no doubt that the requisite records will be forthcoming for review purposes, it seems highly likely that they will reflect not the physicians' actual performance so much as their conception of what is necessary for a record that will at once pass muster and advance their own ends.

Without assuming dishonesty in physicians—indeed, one can assume dedication to serving patient need as the physician sees it—one must nonetheless assume that physicians will not always passively create records, merely to faithfully reflect their activities. Even more than most workers, all of whom struggle to control elements of their work on their own terms, physicians seek to use their own independent judgment in work, and they assign that freedom greater priority than administrative needs. Thus, producing a record for administrative purposes will be less important than doing one's work as one sees fit, so the former will be likely to be manipulated in order to sustain the latter. One must assume that more than one option of what to record will commonly exist and that the physicians will often actively select out of their activities those recordable options that will advance their ends as their judgment determines. In some cases, personal economic ends may be involved; in others, ends of personal convenience in management; in still others, ends of patient benefit as judged by the physician. The record on which the system will rely, therefore, will likely reflect the various stances the physicians assume when they transform their actions into an official set of categories, but it cannot determine the choice of stances.

Furthermore, the scheme assumes that decisions to provide service are made on the basis of essentially technical medical criteria that can be judged objectively as medically necessary and medically unnecessary. But, as we saw in Part II, services can be as much methods of managing patients and colleagues as methods of technical treatment. Medical practice is socially organized work and not simply a technical process. Services are provided as a way of coping with social problems of supply and of demand. While some services were not, by strict technical criteria, medically necessary, at least some physicians considered them to be management devices without the use of which they would be subjected to demands that they did not feel capable of satisfying. The need for such social and psychological safety valves should, in the absence of any really basic changes in practice which could provide alternative management devices, lead to the construction of records in such a way as to justify their use—presumably by the choice of a diagnosis from which justified services follow.

However, such construction may not be necessary if it happens that the norms and standards for acceptable practice laid down by the PSROs are very permissive. Certainly some diagnostic categories, probably only those entailing the most conspicuously expensive services, will be narrowly constrained by standards. Remembering the discussion of mistakes in Chapter Eight, we can also assume that the norms or standards will certainly exclude the blatant, gross, or obvious deviations from common knowledge and practice. But there are likely to be wide limits nonetheless. Provided that these limits are not too narrow, the prudent physician will "naturally" adjust his practice (and claims) accordingly and will do his best to stay within them in order to avoid the inconvenience and embarrassment of having to justify deviation in a direct confrontation with the review group.

Above all, the system, being indirect and dependent on a constructed record, cannot control the stances the physicians take toward their work. Since services will be provided on a fee basis, it will be possible for decisions to be made on the basis of all three of the stances I described earlier in this book. The review system will establish upper and lower statistical limits of acceptable claims, but it will not be able to control how the decision is made to produce records that fall within those limits. The stances I have described may be seen as guiding the physicians' approach to work and choice among alternatives both in performing the work and in constructing its record. Paradoxically, the system will be such that the physicians most likely to run afoul of it will be not only the very small number who are simply stupid, incompetent, or unbalanced but also the physician-expert, who feels obliged to dwell on each case for its own sake, irrespective of gain, rules, and standards. The merchant and the official should be able to adapt without serious difficulty, each on the basis of his own criteria.

No system that cannot strongly reinforce the expert stance is likely to be one fitted to treat human beings as human beings rather than as standardized diagnostic categories. But by its nature the present scheme, using indirect measures of performance created by the participants, cannot determine what spirit the work is performed in, what stance is taken toward the human beings being served. It must be satisfied to deal with the outcome of a process of consultative interaction in the course of which examination takes place and decision rules chosen by which to produce that outcome. But in Part II of this book we saw how the same service-unit outcome could be created by interactions of markedly different qualities, with differences of great importance for the human beings involved. The service-record outcomes of a housecall provided, a diagnosis made, a procedure performed, and a prescription written do not reflect any of the elements involved in the physicians' manner of choosing to provide rather than refuse a service and their manner of presenting their choice to the patient in the light of the context of the patient's request. The service or claim record does not measure the quality of a human encounter: it is too indirect and abstract for that. Only the concrete "examination of [actual] performance . . . provides direct evidence on which to base a performance evaluation, whereas the examination of outcome . . . provides only indirect evidence as to the quality of the performance" (Dornbusch & Scott, 1975:141). In the case of health care, the quality of performance is too important to leave unexamined and unaccountable. A truly adequate system for controlling a service to human beings must be able to control the spirit in which performance is given, the stance toward work. But how could that be done?

ALTERNATIVE METHODS OF CONTROL

Absolute control by an administration over tasks it wishes performed is possible only by elimination of human performers. This, in fact, is one logically possible solution to the problem of controlling the performance of health care—care can be just about completely mechanized. Present-day technology makes this solution possible. Computers could record and analyze the technical substance of patients' complaints and symptoms, could question patients systematically in the course of taking a general health history and a history of the particular complaint, could order and interpret necessary diagnostic tests, and could prescribe necessary drugs even if not, perhaps, actually perform necessary surgery. Programmed on the basis of established standards, a computer would perform exactly as intended, and the records it would keep would be absolutely reliable. The stance would be as programmed.

But such a technically feasible solution is obviously not acceptable on social grounds. Its virtue is only that it carries our thought to a logical extreme by representing the end result of thinking about health care in terms involving the enforcement and control of purely technical standards. Rightly or wrongly, necessarily or unnecessarily, human health care serves diffuse human needs for being comforted and cared for as much as if not more than it serves organic, technically defined needs (cf. Mechanic, 1972:69; Fuchs, 1974:64–67). If the comfort of human interaction were removed from health care by mechanization and patients were treated as mere bodies in the course of such mechanization, medical care would no longer serve most of the needs of today's patients.

The same may be said for a second method by which the performance of medical work could be controlled directly—the retention of human workers while ordering their activities by essentially mechanical principles. There, the bureaucratic principle of rationalized control would be extended directly down into the performance of the concrete tasks of medical care, with every task defined and specified precisely and individual tasks or clusters of tasks arrayed into jobs with identifying job titles and training prerequisites. (For a review of methods of job design and analysis, see Zedeck and Blood, 1974.) Individuals with defined training (most desirably, brief and on-the-job) could be recruited for each job title and assigned to perform their tasks within the limits defined by job description and the operating rules. Careful provision could be made for overseeing their performance by the assignment of supervisors and the requirement of systematic reporting. Even the spirit in which each worker's bit of service was provided to patients could be monitored directly by audiovisual devices, sampled by a special corps of supervisors masquerading as patients, and surveyed by other techniques currently used by commercial service organizations.

Just as the industrialization of the production of material goods destroyed previously skilled jobs and created unskilled and semiskilled jobs, so would the industrialization of health services do the same. And, while industrialization would likely reduce the cost of the production of services, it could do so only by changing the nature of the services. Machine-made shoes are not the same as custom-made shoes any more than the "friendly" manner of a well-trained and supervised flight attendant on a "friendly" airline is the same as the manner of a friend. Life careers in skilled jobs and the special kind of personal commitment that goes with them would be lost, the work itself would become meaningless to those who did it, and the service would be changed to one in which patient needs were categorized and predefined so that services could be applied to them on a categorical basis and in a predictable manner. To my mind, the benefit in efficiency would be less than is warranted by the human cost of turning the patient into an industrial product. In fact, I would argue that only a form of organizing care that permits discretion can constitute a truly human service.

THE IMPORTANCE OF DISCRETION

As Zedeck and Blood (1974:61) put it, "the most important of [organizational policies of job definition] are . . . about the amount of discretion a worker should have in the performance of his task." Discretion is worker control, the antithesis of administrative control. In the automation of tasks, discretion is eliminated; in the industrialization of jobs, discretion is contained within comparatively narrow limits; in the bureaucratization of payment and consultative relationships, as in the medical group, discretion is more free and broad-ranging, though still within defined limits. Discretion represents the degree of freedom and responsibility workers can have in performing their work and is connected with the degree to which they are likely to be alienated from and uncommitted to their work (cf. Blauner, 1964).

Only where there is discretion it is possible to treat each task as an idiosyncratic rather than a standardized problem. In the case of health services, the human patient is the problem whose needs set the task. The amount of discretion granted workers in health care not only reflects a particular conception of their task but also reflects a particular conception of the patient. To the extent that work with patients is reduced to semiskilled tasks defined and governed by formally sustained rules, the patient is reduced to a categorized object. Some degree of objectification or de-individualization in any regular activity such as work is unavoidable (as is some degree of discretion), but only the exercise of discretion allows individualization of the patient. Insofar as we agree that respect for and attention to the dignity and individuality of each patient seeking help is essential to a critical service to human beings such as health care, then we must attempt to maximize, not minimize, the discretion of the health worker.

Discretion on the part of the health worker rather than on the part of those who administer work may thus be taken to be the prerequisite for providing a truly human service. It alone is flexible enough to serve as faithfully as possible the needs of varied individual patients, recognizing and respecting their individuality. But discretion has, as we saw, its dangers. It is more easily subject to abuse than is formally regulated behavior. With the opportunity for discretion goes the possibility of exploitation of the patient, the equal possibilities of being a merchant or an official instead of being an expert or a craftsman. Discretion must, while remaining the core of service, nonetheless be disciplined by a concern for the quality of work in light of the general public and particular patient interest. It cannot be disciplined by administrative rules because such rules either destroy it in the course of regulating it or drive it underground where it cannot be controlled. What is needed for optimal service to human beings is thus not more elaborate and constraining administrative schemes but rather some way of getting workers to discipline themselves in light of the public interest. That is the optimal alternative.

HUMAN SERVICE AND THE FATE OF THE COLLEGIUM

There is a curiously inconsistent quality to many contemporary discussions of health care policies. On the one hand, most cite the strategic role physicians play in providing or controlling the bulk of health services. Fuchs, for example, asserted that "it is impossible to make significant changes in the medical field without changing physician behavior" (Fuchs, 1974:56). In spite of that, however, policy recommendations nonetheless stress *indirect* means of social control that are unlikely to have any significant impact on physician behavior (e.g., the recommendations in Fuchs, 1974: 149–151). "Solutions" are created on the basis of building administrative frameworks *around* that behavior. But it has been apparent for some time that even such a relatively constraining framework as is represented by prepaid group practice fails to control such a critical element of health care as the spirit in which it is provided. Thus, in his sympathetic evaluation of prepaid group practice, Donabedian stated that

> There are two problems that have not been fully solved: how to promote the full flowering of the professional spirit and how to nurture the sensitive personal relationships between professionals and their clients in complex bureaucracies that are governed by impersonal exigencies of their own. (DONABEDIAN, 1969: 25)

I suggest that no formal method of organizing the financing and presentation of health care can solve these problems because, by their nature, formal methods either destroy the possibility for sustaining "sensitive personal relationships" (as is the case in automation or industrialization) or allow discretion without being able to control how it is exercised (as is the case in virtually all present policy schemes in the United States). Formal methods of control rely on formal modes of accounting underneath which can flourish a variety of stances and relationships.

What, then, can be done? Certainly no solution lies in a return to the traditional system of a nominally free market of services within the confines of a medical monopoly. Formal planning of administrative controls over the financing, distribution, and accountability of health service remains necessary and desirable. Also necessary and desirable are a variety of devices designed to provide formal assurance of greater consumer influence on policy-making and day-to-day operation of health care organizations. Both modes of control are likely to improve the *form* of health service. The *spirit* of service, however, can be improved only by changes in those aspects of the everyday milieu of health care which mobilize, activate, and guide the health workers' own unique capacities to exercise collective discipline over their discretionary work.

If the essential criteria of work are qualitative, emphasizing discretion to better serve individual patients, then *direct* observation and control are essential. The collegium, organized collaboratively in a division of labor, has far more potential for undertaking the routine, direct observation of its own performance than does any device of administrative supervision. It is possible for the collegium to exercise supervision as part of its normal work activity. Furthermore, it can do so directly, in the same qualitative terms as work takes place, without the distorting use of administrative artifacts. But, as we have seen, the possibility has not been acted upon. Historically, neither professions nor crafts have been eager to discipline themselves, and they have emphasized more the need for discretion and freedom from interference than the obligation to exercise internal discipline. In order for health workers themselves to serve as the direct source of discipline over discretionary service, within limits properly laid down by public authority, both the organization and the normative foundation of the collegium must be drastically altered.

A group of workers capable of responsibly disciplining their discretionary work must have the commitments often claimed but rarely demonstrated—commitment to using and improving a set of skills and commitment to the use of these skills to advance the public interest. These commitments are mere pieties unless they are accompanied by an additional commitment to carry out an adequate mode of disciplining discretion. Individual self-discipline, often claimed to exist among professionals, is not enough. Without *collective* evaluation and restraint, individual self-discipline is a treacherous foundation for responsible social control. As we have seen, reliance on individual self-discipline easily degenerates into an anarchy of individual opinions, all acceptable because they are said to stem from presumptively conscientious and competent individuals. Neither the standards of good work nor the substance of the public interest are so self-evident that we can assume that well-intentioned persons will individually always make the best choices. *Collective* evaluation is needed for a true system of collegial social control.

As the analytical description of Part III should have demonstrated, however, a collegial system of social control is far more complicated than may at first appear. It has a number of dimensions, including a number of basic, common-sense rules and norms. In contrast to the delinquent community, and its deliberately uncritical and permissive individualism, and to the administrative order, and its formal set of written contracts and work rules, an effective collegial system of social control must involve the formation of a dynamic consensus among colleagues about the boundaries of discretion, a consensus formed in the course of constant interaction over differences of opinion about proper performance. Believing that the free exercise of judgment is necessary for work that serves the requirements of individual patients, the workers must believe also that they are obligated to keep each free judgment honest by keeping it accountable to others and keeping it within collectively determined boundaries that are considerably narrower than expressions of good intent.

Given a set of technical standards and conceptions of mistakes that are sufficiently narrow to avoid protective permissiveness but sufficiently broad to allow discretion, the obligation of a collegium responsible enough for self-government must be both to do its work well and conscientiously as each individual sees it and to be involved in a collective effort to improve the level and direction of everyone's performance. Thus, its legitimate work cannot be solely that of performing technical tasks: collective participation in governing that work is as essential as performing it. It is only a technician who defines his job as simply doing his work. A self-governing worker must consider it to be part of his work to attend to the work of his colleagues while keeping his own work visible to them. Thus, deliberate mutual observation and evaluation of performance must be a legitimate part of responsible etiquette, as must be the obligation to discuss one's observations and evaluations with others. Since they are central to the integrity of the craft and its practice, evaluations must be a matter of open discussion and debate. However, criticism would be simply divisive and destructive if it were carried out in a fashion that attacked an offender's sense of integrity and set him apart from the collegium. Carried out in what some of the group physicians characterized as an educational spirit, aimed at self- and collective improvement for the public good and sustained by the committed climate of the collegium itself, the process could become a type of direct social control that both seeks out and corrects deviation without destroying either discretion or commitment.

My suggestion of how a collegium could operate as a truly responsible, self-governing body can be made only briefly here, for my intent has been less to draw a blueprint than to draw a moral. Certainly a blueprint would have to do more than point out that a new, socially responsible etiquette must replace traditional medical etiquette based on entrepreneurial practice. It would have to contend with the fact that all kinds of specialists—planners and administrators no less than doctors—have a tendency to "confuse the section of reality on which [they are] working with reality itself" (Mannheim, 1948:29). A blueprint would thus have to include provision for the participation of the public in the dynamic interaction of self-governance. It would also have to recognize that the boundaries of health care are not synonymous with the occupational boundaries of medicine and would have to provide for the participation of all members of the health division of labor in the process of mutual evaluation and correction. Furthermore, a blueprint for the transformation of the collegium of health workers would be enhanced by elaboration of a theoretical foundation based on present-day developments in organizational theory which raise critical questions about the adequacy of traditional administrative methods of motivating and controlling performance (e.g., Thompson, 1967; Bennis, 1966; Cartwright, 1965; and Whyte, 1973).

But such detail has no place here, where detail has been used instead to demonstrate that a new blueprint is needed. It has been demonstrated how, underneath the surface of formal frameworks purporting to order performance, performance nonetheless varies in ways crucial to a humane health service. Detail has also been used to demonstrate how, below the purview of formal accounting procedures—at the level of concrete, everyday work—a systematic but uncodified set of habitual understandings and conceptions shared by the participants sustains a process of social control which permits, and even encourages, performance undesired by formal plans. It is on the basis of such detail that the moral is drawn: The quality of health care can be truly transformed only by transforming the process by which health workers exercise everyday control over their own work.

*

Appendixes on the Study

The Study of a Group Practice

The study I report here was a qualitative study, a study in depth rather than a broad survey. As such, its evaluation poses a problem to the reader. Insofar as the study was qualitative, my report of it must by the nature of the case be in a form that can easily appear to be merely anecdotal—that is to say, a form that can be discounted as being arbitrary in its selection of information to report, as being no better than the special pleading of ideologues and official spokesmen. And insofar as some of the substance of what it reports contradicts the cherished assumptions or assertions of persons committed to one or another policy alternative, it can easily appear to be merely "muckraking"—that is to say, an unbalanced or biased report deliberately designed to display the vices of an institution without sufficient regard for its virtues.

It is for this reason that a discussion of my methods of research, analysis, and reporting is essential. Only by becoming familiar with my methods of collecting data can readers evaluate how much to believe what they read—how much is avoidable bias and subjectivity and how much is in all likelihood true. Thus, reading my description of the development of the study, they will be able to see that, while there were some preexisting ideas brought to the study, the questions that were asked of the physicians were more often than not based on comments and problems that the physicians, not the researchers, raised. A serious attempt was made to allow the physicians themselves to define the issues to be probed in detail in the interviews. This was one reason why the original research proposal to study group practice did not reflect in very great detail what it was that was actually studied.

By the same token, only by attending to my method of analyzing the data can readers be in a position to evaluate honestly the extent to which the exposition is representative of the information collected or is merely anecdotal. Thus, in my description of the method of analyzing and reporting the data, readers will see that while there was necessary selectivity in displaying of data (as there is in presenting only a few statistical tables out of the hundreds available to survey studies), there was a systematic method of attempting to avoid arbitrary selection. Ultimately, of course, just as readers of reports of quantitative studies must have faith that the few tables of statistics that have been presented to represent the main findings are neither invented nor unrepresentative, so readers must have faith here. They have a better foundation for such faith, however, when they have been able to understand exactly how I collected information and later analyzed it. This method is what I shall describe now.

THE GENESIS OF THE STUDY

To be able to study group practice requires a point of access to a concrete institution. I was lucky enough to have developed a friendly relationship with two men who were able to serve as sponsors and gain me access to two separate medical groups, one urban and the other rural. On the strength of that contact, I carried out some exploratory interviews with a few physicians in the groups and then applied for federal support in 1960. After revisions recommended by the research grant review committee—revisions that stressed the exploratory character of the proposed study—the revised proposal, which appears as Appendix A, was approved and funded. Work on the study was begun in January 1961.

Initially, I attempted to get an overall picture of both medical groups by interviewing key administrative personnel at some length about group operations and in the urban medical group, to which I could easily commute, by beginning to observe as many meetings of the group physicians as I could find out about and to which I could gain access. In the interviews with the administrative personnel, I moved as quickly as I could from the role of a fairly passive but appreciative and sympathetic listener who had to occasionally ask questions because of his ignorance of fundamental information about the operation of the medical group to the role of a rather more active questioner, probing behind comments that did not seem consistent with what I had already heard. In attending physician meetings, I served almost entirely as a passive observer, taking notes on the spot where possible or otherwise retiring to write notes immediately after the meeting's end. As an observer, I tried to become familiar with group affairs and to learn the names and the idiosyncracies of the various physicians present. I routinely mapped seating arrangements and interaction patterns in my notebook so as to get some hint of friendships and alliances among the physicians.

As it happened, the rural medical group went through an organizational crisis that led to the suggestion that I delay my study until such time as things quieted down. This suggestion was received with relief, for it was a long drive and I had no funds to allow me to stay overnight. Once the magnitude of the task of doing a field study of the urban medical group became apparent, I gave up any idea at all of returning to the rural group. The project, then, was reduced to the study of one large urban medical group with a prepaid-service-contract plan.

THE INTERVIEWS

After three months of attending meetings, listening to physicians talk over lunch, interviewing key administrative personnel, and gaining familiarity with and recognition from many of the physicians in the group, it seemed time to begin formal interviews. The full-time physicians engaged in primary practice—pediatricians and internists by training, all eligible for specialty board certification even if some had not yet been certified—were clearly those in the first line of practice in that most patients saw them initially, and theirs was the task to refer patients to virtually all of the other specialists who served as consultants. Most of them, furthermore, were full time, unlike the consultants. They were the logical physicians to start with.

The first interview schedule was designed to get the physicians interested in talking to me, to obtain information about them as individuals, and, most important of all, to gain some preliminary idea of the work problems that concerned them the most along with hints of how I should explore them in later interviews. At this time and on subsequent occasions, the sequence of individuals to be interviewed was established largely on the basis of my estimate of their willingness to be interviewed and their friendliness, articulateness, and frankness. I felt that the less accessible physicians would be easier to interview after I had refined the interview and gotten familiar with the subject matter and after they had learned that many of their colleagues had already been interviewed.

Virtually every interview was tape-recorded, always with the physician's knowledge and consent. The interviews were not literally transcribed, however, both to avoid the transcription of identifying material and to cope with the fact that technical recording conditions were often very poor. Instead, while listening to the interview through headphones, I (and later also my colleague, Buford Rhea) would dictate it into a transcription machine. The rule of dictation was to reproduce the original interview as literally and passively as possible while changing the names of individuals into predetermined code numbers so that the typescript of the interviews could contain no identifying information. The interview schedule used for this first step in the process of obtaining systematic empirical information from the physicians appears in Appendix B, along with those interview schedules that followed it during the course of the study.

Buford Rhea joined the study as my research associate at about the time of my completing the first interviews of the primary practitioners. Upon beginning to interview the consultants, all of whom were part time, unlike most of the primary practitioners, we discovered that because they were part time they had comparatively little to say about their careers in group practice or even about problems of work in the medical group. This fact provided us with time and opportunity to probe further on problems with patients, doing so on the basis of what we were learning from reading and discussing the earlier interviews and attending meetings and luncheon conversations.

The first interview with the consultants provided us with enough material to be able to move directly into the second interview with the primary practitioners, an interview devoted almost entirely to problems of patient management. After sending a memorandum notifying the doctors that we would call them again shortly and that we would be asking about problems of patient management, we launched directly into the series of interviews. By this time, Buford Rhea and I were dividing the load of interviewing equally, selecting the individuals each would interview on the basis of our judgement of compatibility or effectiveness.

By the nature of the case, as we probed problems with patients we inevitably elicited much material about the insuring organization, what we call pseudonymously in this book the "medical-surgical plan," or MSP. Patients could complain to or threaten to complain to the insurance office, and the latter could in turn seek an explanation from the medical group and the physician involved. We examined the insurance contract on the basis of which patients could insist on their rights, and we obtained information from the administration of the medical group about its experience with patient complaints. Such material, in conjunction with the physicians' spontaneous remarks about the problem of patient complaints, prepared us for formulating a third set of interviews for the primary practitioners which focused on their view of and response to the role of formal contractual and administrative elements in their work. The third set of interviews also focused on what was becoming the central issue of our study—the supervision and control of physician performance.

Prior to formulating the interview schedule on administrative relations, however, it seemed time for us to begin digging more aggressively into some of the more delicate issues of the medical group. For over six months we had been attending Executive Committee meetings and almost all formal family doctor (internist) meetings. At these meetings, issues occasionally involving the competence, but more often the conscientiousness, of individual physicians were sometimes brought up and discussed. In the course of formal interviews and informal discussion at lunch, we heard and recorded gossip about incidents not dealt with at meetings. We had by then examined confidential records and the patient complaint files. More and more we began to feel that our information about what went on in the group was reliable and that we had an accurate sense of how the group actually operated. But the question of validity remained nonetheless. It was possible that we were obtaining superficial information. Certainly we felt that not every physician we spoke to had been entirely open and frank, particularly when it came to discussing colleague performance. Not only were we rather unsure about the method we should use in interviewing the physicians about such delicate topics as supervision, discipline, mistakes at work, ethical lapses, and their evaluation of their colleagues, but also we were unsure about our capacity to judge whether or not individuals were being frank and open. We felt the need for an independent source of information to allow us to judge better the information we got from within the group and for a proving ground for the interviews we wanted to conduct.

Physicians who had once worked in the group but had then left were seen as a potential source of validation of our data and our interview methods. Since they were no longer connected with the group, some having been encouraged to leave and others having left for personal reasons that did not reflect on them or the group, we felt that from them we could obtain a somewhat less defensive picture of group work. Some might even be hostile about the shortcomings they perceived in group

practice or about the way they themselves were treated by their colleagues: those interested in giving us "the dirt" might produce information we had not obtained from physicians inside. In short, we reasoned
that if the physicians we interviewed in the group were glossing over
much of what went on, defensively giving only the "official" picture, at
least some of the physicians who had left the group were likely to be
more open and critical. Furthermore, while interviewing those who had
left the group, we could try out various methods of probing and of
seeking evaluations of the administration and their former colleagues
without fear that our initial ineptitude might lead to repercussions
against our study within the medical group.

The names of all those who had been members of the medical group
for at least a year were collected. We prepared an interview schedule (a
copy of which is in Appendix B, with the other schedules) for them
which attempted to obtain an abbreviated view of their careers, the
reasons why they left the group, the circumstances surrounding their
departure, their problems of patient management in the group, their
evaluation of the administration and its role in governing the group, and
their view of colleague interaction, both in the form of referrals and
consultation and in their evaluation of their former colleagues' performance. While it was sometimes arduous, we were successful in interviewing all but 4 of the 35 former group members that we could locate in
the metropolitan area.

On the whole, the interviews with those physicians who had left the
group did not yield any startling new material. On occasion individuals
provided us with new insights and ideas, but by and large they yielded
rather little more than what we had already learned. Their evaluation of
work in the medical group was very much like that of those who remained in the group. Thus, we felt more secure about the accuracy of
the material we had collected within the medical group and about the
quality of our rapport with group physicians. The experience we got in
probing delicate issues also led us to feel that we were reasonably well
prepared to avoid serious incidents in the remainder of the study. After
completing our interviews with the physicians who had left the group,
therefore, we formulated a new schedule and launched directly into
discussions with the group doctors designed to deal more directly and at
greater length and depth with the role of the administration in regulating
the affairs of the group. As had become our custom, we asked questions
toward the end of the interview which dealt with the issues we planned

to take up in the next interview. The schedule prepared for the consultants was very much the same as the one for the primary practitioners, modified slightly to reflect their different work problems.

By the time these interviews were completed, we were into the second year of fieldwork. Everyone in the medical group knew who we were, and some group physicians tried to enlist us as allies or consultants for one or another issue. Most of the doctors had come to trust our ability to keep secrets, though one or two continued to the very end of the study to call our tape recorders "blackmail boxes" and to ask jocularly whether or not we had "bugged" their offices. We could no longer rely on asserting our ignorance in order to gain the right to ask for detailed explanations and concrete examples. On the whole, we had to shift to a quasi-colleague role that allowed us to challenge facts asserted in conversation or interview, tease gently when we felt evasiveness was obvious, and even bully a bit to obtain direct answers.

Nonetheless, we were quite anxious about the last interview we planned, since it focused on matters about which physicians feel the greatest sensitivity—their evaluation and control of the quality of the performance of their colleagues, and vice versa. We were concerned lest a wrong step on our part stimulate general outrage among the physicians of the group which could lead to refusal to be interviewed further. So in spite of our feeling of rapport with the group physicians at this point, we prepared as carefully as we could for the final interview, trying out ideas and techniques on those physicians we could be sure of, dividing up the interview load on the basis of our agreement as to which of us might be able to deal with which physicians most effectively, and planning the sequence of individuals to be interviewed so that the most cooperative and most strategically located physicians would be interviewed first, thereby minimizing the possibility of unpleasant incidents as well as the number of interviews that would be lost should the study collapse. In an effort to prevent the circulation of disturbing rumors about what we were asking in that final interview, we requested of physicians we spoke to that they not tell their colleagues what was discussed. And so, about a year after beginning the first interviews, we launched into the last.

The final interviews went without incident, in spite of our fears. In more cases than we found plausible, however, there was expression of ignorance about colleagues which was used to justify failure to answer many of our questions. We tried to overcome these expressions of ignorance by asking the physicians to make guesses when they were unsure, but we felt we could not push very hard because ignorance was in fact a genuine and informative possibility. So ended the final interviewing of the field study, though field observations and informal interviewing continued into 1963.

PROCESSING THE INTERVIEW DATA FOR ANALYSIS

By the end of the period of interviewing, we had carried out some 200 separate interviews with physicians and had had them transcribed into typescript. Something had to be done to these thousands of pages of typescript so as to make them available for systematic rather than anecdotal analysis and reporting. Each of the interviews was read, and sections of them which seemed to be distinct incidents, anecdotes, or stated opinions about discrete topics were dictated literally from the interview onto tape along with identification in code of the persons being interviewed, the interview number, and the page number of the typescript so that the context of the selection could be returned to and examined in case of doubts about its meaning. These dictated sections were then typed on 5 × 7 McBee-Keysort cards on which were printed general topical categories to guide coding. Buford Rhea then read all the cards and tentatively classified them into the simple content categories we had decided on in advance. He then read them again so as to test, revise, and refine the initial gross classification as well as to classify them into finer subcategories. The cards were reviewed once again, and then they were punched.

Developing categories for content analysis is an essentially arbitrary process. We deliberately chose redundancy and multiple classification in order to avoid the possibility of excluding potentially relevant material by overnarrow and overrefined coding. Once punched, the cards could be sorted fairly rapidly, and we could be fairly certain that we would not miss anything said in the interviews about some particular topic even if we had to pay the price of having to go over many more cards for some particular topic than would be the case if we were to have used a less gross form of categorization. In any event, it should be remembered that, in the analysis of this book, the cards rather than the typescript of the interviews were used, for by use of the cards we could be systematic and minimize subjectivity and bias in collating and reporting the data.

CREATING THE EXPOSITION

In the preparation of this book, all cards bearing on some general substantive topic such as "patient relations" were removed from the total set of cards and put together in a pack. All the cards in that large pack of between 800 and 1,200 were then read one by one. Notes were taken on the content so that the total range of data they conveyed would be recorded. And as they were read, the cards were sorted into preliminary topical files. They were then read again, each pile "cleaned" by resorting of cards where appropriate or simply shuffling them back into the general topical deck to be examined again. The resultant piles were read again and reclassified and at the same time divided into subcategories or subpiles. They were then read through another time, odds and ends were cleaned up, and the cards were arranged as piles in the form of a topical exposition of what was said by the physicians. In some cases, of course, a card could contain material that was equally relevant to more than one topic. Such cards were marked by a paper clip so that, once used for one topic, they could be placed in the other pile to which they were relevant and their information included.

The piles of cards were then arranged into a descriptive exposition, and a rough draft of summary and connective exposition was written. Many of the cards, though not all, were xeroxed and pasted into the expository text to serve as evidence of the data upon which the summary exposition was based. All statements in all the exposition could thus be made with the assurance that interview material existed to sustain them. The evidence for any exceptions to a statement was also at hand for inspection and, where appropriate, for presentation and discussion. More than half of this first, basic draft was composed of the raw interview material, the first draft chapters being over 100 pages in length. These chapters constituted the working draft from which this book developed.

The procedure for developing this book lay largely in rearrangement of sections, drastic reduction in the raw interview material quoted, and supplementation of the interview data by observational, documentary, and other available material. Only a minute fraction of available quotations from the field material has been preserved in the exposition. In

choosing what to include I have followed the rule that no quotation
would be used more than once and that the quotation to be used would
be chosen on the basis of its unusual articulateness in expressing a view
that is representative of the group for which the individual speaks. The
quotations in the text, therefore, are at best token evidence of the material on which the exposition is based. Given the systematic manner by
which the data were sorted and arrayed, however, the illustrative quotations may be taken express the character of the evidence collected by
the field study.

THE VALIDITY OF THE STUDY

Finally, it is necessary to address the question of how far one can
believe this book and how relevant it is to today's issues. The study is
not, after all, a sample survey that can claim statistical representativeness for its subjects and that can present its data in a rhetorically impres-
sive quantitative form. Furthermore, its data were collected more than
10 years before its date of publication. Does the study have any relevance for today, or is it merely history?

There is first the issue of representativeness. Assuming that I have
been careful enough and systematic enough to have gained a true picture
of the way the physicians I studied conceived of their problems of work
and sought to cope with them, can that picture be taken to portray how
other physicians, who were not studied, respond to their work? In the
strictly statistical sense, the answer can only be negative. The medical
group was studied because it represented a comparatively rare type
lauded by the avant-garde of medical policy-makers and because I happened to be able to gain access to it. The medical group was not randomly drawn as a sample of a defined universe nor can its physicians be
considered to be statistically representative of all those who work in such
a special kind of practice, let alone all physicians in practice.

There is more to truth or validity than statistical representativeness,
however. Statistical representativeness merely attempts to provide assurance that the entire variety of persons in a universe is sampled, with
the criteria by which that variety is defined—that is, the basis for
sampling—depending on the purpose of the study. In some cases, the
assumption is that one is studying basic processes common to all human
being or all primates or all vertebrates—as in much psychological and

biological research—and sampling is considered unimportant. Only when one assumes significant variation among individuals and when one is concerned with describing that range of variation accurately is sampling necessary.

In this study I am less concerned with describing the range of variation than I am with describing in the detail what survey questionnaire methods do not permit to be described—the assumptions, behavior, and attitudes of a very special set of physicians. They are interesting *because* they were special. They were better trained than average and, what is more important, most were committed to a form of practice that was in the avant-garde of social policy. In this sense, how they coped with their problems and how they exercised social control over one another's performance might be taken to represent something close to the characteristic orientations of the most cooperative and most committed of the physicians who are now carrying out progressive social programs. The medical group was studied before Medicare legislation was passed, at a time when most community physicians served patients who were not insured for out-of-hospital health services and who therefore paid the doctor out of their own pockets. Prepaid group practices were surrounded by hostile, entrepreneurial colleagues and often were harassed by local medical societies as being a form of unfair competition. Some of the group physicians ascribed the loss of some of their erstwhile physician friends to disapproval of prepaid practice as "socialism."

The climate for prepaid group practice in the medical community today is considerably more temperate, even if not exactly enthusiastic. And those physicians who routinely deal with Medicare and Medicaid patients today are considerably more accustomed to and accepting of bureaucratic modes of billing and payment than they were in the early 1960s. Furthermore, it is claimed that the young physicians of today, who finished their training in the late 1960s, are more socially conscious—that they are a new breed that is likely to respond to new modes of medical practice in a markedly different way than did earlier generations, including the generation I studied. Even if we assume this to be true—and the evidence to support it is rather modest (cf. Goldman, 1974; Colombotos, 1975)—we must recall that the majority of the physicians I studied joined the medical group and stayed precisely because they approved of its humane and rational principles of financing and organizing care. In this sense, if the newest generation of physicians is in fact much more socially conscious than the older generation, more open to government programs and to peer-review processes, then the physicians of the medical group were precursors of the new rather than representatives of the old. Thus, I would argue that my findings have reasonable grounds for relevance to the present decade.

If one can accept this study for the strategic rather than representative value of the case it focuses on, one is still left with questions about the accuracy and faithfulness of the analysis. Some of these questions can be resolved by assessing my description of our method of collecting, analyzing, and reporting it as well as by critically reading the report itself for the internal consistency of its content. To assess the validity of what I report for physicians *other than* those I studied requires rather different evidence, however. Essentially, it requires comparing what I report for those I studied with the reports of others who have studied other physicians and practices.

Throughout this book I have attempted to assess the validity and relevance of my findings by referring to the information about physicians which became available since the study was concluded. I argue that the evidence that does exist largely supports the generalizability and relevance of my findings to today's issues. Unfortunately, however, while some excellent empirical studies have appeared, there is still a paucity of systematically collected information about the psychology and sociology of everyday community medical practice. I cited those studies that have comparative information, but on the whole the kind of data I present stand alone. In this sense, there is often no other available evidence by which to either confirm or contradict my findings. I have done the best I could to display my evidence here. It might be hoped, therefore, that those who would take issue with it can supply the systematic and reliable evidence that supports their views.

DEVICES FOR PROTECTING IDENTITY

I gained the cooperation of the physicians who were studied by assuring that their identities would be protected. In writing this book, therefore, all identifying materials have been either eliminated or systematically altered or, in special cases, randomly altered. The physicians were assigned code numbers at the time of their first interview. Throughout the text, code numbers rather than names are used. (Code numbers preceded by "L," incidentally, refer to physicians who had left the group.) In general, one can put together the collection of quotations ascribed to one code number and get a faithful picture of the style and range of an individual's response to group practice. But on some occasions in which material reflects negatively on an individual and the individual is still alive and associated with the medical group, I have not hesitated to falsify code numbers and jumble the events described so as to prevent positive identification by readers in and around the medical group. Sex has been disguised in order to avoid identification of the minority of female physicians. I have also avoided identifying individual specialties, if only because in many cases only one or two persons served as consultants in particular specialties. Only the distinction between primary practitioners (internists and pediatricians) and consultants (other specialists) is made in the text, though some cited interview material clearly identifying specialty was let stand when it seemed harmless.

APPENDIX A:
Proposal to Study Group Practice

---

1. RESEARCH PLAN[1]

a. Specific Aims

The proposed research is aimed at exploring the significance of informal organization among physicians to the practice of medicine in two medical groups. "Informal organization" designates aspects of organization that are independent of official administrative authority. Informal organization is manifested both in the existence of patterns of informal interaction that are independent of official positions and "channels," and in attitudes towards work and procedures used in work that are shared by members of those informal groups but that may be unknown to or unrecognized by the official spokesmen for the organization. It is proposed to do an exploratory study of such informal organization in two medical groups so as to be able to determine the value of more extensive future study. The proposed exploratory study will try to answer the questions: In what areas of the group practices studied is informal organization most important in influencing physician behavior? How does informal organization bear on the exchange of medical information among colleagues and in this sense on the technical medical procedures used for particular illnesses or complaints? Most particularly to be emphasized: How does informal organization bear on the physicians' attitudes towards patients and the way they deal with them—that is, bear on patient care?

b. Methods of Procedure

Two medical groups to which access has already been obtained and cooperation assured will be studied—one an urban, prepayment-

---

[1]This is an exact copy of the original proposal, in the form and with the headings suggested by the granting agency.

276

service-contract group and the other a semirural fee-for-service group. Both groups offer a full range of medical services, and in both the physicians are salaried. The differences between these two groups are considered to be particularly valuable for exploratory study, for they should yield some hints of how the significance of informal organization may vary under one circumstance or another. Such a view of potential variety will be invaluable in the planning of a future proposed questionnaire study of a larger number of group practices.

The major method of study to be used will be the focused interview. The interview will cover a number of areas.

(1) Physicians of the groups will be interviewed at some length and depth about their careers in the medical group. They will be asked, for example, how they came to join the group, what other career alternatives were considered, and what consequences they felt their choice has had on their relations with physicians and institutions outside the medical group. Such questions as these will establish a broad context for the understanding of their relations with their colleagues within the group and attitudes towards the group and group practice. The questions will be significant to the study because it is expected that commitment to group practice will vary considerably among the physicians and will play some part in their association with other physicians and their attitude towards and practice of their work.

(2) The greatest amount of attention in the interviews will be focused on the range of problems the physicians perceive in their work—in the use of technical facilities, in formal consultation and referral, in diagnosis and treatment, and most particularly in management of patients. In this last instance, it is expected that patients' requests for housecalls and emergency consultations will be considered to be something of a problem, as will the management of so-called demanding or overanxious patients. How such problems are viewed and handled seems important to any assessment of the quality of patient care. In the case of each problem the physician may discuss, he will be asked to give a concrete example so that vague generalities are avoided and discussion of the full implications of the problem is encouraged. The physician will be asked how he dealt with that concrete problem at the time and how he thinks his colleagues deal with the problem. He will also be asked what he believes to be the cause of the problem, insofar as it is not purely medical or technical.

These questions on the physician's problems of practice will establish the areas of work in which arises the *content* of informal organization—the attitudes and procedures for dealing with problems that are unrecognized or not solved by the officially stated aims and procedures of the administrative organization. When a number of physicians are found to perceive the same problems and to solve them in the same way—that is, when we find shared norms—it will become possible to begin outlining the informal organization of the medical group.

(3) Additional questions in these focused interviews will seek information on the physician's relation to his colleagues. The physician will be asked with whom he discusses—not only in formal consultation, but as well in informal chats during working and leisure hours—the problems he mentioned. He will also be asked who his friends are among physicians outside the group. Answers to such questions as these will make it possible to establish the *structure* of informal organization that sustains and reinforces its content.

To summarize, two essential variables will be explored by means of the focused interview: (1) What are hypothesized to be dependent variables consist in the way in which physicians perceive and attempt to solve their problems of practice in two medical groups. The interviews are designed to explore in depth precisely what these problems and solutions are and in particular what their implications are for the quality of patient care. (2) What are hypothesized to be independent variables consist in the informal relation of the group physician to his colleagues, a relation that in an industrial context has proved to explain much of the process by which the perception and solutions of problems of work emerge and come to be shared by the workers. The interviews are designed to explore the ramifications of informal colleague relations to the way in which group medicine is practiced.

Very little is known in depth about group medical practice. The lengthy focused interviews of the proposed research are designed to yield a portion of such intensive knowledge. That knowledge of the problems of practice and the range of physician attitudes towards these problems in two medical groups will provide a basic body of descriptive information and analytical insight. During the first year this necessary body of data will be recorded, transcribed, coded, analyzed, and independently checked by observation of staff meetings, small staff groups at lunch, administrative records, and the like. Once this is done, it will be possible to construct a questionnaire designed to subject hypotheses about the significance of informal organization to quantitative test. This is the second step, scheduled for the second year of the proposed research.

The questionnaire will gather three basic groups of information for attempted statistical correlation: (1) information on the background and training of the physician; (2) using sociometric techniques, information on the relation of the physician to his colleagues—whom he is close to, whom he seeks advice from, and so on; (3) using the critical incident technique (by which a plausible problem situation is described and the physician asked how he would handle it) as well as direct questions about his attitudes towards his patients, colleagues, and medical group, the physician's way of perceiving and coping with his problems of practice will be elicited. Since the content of the questionnaire depends upon the exploratory interviews, the precise hypotheses to be tested cannot be specified realistically at this time. This will be done at the time of our anticipated request for continuation of funds. At present, however, the three categories of information above should indicate the areas in which hypotheses can be formulated and tested.

The first year of the proposed research will be spent in interviewing at some length all the physicians in both of the medical groups (about 75 in all), a sample of 25 to 50 physicians who have left the medical groups, and some of the administrative personnel. Time will also be consumed by coding and analyzing of the interview material. If the results of that exploratory research are encouraging, and if it seems likely that the findings of the study may have relevance to the practice of medicine in other medical groups, application will be made for continuation of funds. We will ask for such continuation in order to develop the questionnaire described above and to use it to make a study of the role of informal organization in group medical practice in a considerably greater number and variety of medical groups.

c. Significance of This Research

In sociological studies of a variety of work organizations, the nature of the informal organization of work has proved to be as significant as or even more significant to the quantitative and qualitative character of production than have such formal factors as the mode of compensation, the table of organization, and other aspects of the formal or official organization of authority and responsibility. If informal organization is found to be a significant variable in group medical practice, then it follows that, in order to create or maintain practices that produce what is believed to be a high quality of patient care, it will be necessary to penetrate the formal selective and administrative devices of the medical group by focusing on those sub-official aspects of group practice that stimulate the development of the kind of behavior that sustains high quality. The exploratory research proposed here, while it is hardly able to take all possible variables into consideration, would allow a tentative assessment of the potential importance of informal organization to group medical practice and tentative suggestion of ways of using informal organization to maintain a high quality of patient care in the two groups studied. The research that may follow the exploratory study should allow even more precision in such assessment and suggestion.

APPENDIX B:
Interview Schedules

April 1961

First Interview, Primary Practitioners: BACKGROUND

Introduce tape recorder and method of preserving confidence.

1. Where did you go to medical school? Date of graduation. Where intern (dates, type)? Where resident (dates, type)? Any practice before joining medical group? Describe.
2. Career alternatives considered in med school, intern, residency.
3. Events surrounding choice made. If not medical group initially, events leading up to med gp job. What did you hear about the group, from whom? How about its MSP connection—what did you know about that?
4. What did you actually expect when you took the job with the group—what kind of patients did you think you'd have, what kind of colleagues, what kind of educational and clinical opportunities, what were the problems you expected to have? On what basis did you have that expectation—who told you, etc.?
5. Considering your experience and what you expected, in what ways were you "green" when you joined the group? What techniques did you have to learn, and what did you have to learn to adjust to?
6. Now full-time? If not, ever full-time? If not, what proportion time in group? Why do you keep it? If full-time, gross annual income from FFS patients. Has it grown or slackened over time?
7. What's your hospital rank? Should it really be higher now? If yes, to what do you ascribe that?
8. Ever met hostility in hospital because of your group job? Describe concretely. How about hostility from other medical people you meet outside the hospital? Describe completely.
9. Do you have any good friends who are in solo practice? Local? How do they look on your MSP affiliation and group job? Have you ever had to defend gp practice to them? Have you ever tried to sell them on group practice? Situation in which you defended and/or sold. Do they seem to have any problems in their practice? What are they?

10. Present satisfaction with MG job. What's the worst side of working here? What's the best part? Do you plan to stay? Hopes for future?

June 1961

First Interview, Consultants

Confidentiality, permission to tape.

1. Events leading up to medical group job. Initial private practice and its problems. What did you take into consideration before joining the group? MSP an element?
2. What didn't you anticipate about work in the group? What adjustments required? Probe thoroughly.
3. What proportion of your time is presently with the group? Proportion of annual income from group? Plan to stay?
4. Ever met hostility because of your group affiliation? Hospital? Outside? Examples. Probe. Does your group affiliation mean referrals from some physicians are lacking?
5. All things considered, advantages and disadvantages of solo practice. Group practice. Do you think your colleagues by and large share your views? Any problems in each unique to your specialty? Examples.
6. What's the most upsetting (annoying) experience you've ever had with a patient in the group?
7. Which of the below have you experienced? Often? Give examples of such patient behavior and tell how you handled the situation.
    a. Called in an outside doctor for another opinion. How did you find out?
    b. Came in asking for a test or procedure ordered by an outside doctor.
    c. Tried to insist on an emergency appointment even though you didn't think it was an emergency.
    d. Complained to you he was kept waiting too long.
    e. Tried to get you to prescribe what he wanted.
    f. Asked for a consult with another doctor in your specialty.
    g. Kept insisting he needed diagnostic tests or procedures you didn't think necessary.
    h. Began complaining about his family doctor or pediatrician to you.
    i. Threatened to complain to MSP about your treatment.
8. Have you ever asked a patient to leave your office? Describe incident. Example of patients you wish wouldn't come but do. How do you try to discourage them?

9. Compared to other doctors in your specialty, do you think you have more or less trouble handling patients? On what basis do you have your impression?

August 1961

SECOND INTERVIEW, PRIMARY PRACTITIONERS: PATIENT RELATIONS

1. What's the most upsetting experience you've ever had with a patient? Probe.
2. The following have sometimes upset physicians. Which have you experienced? In each case give detailed examples of how you handled the situation.
   a. Tried to insist you make a housecall you didn't think necessary.
   b. Tried to insist on an immediate appointment even though you didn't think it an emergency.
   c. Came in complaining you kept him waiting too long.
   d. Called in an outside doctor for a housecall after you said it was unnecessary. How did you find out?
   e. Called in an outside doctor for another opinion. How did you find out?
   f. Came in for you to authorize a test ordered by an outside doctor.
   g. Kept saying he needed penicillin or in some other way tried to get you to prescribe what he wanted.
   h. Kept feeling he needed lab tests you didn't think necessary.
   i. Kept feeling he needed a consult with specialist you didn't think necessary; immediate specialist consult without your work-up.
   j. Asked for a consult with another doctor in your own specialty.
   k. The above have been examples of how the patient might try to get you to do what he wants, but I imagine you might sometimes have problems getting patients to do what you want—resistant patients who simply won't follow your advice even when you know it's dangerous for them. How do you handle them? Examples.
3. Have you ever asked a patient to leave your office? Your panel? Describe incidents. Example of patients you wish would leave but don't. How do you try to discourage them?
4. Ever asked to make a housecall or see a patient of a colleague? Who asked you? What was the problem? Did you discuss it with the colleague? Did you see the patient? How did you manage him?
5. Sometimes when a patient complaint is received in the office, the doctor is asked to call the patient and cool him off. Have you ever been asked to do this? Describe the incident in detail.

6. By and large, do you get along well with your patients? Do you get many gifts from them? Probe. Complaints? Probe.
7. Have you asked people in the front office to let you know when any patient complains or requests transfer out of your panel? Probe.
8. How would you solve the housecall problem in the group?

October 1961

INTERVIEW SCHEDULE FOR PHYSICIANS WHO HAVE LEFT THE GROUP

1. Sketch your medical career to date: medical school, internships, residencies, etc. How did you come to join the group? Was group practice what you expected it to be? Were there any problems of adjustment?
2. Why did you leave the group? What factors were most important in reaching your decision? Who influenced you? Was there anything about the group that you were reluctant to leave? How did your colleagues react to your decision? The administration? Looking back, is there anything you miss about group practice? What would induce you to go back? Knowing what you know now, would you join again if you were in the same situation as when you first joined?
3. Did you have any problems with patients which you felt were functions of the group situation itself? What was your most annoying experience with patients? How was it handled? Did patients ever complain about you? What were the complaints typically about? Do things like that happen in your private practice? (Probe: Is this due to group practice or prepayment?)
4. How well do you think the administration handled these patient problems? (Grade.) Were they ever useful to you? Did they ever put pressure on you to satisfy patient demands? Did MSP? Did the group knuckle under to MSP pressures? Did the administration ever intrude into purely medical affairs?
5. In general, did the existence of an administrative set-up have any influence on the way you practice? Were there any ways that the administration could check up on you? (Probe: How about audit of charts?) Do you think there should be more or less of these kinds of control? Do you think the administration had a fairly accurate idea of what sort of work you were doing? How did they know? (Or why didn't they?) How would you grade the administration on encouraging high quality of medical care?
6. How responsive was the administration to physicians' suggestions and complaints? (Grade.) Did the Executive Committee have any

influence? What did it do? What should it have done? What issues were most important while you were there? Did factions form? Who led them? Were there "ins" and "outs" among the physicians? (Probe: What did in or out entail?)

7. Here are some other problems which may arise when a group of physicians must work together. Did you ever encounter any of them? Examples. What did you do about it? (Probe: Who did you discuss it with? To whom did you complain publicly or privately?) Were there any other such problems?
   a. Referrals: Is it true that family doctors and pediatricians are inclined to fob patients off on specialists? Did specialists resist?
   b. Exchange of information: Did specialists keep family doctors informed? Did family doctors give adequate work-ups?
   c. Advice and assistance (including consultations) from colleagues.
   d. Sloughing off work on colleagues: postponing housecalls until off duty, getting difficult patients to transfer to someone else's panel, etc. (Probe for varieties.)

8. Physicians obviously differ in a great many ways. I am interested in just how judgments are formed about group doctors: what things are important and how you get information about them. For example, how were you able to evaluate the technical ability of other doctors? (Probe: Did this influence the way you yourself behaved?) Were comparisons made of number of housecalls? Punctuality? Speed of processing patients? How well physicians got along with their patients? What else?

9. Summing up, what kind of person is likely to be attracted to working in a group? What criteria would you see if you were hiring physicians for a medical group? (Probe: Would you give technical brilliance priority over ability to get along with patients? With colleagues?)

November 1961

THIRD INTERVIEW, PRIMARY PRACTITIONERS: ADMINISTRATION

1. What's the administration for? What are the most important problems you have taken up with any of the administrative personnel— director, assistant director, business manager, etc.? (Probe for details.) What problems *should* you be able to take to them?

2. Here is a list of typical patient complaints. In each case I would like to know how the people in the front office *should* handle them: Should an investigation be made of the complaint before its final disposition, and if so, who should do the investigating first? Should

the doctor be asked for an explanation, or should the investigation be confined to a check of the records? If an investigation is not in order, what do you think should be done? (Apologize? Give the patient what he wants? Ask him to leave the group?)

a. Doctor late for appointment or cancelled.
b. Unable to get an immediate appointment. (Doctor didn't think an emergency.)
c. No housecall: no temperature, but patient afraid to go out in bad weather.
d. No housecall: temperature 103°.
e. Doctor won't refer to specialist or hospitalize.
f. Doctor won't repeat diagnostic procedure, e.g., EKG.
g. Doctor rude and unsympathetic.
h. Outside doctor's diagnosis or therapy implies group doctor's mis-diagnosis or mistreatment.
i. Doctor asked patient to leave his panel; patient wants to stay.

Do you think a patient is more likely to get satisfaction from the group if he complains directly to MSP instead of the group?

3. How responsive is the administration to *physicians'* complaints? Does the administration do an adequate job protecting the physician from patient pressures? From other external pressures, e.g., union? From hospital influences? Examples.

4. How about the Executive Committee: What is it for? What should its functions be?

5. Here are some problems that have come up in various meetings over the years. In each case, do you think it is an administrative problem, a collegial problem, or some combination? (Probe.)

a. Reducing the utilization of lab and X-ray services.
b. Setting priorities for scarce items, e.g., flu vaccine, hospital beds.
c. Setting walk-in and/or housecall policy.
d. Selecting patients for reassignment when a physician's panel is reduced.
e. Controlling unnecessary referrals to specialists.
f. Setting up standard procedures, e.g., for general physical.
g. Firing physician.

6. In most organizations, one of the administration's jobs is to super-vise employees. Is that done here? How? How do you feel about it?

a. Making sure physicians keep scheduled hours.
b. Checking on number of services rendered. (Probe: check on elective procedures.)

   c. Adhering to standard examination procedures.

   d. Making sure physicians don't slough work off on colleagues, e.g., delaying housecalls, unloading undesirable patients.

   e. Making sure physicians aren't rude to patients or otherwise treat them badly.

   f. Making sure physicians aren't rude to *other* physicians' patients, e.g., when on call.

7. Do people in the front office have an accurate idea of the *quality* of medical care given by individual physicians? (In consulting room? Over the phone? In patients' homes?) How do they know? Do you think a continuing audit of charts is useful or necessary for maintaining high quality of care in the group? If so, what elements should be included? Who should do it? If not, what does keep a doctor on his toes?

8. Do your colleagues have an accurate idea of the quality of your practice? More or less than the administration? How do they know? How do you learn about your colleagues? Should physicians' performances be posted and identified by name? (E.g., number of patient complaints per month, number of transfers, proportion of housecalls to office visits, proportion of lab orders, etc.)

November 1961

SECOND INTERVIEW, CONSULTANTS: ADMINISTRATION

1. From your own experience with the front office, how would you grade their performance in these areas, using A, B, C, D, F, as your grades and maximization of the physician's effectiveness as your criterion:

   a. Handling patient complaints.

   b. Scheduling physician time—hours, vacations, etc.

   c. Maintaining and transmitting records.

   d. Maintaining the physical plant.

   e. Obtaining competent auxiliary help.

   f. Encouraging a high quality of medical care.

   g. Responding to physician suggestions and complaints.

2. Have you ever been called by someone down in the office about a complaint a patient made about you? Recently? Describe incident—what was involved, how it got to the office, who called you, what was said, etc. Whose side did the person in the front office

seem to be on? What was the role of MSP in the matter? Should the situation have been handled differently?

3. What's the administration actually for? For example, what matters have you had on occasion to go to any of the administrative personnel about? Director, assistant director, administrator, etc.? Give details. What matters would you like to be able to take to them but feel you can't or are too hopeless to bother about?

4. How about the Executive Committee? What's it for? What is its actual function? Probe extensively on executive and representative functions. What *should* its functions be?

5. Are there any ways the front office has of checking up on your performance as a doctor? Hours, number of services rendered, of course, but how about the quality of the medicine you practice and the quality of attention you give your patients? Do you think people down at the office have a fairly accurate idea of what goes on in your consulting room and over the phone? More or less accurate than your colleagues? How do they know what they know? How do you learn about your colleagues?

6. What actually does keep the doctors in the group on their toes? How are you kept on your toes? Examples. How do you keep others on their toes? Examples.

7. Do you think a continuing audit of charts is useful or necessary for maintaining a high quality of medical care in the group? If so, who should do the audit and how confidential should it be? An active committee within the group to review charts and talk to doctors? How about an audit from outside, like the MSP committee?

8. The group circulates a number of standards for practice—e.g., procedures for the general health exam by pediatricians and family doctors. Should more such lists be made for more areas of practice (presumably paralleling the opinion of major medical authorities)? Even if no more than what is presently established were involved, should a committee sample charts to see that those procedures are really followed?

9. How about lab services? Should there be more effort to see that they are not overutilized (as a substitute for careful clinical judgment)? If no, why not? If yes, how?

10. How about specialist services? Should there be more effort to see that they are not abused—referrals without work-ups, referrals made as placebos, etc.? If yes, how could this be done?

May 1962

FINAL INTERVIEW, ALL PHYSICIANS: COLLEAGUE RELATIONS

1. As part of our study of the group, we have been trying to determine what the doctors exchange information about and what not. We've made a list of topics you might discuss. In each case, may we have an example from your experience and indication of the people with whom you've discussed it and similar topics—colleagues in general, close colleagues only, no one, etc.?
   a. Everyone needs advice in handling a case sometimes. Describe a recent instance in which you discussed the *technical* aspects of a case with someone else. Who was it? How was discussion initiated? Probe variation in technical problem, person consulted, circumstance of consultation.
   b. Doctors can make *mistakes*, some serious, some trivial. Example. Probe.
   c. Doctors can become concerned about the *propriety* of their actions—ethical.
   d. There are little *tricks* doctors learn after finishing training—e.g., handling a large volume of patients when things pile up. Example. How and from whom did you learn it? Ever teach it to someone?
   e. There are questions concerning your *personal career*—e.g., whether or not to stay in the group.
   f. There are questions about *another doctor's* good taste, ethics, competence.
2. (General doctors only) When referring patients, are there occasions when you've felt it necessary to refer to an individual rather than a service? Example. Probe for reasons—patient relations, information feedback, consideration of service to patient.
3. (Family doctors only) Who do you usually use for consultation in cardiology? Chest? Endocrinology? Internal medicine as such?
4. Who are your two closest physician friends? Where do they work? Of the doctors in the group, with whom are you most friendly? Who do you see after hours, socially? Who do you usually cover for?
5. We've heard that a physician's technical competence quickly becomes known. We'd like to find out just how it becomes known: Consider the group doctor you think most highly of technically. His name is unimportant. Can you recall in as much detail as possible just how you arrived at your evaluation—chronicle of personal impressions, incidents, comments by others, knowledge of his work,

etc., that influenced your evaluation? Now, could you do the same for a doctor you think less highly of? How you came to think so?

6. We've heard that a doctor's style of practice becomes fairly well known after a time in the group. It's often said that you can tell a patient's doctor after a minute's conversation with the patient. We've gathered the available statistical material measuring several aspects of style of practice. Now we'd like to find out whether or not doctors' judgments agree with the statistics.

   a. For example, doctors vary widely according to the number of housecalls they make. Here's a list of all the family doctors and pediatricians in the group. Please rate each according to whether he is more or less likely to make housecalls compared with the other doctors in the group. Use a plus for more, a minus for less and "A" for average. A question mark if you don't know enough to rate an individual. (Probe for source of information.)

   b. Who is more or less likely to keep patients happy? (Our measure here is patient complaints.) (Probe for source of information.)

   c. Who is more or less likely to finish on time, handle a large number of patients quickly? (Probe for source of information.)

   d. Who is more or less likely to refer his patients out to the consulting specialists? (*For specialists*: Who is more or less likely to refer patients only after examining them thoroughly, etc.?) (Probe for source of information.)

   e. (*For specialists only*.) Who is more or less likely to want to keep close tabs on cases he refers to you?

7. *Optional, if time*. We've heard that some people have more influence on group policy than others—that there are "ins" and "outs." We'd like to find out how much consensus there is about this in the group. Here is a list of all the doctors in the group. Please mark each name "I" (in), "O" (out) or "?" (don't know). Probe.]

8. Finally, we are interested in the way your judgment about the quality of care agrees with that of your colleagues. Here is a list of all the specialties in the group. Using the average level of *group* quality as your base, rate each service as above, average, or below in *technical quality*. Now to the left of those ratings, do the same thing for the level of patient satisfaction with the specialty's services.

9. Here is a list of all the doctors in the group. Please rate each one for technical quality.

References

Babbie, Earl R. *Science and Morality in Medicine*. Berkeley: University of California Press, 1970.

Barber, Bernard. *Science and the Social Order*. New York: Collier Books, 1952.

———— et al. *Research on Human Subjects*. New York: Russell Sage Foundation, 1973.

Bechhofer, Frank and Brian Elliott. "An Approach to a Study of Small Shopkeepers and the Class Structure." *Archives Européennes de Sociologie* 9 (1968): 180–202.

Becker, Howard S. *Sociological Work*. Chicago: Aldine Publishing Co., 1970.

———— et al. *Boys in White*. Chicago: University of Chicago Press, 1961.

Bennis, Warren. *Changing Organizations*. New York: McGraw-Hill Book Co., 1966.

Bensman, Joseph and Robert Lilienfeld. *Craft and Consciousness*. New York: John Wiley & Sons, 1973.

Benson, J. Kenneth. "The Analysis of Bureaucratic-Professional Conflict: Functional versus Dialectical Approaches." *The Sociological Quarterly* 14 (Summer 1973): 376–394.

Blau, Peter. *The Dynamics of Bureaucracy*. Chicago: University of Chicago Press, 1955.

———— and Richard A. Schoenherr. *The Structure of Organizations*. New York: Basic Books, 1971.

Blauner, Robert. *Alienation and Freedom*. Chicago: University of Chicago Press, 1964.

Bucher, Rue and Anselm Strauss. "Professions in Process." *American Journal of Sociology* 66 (January 1961): 325–334.

Burkett, Gary and Kathleen Knafl. "Judgment and Decision-making in a Medical Specialty." *Sociology of Work and Occupations* 1 (February 1974): 82–109.

Carlin, Jerome. *Lawyers' Ethics, A Survey of the New York City Bar*. New York: Russell Sage Foundation, 1966.

Cartwright, Dorwin. "Influence, Leadership and Control." In J. G. March, ed. *Handbook of Organizations*. Chicago: Rand McNally & Co., 1965, pp. 1–47.

Colombotos, John. Personal communication, 1975.

Committee on Finance, U.S. Senate. *Report 92-1230*, pp. 254–269, September 26, 1972.

Crozier, Michel. *The Bureaucratic Phenomenon*. Chicago: University of Chicago Press, 1964.

Daniels, Arlene K. "How Free Should Professions Be?" In Eliot Friedson, ed. *The Professions and Their Prospects*. Beverly Hills: Sage Publications, 1973, pp. 39–57.

Denzin, Norman K. "Rules of Conduct and the Study of Deviant Behavior: Some Notes on the Social Relationship." In Jack D. Douglas, ed. *Deviance and Respectability*. New York: Basic Books, 1970, pp. 120–159.

Derbyshire, Robert C. *Medical Licensure and Discipline in the United States*. Baltimore: The Johns Hopkins Press, 1969.

Dibble, Vernon K. "What Is and What Ought to Be: A Comparison of Certain Characteristics of the Ideological and Legal Styles of Thought." *American Journal of Sociology* 79 (November 1973): 511–549.

Donabedian, Avedis. "An Evaluation of Prepaid Group Practice." *Inquiry* 6 (September 1969): 3–27.

Dornbusch, Sanford M. and W. Richard Scott. *Evaluation and the Exercise of Authority*. San Francisco: Jossey Bass Publishers, 1975.

Eilers, Robert D. and Sue S. Moyerman, eds. *National Health Insurance*. Homewood, Illinois: Richard D. Irwin, 1971.

Ellul, Jacques. *The Technological Society*. New York: Vintage Books, 1964.

Etzioni, Amitai. "Social Control: Organizational Aspects." In D. L. Sills, ed. *International Encyclopedia of the Social Sciences*, vol. 14. New York: Free Press and Macmillan, 1968, pp. 396–402.

Feinstein, Alvan R. *Clinical Judgment*. Baltimore: Williams and Wilkins Co., 1967.

Freidson, Eliot. *Patients' Views of Medical Practice*. New York: Russell Sage Foundation, 1961.

———. *Professional Dominance*. New York: Atherton Press, 1970.

———. *Profession of Medicine*. New York: Dodd, Mead & Co., 1970.

———. "Professions and the Occupational Principle." In Eliot Freidson, ed. *The Professions and Their Prospects*. Beverly Hills, Calif.: Sage Publications, 1973, pp. 19–38.

——— and John H. Mann. "Organizational Dimensions of Large-Scale Group Medical Practice." *American Journal of Public Health* 61 (April 1971): 786–795.

——— and Buford Rhea. "Processes of Control in a Company of Equals." *Social Problems* 11 (Fall 1963): 119–131.

———. "Physicians in Large Medical Groups." *Journal of Chronic Disease* 17 (1964): 827–836.

———. "Knowledge and Judgment in Professional Evaluations." *Administrative Science Quarterly* 10 (June 1965): 107–124.

Fuchs, Victor R. *Who Shall Live?* New York: Basic Books, 1974.

Garfield, S. R. "The Delivery of Medical Care." *Scientific American* 222 (1970): 15–23.

Garfinkel, Harold. *Studies in Ethnomethodology*. Englewood Cliffs, N.J.: Prentice-Hall, Inc., 1967.

Gibbs, Jack P. "Social Control." *Warner Modular Publications*, Module 1 (1972): 1–17.

Gilb, Corinne Lathrop. *Hidden Hierarchies: The Professions and Government*. New York: Harper and Row, 1966.

Glaser, William A. *Paying the Doctor: Systems of Remuneration and Their Effects*. Baltimore: The Johns Hopkins Press, 1970.

Goldman, Lee. "Factors Related to Physicians' Medical and Political Attitudes: A Documentation of Intraprofessional Variations." *Journal of Health and Social Behavior* 15 (September 1974): 177–187.

Goode, William J. "Community Within a Community: The Professions." *American Sociological Review* 22 (April 1957): 194–200.

———. "The Theoretical Limits of Professionalization." In Amitai Etzioni, ed. *The Semi-Professions and Their Organization*. New York: The Free Press, 1969, pp. 266–313.

Goran, Michael J. et al. "The PSRO Hospital Review System." *Medical Care* 13 (April 1975): 1–33.

Goss, Mary E. W. "Physicians in Bureaucracy: A Case Study of Professional Pressures on Organizational Roles." Unpublished Ph.D. dissertation, Columbia University, 1959.

———. "Influence and Authority Among Physicians in an Outpatient Clinic." *American Sociological Review* 26 (February 1961): 39–50.

———. "Patterns of Bureaucracy Among Hospital Staff Physicians." In Eliot Freidson, ed. *The Hospital in Modern Society*. New York: The Free Press, 1963, pp. 176–179.

Gouldner, Alvin W. *Patterns of Industrial Bureaucracy*. New York: The Free Press, 1954.

Gray, Bradford H. *Human Subjects in Medical Experimentation*. New York: John Wiley & Sons, 1975.

Greenlick, Merwyn R. "The Impact of Prepaid Group Practice on American Medical Care: A Critical Evaluation." *The Annals of the American Academy of Political and Social Science* 399 (January 1972): 100–113.

Harris, Richard. *A Sacred Trust*. Baltimore: Penguin Books, 1966.

Haug, Marie R. and M. B. Sussman. "Professional Autonomy and the Revolt of the Client." *Social Problems* 17 (Fall 1969): 153–161.

Heydebrand, Wolf V. and James J. Noell. "Task Structure and Innovation in Professional Organizations." In Wolf V. Heydebrand, ed. *Comparative Organizations*. Englewood Cliffs, N.J.: Prentice-Hall, Inc., 1973, pp. 294–322.

Horn, Joshua S. *Away with All Pests*. New York: Monthly Review Press, 1969.

Hughes, Everett C. *The Sociological Eye*. Chicago: Aldine Publishing Co., 1971.

Hummel, Hans J. et al. "The Referring of Patients as a Component of the Medical Interaction System." *Social Science and Medicine* 3 (April 1970): 597–607.

Johnson, Terence J. *Professions and Power*. London: Macmillan and Co., 1972.

Katz, Jay, ed. *Experimentation with Human Beings*. New York: Russell Sage Foundation, 1972.

Lewis, H. R. and M. E. Lewis. *The Medical Offenders*. New York: Simon and Schuster, 1970.

Mannheim, Karl. *Man and Society in an Age of Reconstruction*. London: Rout-
ledge & Kegan Paul, 1948.

Marcus, Philip M. "Schoolteachers and Militant Conservatism." In Eliot
Freidson, ed. *The Professions and Their Prospects*. Beverly Hills, Calif.:
Sage Publications, 1973, pp. 191–216.

Marmor, Theodore. *The Politics of Medicare*. Chicago: Aldine Publishing Co.,
1973.

McNamara, Mary and Clifford Todd. "A Survey of Group Practice in the
U.S." *American Journal of Public Health* 60 (1970): 1303–1313.

Mechanic, David. *Public Expectations and Health Care*. New York: Wiley-
Interscience, 1972.

———. *Politics, Medicine, and Social Science*. New York: Wiley-Interscience,
1974.

Mencher, Samuel. *British Private Medical Practice and the National Health
Service*. Pittsburgh: University of Pittsburgh Press, 1968.

Moore, Wilbert E. *The Professions: Roles and Rules*. New York: Russell Sage
Foundation, 1970.

Mumford, Emily. *Interns: From Students to Physicians*. Cambridge: Harvard
University Press, 1970.

Nathanson, Constance A. and Marshall H. Becker. "Doctors, Nurses and Clinical Records." *Medical Care* 11 (May–June 1973): 214–223.

Parsons, Talcott. *The Social System*. New York: The Free Press, 1951.

———. "Professions." In David L. Sills, ed. *International Encyclopedia of the
Social Sciences*, vol. 12. New York: The Free Press and Macmillan, 1968,
pp. 536–547.

Perrow, Charles. *Organizational Analysis—A Sociological View*. Belmont,
Calif.: Wadsworth Publishing Co., 1970.

Pitts, Jesse R. "Continuity and Change in Bourgeois France." In Stanley
Hoffman et al. *In Search of France*. Cambridge: Harvard University Press,
1963, pp. 235–304.

———. "Social Control: The Concept." In David L. Sills, ed. *International
Encyclopedia of the Social Sciences*, vol. 14. New York: The Free Press and
Macmillan, 1968, pp. 381–396.

Platt, Anthony M. *The Child Savers—The Invention of Delinquency*. Chicago:
University of Chicago Press, 1969.

Rayack, Elton. *Professional Power and American Medicine*. Cleveland: World
Publishing Co., 1967.

Roemer, Milton I. and William Shonick. "HMO Performance: The Recent
Evidence." *The Milbank Memorial Fund Quarterly/Health and Society* 51
(Summer 1973): 271–317.

Ruzek, Sheryl K. "Making Social Work Accountable." In Eliot Freidson, ed.
The Professions and Their Prospects. Beverly Hills: Sage Publications, 1973,
pp. 217–243.

Saward, Ernest W. et al. "Documentation of Twenty Years of Organizational
Growth of a Prepaid Group Practice Plan." *Medical Care* 6 (May–June
1968): 231–244.

Schurmann, Franz. *Ideology and Organization in Communist China*, 2nd ed. Berkeley: University of California Press, 1968.

Scott, W. Richard. "Reactions to Supervision in a Heteronomous Professional Organization." *Administrative Science Quarterly* 10 (June 1965): 65–81.

Shortell, Stephen M. "A Model of Physician- Referral Behavior: A Test of Exchange Theory in Medical Practice." *Center for Health Administration Studies, University of Chicago, Research Series,* No. 31, n.d.

Smigel, Erwin O. *The Wall Street Lawyer.* New York: The Free Press, 1964.

Smith, Adam. *The Wealth of Nations.* Baltimore: Penguin Books, 1970.

Somers, Anne R., ed. *The Kaiser-Permanente Medical Care Program, A Symposium.* New York: The Commonwealth Fund, 1971.

Somers, Herman and Anne Somers. *Doctors, Patients and Health Insurance.* Washington: Brookings Institution, 1961.

Stelling, Joan and Rue Bucher. "Vocabularies of Realism in Professional Socialization." *Social Science and Medicine* 7 (September 1973): 661–675.

Stinchcombe, Arthur L. *Creating Efficient Industrial Administrations.* New York: Academic Press, 1974.

Szasz, Thomas. *Law, Liberty and Psychiatry.* New York: The Macmillan Co., 1963.

Tannenbaum, Arnold S. *Control in Organizations.* New York: McGraw-Hill Book Co., 1968.

ten Broek, Jacobus et al., eds. *The Law of the Poor.* San Francisco: Chandler Publishing Co., 1966.

Thompson, James D. *Organizations in Action.* New York: McGraw-Hill Book Co., 1967.

Toren, Nina. "Semi-Professionalism and Social Work: A Theoretical Perspective." In Amitai Etzioni, ed. *The Semi-Professions and Their Organization.* New York: The Free Press, 1969, pp. 141–195.

Veblen, Thorstein. *The Instinct of Workmanship.* New York: W. W. Norton & Co., 1964.

Weber, Max. *The Theory of Social and Economic Organization.* New York: Oxford University Press, 1947.

Weiss, Carol H. "The Politicization of Evaluation Research." *Journal of Social Issues* 26 (1970): 57–68.

Wheeler, Stanton, ed. *On Record: Files and Dossiers in American Life.* New York: Basic Books, 1970.

Whyte, Martin King. "Bureaucratization and Modernization in China: The Maoist Critique." *American Sociological Review* 38 (April 1973): 149–163.

Wolfe, Samuel and Robin F. Badgley. "The Family Doctor." *The Milbank Memorial Fund Quarterly* 50 (April 1972): Part 2.

Zedeck, Sheldon and Milton R. Blood. *Foundations of Behavioral Science Research in Organizations.* Monterey, Calif.: Brooks/Cole Publishing Co., 1974.

Zola, Irving Kenneth and Stephen J. Miller. "The Erosion of Medicine from Within." In Eliot Freidson, ed. *The Professions and Their Prospects.* Beverly Hills: Sage Publications, 1973, pp. 153–172.

Author Index